T0196507

Outside the Lines

*A Personal Journey
From Abuse to Social Work*

KAREN WUSSOW

iUniverse, Inc.
New York Bloomington

Outside the Lines
A Personal Journey from Abuse to Social Work

iUniverse books may be ordered through booksellers or by contacting:

iUniverse
1663 Liberty Drive
Bloomington, IN 47403
www.iuniverse.com
1-800-Authors (1-800-288-4677)

Because of the dynamic nature of the Internet, any Web addresses or links contained in this book may have changed since publication and may no longer be valid. The views expressed in this work are solely those of the author and do not necessarily reflect the views of the publisher, and the publisher hereby disclaims any responsibility for them.

ISBN: 978-1-4502-4763-4 (sc)
ISBN: 978-1-4502-4764-1 (ebook)

Printed in the United States of America

iUniverse rev. date: 8/12/2010

Cover art by: Joan Larson

Dedication

*This book is dedicated
to my three children and grandchildren
for teaching me about the softer side of real life.*

Acknowledgements

My dream of seeing my book to completion would never have happened without the help of many. Although I can't thank everyone individually, there are a few who deserve special mention.

With love and thanks to Grandmother Elma, who looked into my eyes and my heart as a child and made me believe in a touch that didn't hurt.

To Bev S., my college professor, who took time from her busy life to teach me, guide me and support me as a person and a professional for the past eighteen years.

With thanks to Sandy R., my college professor, who supported me on my journey and asks me to speak to her class each year. She is courageous and wise in her teachings, and I am honored to be a part of her curriculum.

For Paula and Carol, the "Grandmas," who taught me that people and life's events are not perfect, but our perception of the world can be. They installed in me the belief that we are where we need to be, therefore, perfect. The world is truly perfect because they are part of it. They graciously shared their love of life, people, and adventure with me and my children. Thank you for listening with your heart and loving me just as I am.

For my granddaughter, who has brought a sparkle to my heart and only sees her grandmother in front of her, not an abuse victim or social worker. She has reminded me how to see with my heart and encourages me to be who I am. Her innocence is a reminder of all that remains to be done for all the children in our communities.

With thanks to Marie, my therapist, who has assisted me during many dark memories of my life. She offered me guidance and understanding. She cried with me as we discussed my abuse, and she has been a strong and honest support for me during my emotional struggles to write this book. She reminds me of a candle of hope ever burning.

Finally, I want to express my gratitude and appreciation to Joan Hasskamp, who took my original draft and molded it into a book. Through this seemingly endless process, she maintained her gentle smile and warm heart. I admire her skills, gentle personality, and love for others. I am awed by her willingness to be a dream builder for others.

Contents

Chapter One
Early Childhood Memories

TODAY IS ANOTHER DAY, a miracle like all others.

I pick up my granddaughter, Kelly, on my way home from work. She lives with her mom Sandy. My daughter is a single parent and her job requires her to travel frequently. Lately she's looked exhausted. The life of a single mom isn't easy. Sandy hugs me and thanks me for helping out with Kelly.

I cherish the time spent with my eight-year-old granddaughter. I marvel at her energy and enthusiasm as she bounds down the street, excitedly telling me about a horse she wants to ride. The bows in her hair perfectly match the color of her shirt and socks. Her blond hair glistens in the sun. Her innocence and joy warms my heart. Watching her I reflect on the stark contrast between her childhood and mine. We arrive home where we discover Adam stretched out on the floor in front of the television, his dog at his side. At sixteen my son is long and lanky. It seems like only yesterday when he was Kelly's age.

I take a minute to quickly call my other daughter, Shawna. She's just been hired as a county probation agent. We talk for a few minutes about her day. She's a newlywed so I don't keep her on the line long. We set up a date to meet over the weekend. I will remind her then of how proud I am of her and how much I love her.

I'm hot and tired after a long day of work so I ask Adam to watch Kelly while I take a quick bath. After dinner, I promise them we will go the Diary Queen.

As I slowly dip into the lukewarm water, I'm reminded of my many blessings. My present life was once only a dream, a distant dream of a very small and frightened little girl. I shut off the tap and begin to shave my leg. Suddenly, memories of my childhood surface as the razor cuts the skin covering the small bone chips on my shin. I shudder at the recollection of my mother and the physical and emotional abuse she inflicted on me as a child.

My earliest significant memory is when I was approximately three years old. Our family lived in a small house in central Minnesota. It contained little furniture or personal belongings. I remember standing in the bathroom adjacent to the living room. My mother was crouched behind the sofa and my father was in the kitchen behind the stove. They were throwing empty beer bottles at each other. Broken glass was flying everywhere. My older brothers and I were terrified. Through our tears we pleaded with them to stop. As I stood in the bathroom crying, a bottle smashed at my feet. I remember making a decision to step on the broken glass in hopes they would cease their fighting.

My five-year old brother, Jerry, came and stood beside me. He hollered that I was hurt and bleeding. It worked. My parents stopped fighting for the moment. Mother staggered over to me, barely able to stand due to the amount of alcohol she had consumed. My father was equally as drunk. Mother reeked of beer as she washed the bottom of my foot and wrapped it in cloth. Father slumped over and fell to the floor. I went to him because he was crying, which made my cry. I assured him I was all right, that it was an accident. Amid sobs, he said life was hard. I could tell by the way he smelled of alcohol and the way he was crying and carrying on that he was sad about how things were. The alcohol affected my father that way.

Several years later I experienced my first feeling of shame. We had driven to my Aunt Elizabeth's home. My parents were arguing about money in the car. I believe they wanted to borrow money from her. My father asked me to go to the door to see if she was home. When I knocked, a girl almost the same age as me answered. She was my cousin and I stood there in awe of her. Her hair was up in ponytails above her ears, and the ponytails had little curly ringlets that were tied with pretty pink ribbons. She wore a pretty pink robe and matching fluffy pink slippers. Her ponytails bounced up and down and she smelled really nice. I asked her if her parents were home. She cheerfully said they were and left to find them.

As I stood on the steps and waited, I looked at myself. My pants were dirty and too short, my shirt too big and buttoned crookedly. I used the back of my hand to brush my unkempt hair from my eyes. I ran back to the car, ashamed of my appearance. My father ordered me to wait in the car, which I was more than willing to do, and my mother and father went inside. They were in the house just a few minutes and by the time they returned to the car they were in a foul mood. My dad climbed in, slammed the door and told my mother to sit down and shut up. He stomped on the accelerator sending us kids flying around in the back seat.

This scene played out many times. My parents drank up all the money and then asked family for help. Most family members avoided my parents due to their habit of borrowing money and never paying it back. It didn't take long for them to burn their bridges with everyone. This was one of the reasons our family was so isolated. The other reason was that their drinking and the resulting argumentative and belligerent behavior drove most everyone else away.

Alcohol was a way of life and a constant variable in my growing-up years. The verbal and physical abuse between my parents never stopped. My memories of my childhood are fragmented and scattered, but I have felt strongly about filling in those blank spaces. I have often asked family and friends to fill in the gaps of what happened during my youth—times I cannot remember. The accuracy of the stories I have been able to glean, I cannot say with certainty, but they are all I have.

MY MOTHER, DORIS, WAS FIFTEEN AND PREGNANT with my oldest brother, Duane, by my father, who was twenty-five. My father had completed his time in the military prior to meeting mother. Both my parents had between a sixth and ninth grade education. Mother was sent to live with an older sister when she became pregnant, but my father followed her there, and they continued their relationship. The drinking and physical abuse was predominant even at this early stage of their relationship. Mother was the black sheep of her family. Only three of her siblings remained in consistent contact with her. I met some of her sisters for the first time at her funeral when I was thirty-two years old. They said they had given up hope on our family, that it was simply too painful to see small children so hungry and dirty.

MY PARENTS MARRIED IN THE DAKOTAS in 1955—my mother's mother, Stella, told them either to get married or she'd see to it that my father would be charged with statutory rape. Initially, my parents lived in Minneapolis, near mother's family. Duane was born there. Two years later, Jerry was born. By then the family had moved to the small town in central Minnesota where father was from. They lived in a trailer court. Father worked construction, and mother waitressed. I was told by Aunt Victoria (father's sister) that the first time they saw Jerry after his birth; mother came in with a six-pack of beer in one hand and Jerry in the other. She held him by the corners of the blanket, even though it was the beginning of winter. She had been dropped off by a taxi and already was intoxicated.

I was born in 1959, when mother was twenty years old. I was to be the only girl. Mother had another pregnancy in 1960, but Dawn lived only a few short hours, enough time to be baptized before her death. There was a funeral, but my parents couldn't afford a headstone for her grave. Later, a marker was put on her grave by Aunt Rita and her husband. I was told that mother was drunk when she started hemorrhaging and refused to get medical attention. By the time she was taken to the hospital, she had lost so much blood the baby couldn't be saved. Jerry and I have at times referred to this deceased sister as the lucky one. She didn't have to live through the ugliness of what alcohol did to all of our lives.

When drunk, mother sometimes referred to Dawn, and I suspect this was a traumatic event for her. I have been told that mother had miscarried several times due to alcohol consumption and physical abuse.

During this time, my father's mother, Elma, and his sister Helen were the emotional and financial support for my parents. When mom was in a drunken rage over something or other, she would call her sister Anne and her mother Stella in Minneapolis and ask them to pick us up. He'd come home from work to discover his family missing.

I remember that dad worked for the city and he occasionally gave us rides in a big truck. During the holiday season, he proudly pointed out the decorations that he had put up. While life was better when dad worked, jobs never lasted long due to the alcohol abuse.

Both of my parents came from families that abused alcohol. The only family member that I can remember that didn't was Grandmother Elma. She was a very spiritual woman. She was approximately sixty years old when I was born. Her very presence demanded respect; my mother, who showed little respect to anyone, never challenged grandmother verbally or physically. I spent many days and nights with grandmother. Jerry stayed with grandma's sister, great aunt Helen, and her husband, Ed. Ed and Helen had no children and treated Jerry as if he was their own. They taught him about love and the church. I know he felt special to them. In fact, there were times mother told Jerry to go stay with Ed and Helen after she had been drinking and abusive. Jerry never hesitated; he willingly ran over to Ed and Helen's home and was welcomed in. This was a safe place for him. Likewise, I stayed with my grandma whenever possible.

After Dawn's death in 1960, mother gave birth to Jesse in 1962. My parents separated shortly thereafter. Jesse was born with a variety of physical ailments (heart murmur, enlarged chest, lazy eye, under weight), which most likely were a result of mom's alcohol use during pregnancy. Lenny was born nine months later; he had not been expected to live according to grandma. He was referred to as a "blue baby" and was so small he fit in a tiny shoebox. He was born with a number of health problems as well. During both these pregnancies my father was physically abuse to my mother which may also have contributed in some way to their health issues.

Many of my earliest memories involve the time spent in bars with my parents. I recall them buying the five of us orange pop and cheese popcorn. We often fell asleep in a booth, because my parents usually stayed until closing time. Sometimes father had Duane drive us home, even though he wasn't legal at the age of 9 and could barely see above the dash. Other times, when my parents stopped at the bar for a "quick drink," we'd have to wait in the car for hours. These waits were exhaustingly long, but we knew better than to interrupt them even though we were hungry. Sometimes, father brought us out beef jerky and pop. He'd promise that they'd be out soon, but that never happened. Eventually, hours later they emerged in a state of total intoxication. Oftentimes they invited their drinking buddies over, and the party continued all night long at our house.

Sometimes when they went drinking they dropped us off at Aunt Victoria's house. If we were fortunate, we stayed the night, but if my parents were particularly drunk and belligerent, they'd bust in and drag us home in the middle of the night. Aunt Victoria was very kind and her house was quiet. I remember lying in bed and wishing that my parents wouldn't barge in. I knew if they took us home there'd be no rest because the drinking and fighting didn't end when they left the bar, but continued at home, often becoming more intense and volatile. The result was always the same when they and their friends were drunk—volatile behavior, physical altercations, yelling, hitting and name calling.

When intoxicated, my parents fought continuously. This caused great tension and meant little, if any, sleep for anyone. We faced the constant fear that someone was going to get hurt. Duane, Jerry and I would cry upstairs as we listened to the intense arguing, swearing, and physical threats. On one occasion my mother yelled for us and ordered us to come downstairs. Mom had called her mother and sister in Minneapolis and they were on their way to pick us up. Dad went ballistic and said we weren't going anywhere. The argument escalated until they exchanged blows.

As a general rule, mother wanted us to see father hit her, so we were often forced to be present during the physical altercations. Mother cried during these traumatic events and asked us to hug her, while telling us she loved us. She tended to lean on us emotionally while was drunk. The days all ended the same with the broken beer bottles, yelling, hitting, broken dishes, flipped over chairs, and blood. I remember the multitude of booze bottles and the pervasive smell of alcohol. Our lifestyle was so out of control that nothing could be counted on, except to have this scene replayed over and over.

What did my parents fight about? Surely alcohol manufactured reasons out of nothing, but some of the arguments were because mother liked to accuse father of seeing other women. In retaliation, dad argued that Duane wasn't his child. Other times, there didn't seem to be any real reason for the arguing; they just argued. Mother was very verbal and vulgar at all times but even more so when drunk. Most often the verbal confrontations escalated into physical altercations.

While dad worked, mother sat at home and drank. She expected him to be home right afterwards but if he wasn't, she turned her rage on us. She was convinced he was cheating on her. She pulled our hair, twisted our arms behind our back and pushed them up towards the back of our heads. If we sensed mother's mood, we left to stay at our safe homes. If we were lucky, we escaped to these safe places before she hurt us, but not always.

I DON'T REMEMBER MANY HOLIDAYS, but I remember one Christmas. We received a large box of toys that had been donated. Most of the toys were broken, but we didn't mind; toys were a luxury in our home. Grandma Elma always had a small box of toys behind her door for me to play with (Old Maid deck of cards, pair of high heels, and a large necklace). She always made me feel special by allowing me to have afternoon coffee with her Sister Helen and their mutual friends. Some of our best times together were when we played Old Maid or other games. She let me climb into bed and sleep with here where I always felt safe. While Grandma doted on me, Duane and Jerry were made to feel special by great aunt Helen and Aunt Victoria. One time, Victoria purchased cowboy outfits for them at a garage sale, and one year, she bought them each a red suit for Christmas to go to church in. These kind and caring relatives offered each of us safe respite from our own chaotic home.

IN 1965, MY PARENTS DIVORCED. The courts offered father custody of Duane, Jerry and me. Father didn't want mother to have Lenny and Jesse by herself so he declined the arrangement. I suspect he knew the younger boys would never survive without our protection. In the end it was agreed that mother would retain custody of all five of us.

Mother moved us to Minneapolis near her family and father moved to Duluth. There was a great deal of sadness, fear, and anxiety for us, as we left our safe homes behind—Grandmother Elma, Aunt Victoria, and great Aunt Helen. We had no idea when we would see them or our father.

I NEED TO SAY THAT I HAVE some positive memories of my parents. Father was a very active outdoorsman. He loved both deer and bird hunting. He liked to brag that I would make a great grouse hunter because I had a good eye. He also fished, though at times he referred to this as "bottle bass" fishing because most of the time was spent imbibing. Mother didn't approve of his time away from home so this caused many arguments between my parents.

Both of my parents had wonderful senses of humor—when they were sober. On occasion, father would pile us in the car and take us to the gravel pit and let us play. Sometimes he joined us in the dirt; other times he sat in the car and drank beer. My parents usually kept a case of beer in the backseat or trunk of the car; alcohol was never far regardless of what activity was going on.

When father was drunk, he liked to drive us down gravel roads far in excess of the posted speed limit. Flying over hills tickled our tummies, and we all laughed, ignorant of the danger we were in. Sometimes mother and their friends joined us. It was wonderful to laugh with my parents during these outings. Unfortunately, the good times were short-lived.

Because of their bad tempers and heavy drinking, anything could set one of them off. Something as simple as dad wanting mother to sit by him and her refusing could escalate into a physical battle. Dad would try to throw mother out of the car while mother would kick and slap at dad. In an instant, the quality time together would be over.

One time, my father stayed overnight with us in Minneapolis. In the morning, Jerry played a Roger Miller record on a small turntable. In a section of the song, a trumpet played. Dad grabbed an orange plastic hat that belonged to one of my brothers and pretended he was making the trumpet sound by blowing on the bat. Everyone laughed, but it seemed, within an instant, things changed. Mother became enraged about something and began chasing father with a butcher knife around the kitchen table. The laughter vanished, the fear returned, and the drinking and violence continued throughout the day.

Father was very affectionate at times. He gave hugs and kisses and spoke freely of his love for us. We loved him deeply in return. He disliked mother abusing us, and it was apparent he was deeply saddened by our family life. I could see the frustration in his body and in his eyes that he had no control over what the future held for all of us. Father cried and hugged us, and his tears deeply disturbed me because I didn't know how to help him or what to say to make him feel better. I tried to assure him that we were fine and everything was okay, but of course, it really wasn't.

Father was abusive to mother, but he usually needed to be provoked. Mother was good at starting arguments and keeping them going; she was very cruel verbally. Self-control was not my father's strength. He believed in discipline. If we disobeyed him, he didn't hesitate to leave his handprint on our butts. But after the divorce, he changed and rarely disciplined us. He raised his voice but our time with him was so limited that we rarely left his side when we had the opportunity to be with him. Times were more enjoyable when we travelled to visit him, rather than when he came to our apartment. Mother's family would barricade the door when he knocked. We'd try to open it but our attempts were futile. Dad would pound for a long time but eventually he'd give up and walk away. We'd cry for hours afterward, upset that we weren't allowed to spend time with him.

In 1965 we moved in with my Uncle Joe on Penn Avenue in Minneapolis. We lived off of public assistance and mother's part time wages.

We resided in the upstairs portion of Uncle Joe's house. My mother's brother was a kind man; he was not married and worked full time. He frequently lent money to my mom. He was also good friends with dad. Joe liked to drink with my parents, and at times would drink to excess, but he always managed to go to work and offer emotional and financial support to us.

When mother took Duane and Jerry to visit dad in Duluth, my mother's brother Vern babysat Jesse, Lenny and me. He was usually intoxicated. Uncle Vern occasionally wet where he slept. This made my mother very angry, but she also seemed to have compassion for him.

When mother went out drinking, she left us home alone, but Uncle Joe checked on us. Shortly after we moved in, Duane started hanging out with some older cousins. The cousins were about ten years older than Duane. Mother accused Duane of using drugs with them, especially sniffing glue. It was clear that mother didn't approve of Duane spending time there, but she had no control over his actions, and it seemed that he was able to come and go as he pleased by the age of ten.

Mother's abuse was worse when she drank. She'd kick us, hit us, and throw us against walls. She'd grab handfuls of hair, twisting it as she dragged us from one room to the other. When mother was sober, she attempted to keep the apartment clean, but that was difficult considering that she started drinking first thing in the morning. Booze bottles, beer bottles, and full ashtrays littered our apartment. I don't remember being taught about hygiene. We found whatever clothes were lying around and put them on, clean or dirty. I had brothers, so most of my hand-me-downs were boy's clothes. Mother went to Salvation Army for our clothes and to obtain Christmas presents, though I don't ever remember believing in Santa Claus.

Mother became attached to a boyfriend, Don. At first, Don treated us well. He took my older brothers to their first wrestling match and bought me a ballerina outfit, with a tutu and tights. Mother worked part time at White Castle when she dated Don. I'm not sure when mother found out that Don was married and only separated from his wife and children, but when she did, she was livid. They argued incessantly and at times, he was physically abusive to her.

When mother allowed father to visit, it was very strained between my parents. They continued to drink together and with that, inevitably came violence. I often saw father in tears over the divorce and the separation from his children. Anger and violence simmered slightly below the surface. Father disliked the fact that mother had a boyfriend, and he often came to the apartment when he knew Don would be there. The violence I witnessed between those three adults is difficult to describe. I was frightened father would be injured. Mother always ended up hurt. Jerry and I would take Jesse and Lenny into a bedroom and try to distract them from the violence. The night usually ended with a neighbor calling the police.

WE MOVED TO THE HOUSING PROJECTS in the spring of 1966 and stayed there eighteen months. The apartments were inhabited by racially diverse, low-income families. Violence was a daily occurrence, and police were a constant presence. Once I was sitting on the curb with a friend when a police car drove up and parked next to us. I heard the driver say to his partner, "Why should we risk our lives coming here? We should just let them kill each other off, and we'd never get called here again."

Shortly after we moved in, mother entered a chemical dependency treatment center in Willmar, Minnesota. During this time, my grandmother Stella stayed with us. The treatment was unsuccessful. When mother returned home, she commenced drinking almost immediately.

The liquor seemed to be taking its toll on her both physically and emotionally. When home, she walked around in her underclothes, wearing only bra and panties. Unless she was going out, she rarely dressed anymore.

While Duane spent most of his time at our cousin's house, he came to stay with us for a couple of weeks. The neighbor man we shared a concrete patio with had a son the same age as Duane. Mother and the man bet each other that their child was the toughest. Mother forced Duane to fight the boy so she could win the bet. Duane fought hard to make mother proud of him. It was nauseating to watch. Duane was tired, stumbling and bleeding, yet mother goaded him to continue. Mother and the neighbor taunted their sons. "Kick his ass!" or "He's a pussy," they yelled at the boys. I begged mother to call it off. Mother swore at me and told me to shut up and get my ass in the house. She wasn't stopping anything she said, until Duane whipped the other boy's ass. After this incident, Duane rarely came home again.

When mother received her food stamps, she frequently purchased a pack of gum or orange juice and took the rest in change. Then she went to the liquor store to buy vodka. Mother rarely bought any groceries. We never sat down to eat a meal. If there was actually something in the house to eat we just grabbed it and wolfed it down.

Mother frequented the pawn shops on those rare occasions we had anything of value. My grandmother Elma bought me a small turntable with a radio for my birthday once, but within a week, mother had pawned it. Mother never had any intention of retrieving what she pawned. One time, in desperation, she pawned her false teeth for twenty dollars. The pawn shop clerk was certain she would return for them, but as we walked out she said to me the teeth never felt right in her mouth anyway, so they were his.

We lived in a revolving door of behavior that followed a monthly pattern. Life was less stressed once mother received her food stamps and AFDC check at the beginning of the month; but, by the second week, she was looking for money to buy her alcohol, as well as the needed money for rent and food. We knew the cycle well, and our own tensions rose and fell in tune with hers.

I learned to be resourceful and handle everyday occurrences myself. When I chipped my front tooth and split my upper and lower lip, mother didn't notice because I cleaned it up. She lived in constant fear that Social Services would become suspicious of our living situation and we'd be removed from her. She said it would be our fault if that happened so we became very adept at hiding injuries from her. If she did notice an injury, her wrath was severe.

I made friends with a black girl in the neighborhood. We liked to walk to school together. One morning I entered her house and was startled by the sight of her head planted next to a hot iron on an ironing board. Fearing the worst, I grabbed her hand and said, "Let's run before your mother returns." I panicked, thinking that her mother was going to hit her or burn her, or both. She shook her hand free and asked what was wrong. Breathless, I expressed my desire to protect her. She laughed and then explained that her mother ironed her hair before putting it into pigtails. I was relieved, but a bit confused.

With Don around, mother's drinking increased and so did her bizarre behavior. Once when mother was drunk, she gave Lenny, who was three, vodka. As a result, he couldn't stand up. Mother and Don laughed at his actions. Sickened by their treatment of Lenny, Jerry and I whisked Lenny away. We carried him to the upstairs bathroom where he toppled over. His head crashed into the toilet seat, breaking it. He shook uncontrollably and then vomited. Fortunately, he recovered.

One time, mother and Don took us to a house party. Late into the night after they were done drinking, we walked home. We crossed over a bridge that had a train running below it. Don picked up Jesse by the ankle and he dangled him out over the train and threatened to drop him. Don and mom both laughed while I pleaded for Jesse's life. After begging for what seemed like an eternity, Don brought him back up. I clutched Jesse to my chest but I was so weak from fear and anxiety that I could hardly stand. Jesse cried all the way home.

Mother and Don liked to play cards but one night they were caught cheating by their drinking buddies. Everyone involved was yelling, screaming and swearing. Lying in bed I could hear furniture and beer bottles being thrown and crashing. In the morning we crept downstairs to find the apartment trashed. Amid spilled ashtrays, broken beer bottles, and smashed furniture was mother and Don passed out on the floor. Money lay everywhere. We quickly picked up the money and ran to the Dairy Queen. We were all hungry and knew mother wouldn't be buying food with it. When we returned, mom and Don were awake and sitting on the couch, but the apartment was still a mess. Mom asked me to hold a cold washcloth over Don's broken nose. She always tried to get us to like her boyfriends, but it really never worked. I disliked holding the washcloth on his face; I disliked being near him. He smelled of stale alcohol, cigarette smoke and sweat.

When Don came over, mother sent us upstairs with orders to be quiet. She didn't like to be disturbed when she was with her boyfriends. The only time we were ever sent to bed was if she had a boyfriend over. Otherwise, she really didn't care about our bedtime. One night when she sent us up early, my brothers and I were talking across the hall. Don heard us and marched upstairs. He had a short fuse and from the loudness of his step I could tell we were in trouble. He screamed that if we knew what was good for us we better shut up. Then he went after Duane. Duane's bloodcurdling screams went on for what seemed like an eternity. After Don went downstairs I ran to Duane to see if he was okay. I tried to comfort him the best I could but he sobbed and sobbed. I yelled downstairs that I was telling our dad what Don had done to him so Don better watch out. Mother ordered me to shut my mouth or she would take care of me. We didn't see much of Duane after that incident. If I allow myself to go back to that place in time, I can still hear Duane's screams today.

On another occasion, a different boyfriend of mother's came into my bedroom to say goodnight. I pretended I was sleeping. He removed the covers, kissed my crotch and left. I remember feeling scared and sick to my stomach. I crawled under the bed and slept there the rest of the night. I worried that he would come back but fortunately, he never did. I never told anyone about this incident.

One Friday night mother left to party with this same boyfriend and didn't return until Monday afternoon. It was normal for mother to leave us alone while she went out with boyfriends or girlfriends; but this was the first time she had disappeared for an entire weekend. I didn't feel scared and truthfully, it was a relief not to fear her rage at night. Jerry and I handled things. We gave Jesse and Lenny a bath on Sunday night. I took the boys (three and four) with me to my first grade class on Monday. Jesse and Lenny sat on each side of my desk and went through the lunch line with me. Amazingly, nobody questioned this. When we arrived home from school, mother was there. She said her boyfriend had left her in the woods without any clothes.

Winters were difficult because we never had appropriate clothing. One time I froze my hands on my way to school. A student working in the nurse's office placed them in hot water to warm them up. My screams sent the nurse running in. She quickly removed the hot water and replaced it with lukewarm water. My hands bother me in the winter to this day.

Food was always in short supply and mother rarely cooked. One morning Duane attempted to make Cream of Wheat because we were all hungry, but because he didn't possess any cooking skills, the cereal turned to cement. We were all sad when he threw the pan out on the curb.

When I was seven years old, I stole Twinkies from the store on my way home from school. We were all hungry and needed something for supper. Mother, still drunk, woke to find us kids devouring the Twinkies. She roared that no kid of hers was going to be a thief, so she marched me back to the store to confess my crime to the manager. I explained to him that I didn't mean to be a thief but sometimes we were hungry. I'm not sure what the manager thought about my mother's drunken condition, but he thanked me for coming forward and being honest. As my mother headed for the door, he leaned down to me and softly said, "If you're hungry again, come in and see me, I'll find you something." Then he winked at me. For a long time after that, I worried that grandma Elma would find out that I had stolen. As religious as she was, she wouldn't approve of it. While I never stole again, sometimes when Jerry was really hungry, he would sneak an ice cream bar and eat it in the grocery store.

When mom allowed dad to visit us, he was often taken out of our apartment by the police. With the separation we were super lonesome. When they were both drunk they would fight and mom would call the police. I remember one time the police burst in just as he was kissing me goodnight. They roughly handcuffed him and dragged him out to the police car while I cried.

Mom took me to visit dad in jail which was a very traumatic event for me. Mother said he hadn't paid child support. There was a screen between my father and me. I put my hand on the screen and so did he. We both sobbed.

IN THE FALL OF 1966, MY FATHER moved to Minneapolis to be near us. Dad worked a variety of odd jobs. Mother frequently sent us to his place of employment to borrow money from him. When dad visited our apartment, he often brought groceries or sacks of fast food. Mother cussed at him about the fast food. She referred to it as slop and wouldn't let us eat it. One time she knocked the food out of his hands. Dad retaliated and backhanded her in the face. She lay on her back and kicked him. He grabbed her leg and twisted it until it broke.

IN THE SUMMEAR OF 1967, Jerry and I and sometimes Duane began spending the summers in Alexandria with my dad's family. Those were the wonderful times. I worried about my younger brothers being left alone with mother, but it was a wonderful break for the three of us. Grandma Elma or whatever relative we stayed with fed us regularly. We were never hungry like we were with mother. We felt safe for three months. It was a relief not to live in fear. Grandma taught me about honesty, hygiene and appropriate behavior.

I have very fond memories of Grandmother Elma. She requested I wash up each evening before bed, something I never did at home. Often I said I was clean even if I wasn't. Cleanliness had never been a concern of my mother's. One time grandma checked behind my ears to see if I was telling her the truth, and she found a huge wood tick there. She said, "You lied to me," and I could tell I had deeply disappointed her. I felt sad about disappointing her after all she had done for me. I washed every evening as she requested after that.

One time I swore at some kids in the neighborhood. I had learned some pretty choice words from my parents. Grandma called me into the house and told me my behavior wasn't acceptable. I responded, "It's okay when I'm home with my mother." Grandma held my cheeks in her hand and squeezed. She said, "I don't care where you come from. You can act and behave like a decent human being." I got the message that swearing was not okay.

I possessed poor table manners. I ate wherever I was and with whatever utensils I could find. Once I left the dinner table to go to the bathroom. Grandma frowned at me and said only animals go to the bathroom while they eat. I asked grandma when I was supposed to go to the bathroom, and she advised me of more appropriate behavior.

Aunt Victoria taught me how to wash out my underwear by hand so I could wear clean underwear every day. Again, this was something new to me, but I liked it and used it at home.

One of the final summers I spent with grandma, she had bunion surgery on her feet. I had always slept in the same bed with her but after the surgery she said her sore feet coupled with advancing age meant I'd have to sleep in my own bed. Devastated by this, I pleaded with her to let me stay with her. I always felt safe lying next to her. She agreed to let me sleep on the floor by her bed. She teased me that she was going to step on me in the night. Sometimes I woke up to her rubbing my tummy ever so gently with her feet and we'd laugh. These are wonderful memories of time spent with a grandmother I loved dearly.

One time when we still lived in the same town as grandmother, Jerry and I made mother angry. She chased us five blocks to grandma's house. Jerry dove under grandma's large wooden stove and I ran into the bathroom. Mother was close behind us, but grandma met her at the door and blocked her way. Grandma said to mother, "You will not hurt these children in my presence." Mother turned and marched away. As mad as she was, she didn't cross grandma.

The end of summer was always a very sad time. I shed many tears as the day approached when I had to leave and return to mother. After we returned home, it took us months to make the emotional transition to our regular lifestyle again.

When I think of Grandmother Elma, I think of small chocolate stars, the round peppermint mints she kept by her bed, and Paul Harvey. I can walk down a candy aisle in a store and smell this combination of chocolate and mint, and it brings a sense of calmness and a smile to my heart.

After grandmother's noon meal, she read the bible for about an hour, and it was understood that everyone was to be quiet while she kept in touch with her spirituality and heart. We respected that. She represented strength, kindness, love, and compassion to us, but most of all honesty, respect, and spirituality. She has been and will always remain my role model. Grandmother Elma passed away in 1993. I miss her and her gentle all-knowing smile; however, she remains deeply in my heart. I will continue to do my best each day to make her proud of me.

IN 1969, WHEN I WAS EIGHT, we moved again.

Mother entered treatment two months later. Crystal, an elderly woman who was paid by the county to watch us during this time, was in charge. Crystal was a kind lady, but she struggled to maintain order and discipline. Crystal refused to answer the door when dad came to visit, causing extreme chaos because we wanted to see our father. Her concern was that we would leave with him. She was right; there was a very strong chance that we would have.

Treatment failed. Mother's behavior became more erratic and violent because she no longer just drank beer, but also vodka. The level of abuse escalated. Mother still saw Don plus she dated other men. I didn't like any of them, and her abusive behavior didn't diminish with men present.

One snowy winter night, we woke to mother kicking and swearing at us. Mother forced the boys out of the window and onto the snowy roof with just their underwear on. She closed the window, all the time cussing and swearing at them. Mother got in my face and ordered me not to let them in or I would get it worse. I didn't know what to do. She eventually stumbled away and resumed drinking at the kitchen table. When I thought she had passed out, I tiptoed to the window. She woke up and caught me. She grabbed me by my hair and flung me into the wall, giving me a bloody nose and lip. Then for some unknown reason, she let the boys come back in. Eventually, she passed out. Although the boys shivered for a long time after, they seemed okay the next morning.

Her rages were becoming frequent so it was never safe to go into a deep sleep. Unfortunately for us, most occurred in the middle of the night because she was passed out during the day when we were in school. I was so afraid of falling asleep, I quickly became sleep deprived.

When I was able to fall asleep, I was often awakened by mom grabbing and twisting my hair and dragging me from room to room. It was impossible to resist with her clutching my hair. More than once I landed on my back and had the wind knocked out of me. I'd try to hold on to my hair to keep it from hurting too much, but when she dragged me around, gobs of hair fell out. At times, she held my head down and kicked me in the stomach or face. It was understood between and Jerry and me that we had to keep Jesse and Lenny safe. For that reason we took the beating so they wouldn't have to.

If father stopped over with a meal or some groceries, she kicked us under the table extremely hard if she didn't want us sharing some particular information with him. Mother's frequent kicking of my shins produced loose bone chips that still affect me today.

My father was a short, stocky man, always wanting to prove his strength, especially after he had been drinking. Once he broke a beer can in half with his bare hands to show us how strong he was. The can broke in half and the can's ridges cut deeply into the underside of his forearm from his wrist to the inside of his elbow. Blood was everywhere. We scrambled to give him something to wrap his arm in. Jerry and I begged him to go to the hospital but he laughed us off. To this day, I am amazed he didn't bleed to death.

Father was extremely jealous of mother's boyfriends. If he showed up drunk and one of mom's male friends was there, he would provoke a fight. We didn't have a phone to call for help. One night he broke mother's nose and I ran to the neighbor's to call an ambulance because we didn't have a phone.

One time when I came home from school, I walked into the apartment to find father in the hall lying in his own vomit. For a minute I thought he was dead. I cleaned him up and helped him walk to the couch, where he passed out. Mother wasn't home which meant she was out drinking or trying to borrow money.

One Christmas we had a small tree. It was covered in decorations we made in school. The joy it brought to our home was temporary because during a fight, the tree was knocked over and destroyed. During the scuffle, mother broke her leg. Jerry rode with mom to the emergency room while I stayed behind and tried to console my father and younger brothers. Father cried about how ugly things were between him and mother. I felt helpless because I didn't know how to help. The yelling, hitting, cursing, and physical violence traumatized our family continually.

WE DIDN'T GO TO SCHOOL REGULARLY. I have few memories of being in school, but one memory stands out. I was in second grade and my class was rehearsing Christmas carols. We were singing the song "Silver Bells" when my teacher asked me to go to the office and take a phone call. Fear and dread overwhelmed me. I was certain my mother or father had died. A woman from hospital was on the line. She nonchalantly said, "You need to tell you mother that your father is in the hospital and is not expected to live. He has more alcohol in his body than he has blood."

I was numb and not quite sure what to do with the information. I walked back to class, sat down at my desk and finished out the day in school. Later that evening I told my mother. She said she hoped he died. I never prayed so hard my entire life as I did that night, pleading for my father to live. I wanted to tell him how much we needed him.

Around this time, a Social Worker, Peter Brinda, took an interest in our family. Mother never answered the door when he came around. We always kept our door locked and we'd hide, on mother's orders, whenever any Social Service people showed up. I was often truant because I disliked how the teachers and others whispered about me and the pity I detected in their eyes. I met their gazes with strong defiance.

Many days I took Jesse and Lenny to the park just to get out of the house. Mr. Brinda started showing up with small treats. He'd ask simple questions to earn our trust. I found him to be kind and not at all like mother described Social Service people. He'd ask if we were hungry, when we last ate, or if we had any clothes that fit us. He'd ask why I didn't attend school. He seemed concerned about us and I started to look forward to his company. I didn't share information about myself, but I shared how I felt about my brothers being hungry. I expressed my worry about leaving them home with mom while I was at school because they were not old enough to fend for themselves. He complimented me on what a good sister I was. I felt great pride and assured him I did the best I could to keep the boys fed.

I never shared with mother that I talked frequently with Mr. Brinda. I looked forward to meeting him in the park because of the kindness and compassion he showed to us. Since mother's behavior was becoming increasingly bizarre it was safer to avoid her as much as possible.

Jesse and Lenny became very adept at following my directions. They were quiet when I told them to be quiet, they were still when I told them to be still, and they ran when I told them to run. My role was to keep them safe because if I didn't, who else would? I carried this role into adulthood.

One morning I checked on mother before I left for school. I usually did this to see if she was all right. She was in the guest bedroom, passed out. There was blood everywhere. I tried to wake her, "Mother, wake up! You're hurt! You're bleeding badly. We need to get you to the doctor!" She didn't wake up at first and I became frightened. I cried and yelled louder. Finally she came to and backhanded me, sending me crashing into the wall. I cried and wiped my bloody nose. I asked if she was dying and needed a doctor. Mother shoved me out of the bedroom as she called me names—"Stupid-ass kid, you don't know anything you dumb shit! I have what women get monthly, I'm not dying you dumb ass."

I was sure she didn't realize how hurt she was, which had been true on many other occasions. As I pleaded with her, she became angrier. She hit me again, and this time I landed on the floor. She ordered me to clean my face and get my ass to school before welfare found another reason to come to the house. I left sobbing and crying, afraid that she might die. Instead of going to school, I spent the day in the park.

I remember one time my father brought over raw hamburger and asked that I fry it up into burgers. I found a pan and because I was still pretty small, I stood on a chair to use the gas stove. Dad walked by and tickled me. I jumped off the chair and he chased me and tickled me. It was fun. We were both laughing. Then he put me back on the chair to continue frying the hamburgers. He repeated this game two or three times but the third time he caught me, instead of tickling me, he leaned next to my face and said, "You're just like your mother, you won't do anything without a piece of ass." The mood changed. This was the first time I felt afraid of him, but I didn't know why. I wasn't even sure what he meant, but the way he said it, the look in his eyes and the alcohol on his breath—my senses told me the game was over and something frightening had taken place.

My mother's drinking increased and so did her abusive behavior. We often found her staring at the ceiling in a drunken haze, mumbling incoherently. Up to this point, the really violent behavior occurred in the middle of the night; but now, she started behaving that way when we came home from school. Asking her a simple question could enrage her. Extra caution was required at all times.

It was impossible to please mother. She demanded we make her tomato soup with lots of pepper, then would complain there was too much pepper and not eat it. She had us light her cigarettes on the stove. She smoked Pall Mall cigarettes with no filters. The writing on one end of the cigarette let us know which end to light.

If we lit the wrong end, she became livid and called us names. "How stupid could you be if you don't even know how to light a cigarette?" she would scream. She attempted to hit us, but she would miss because she was so drunk. She mumbled and looked at the ceiling for hours. We were afraid to go to bed with her still awake because she might pass out drunk with the cigarette lit between her fingers.

One night I sat in the bathroom and watched mother get ready to go out. I thought she was so beautiful. She put her shoulder-length hair in pin curls and this left her hair wavy and lovely. Mother had coal-black hair and a perfect complexion. The only make-up she wore, and all that she really needed, was lipstick. With a pretty dress on she looked beautiful. I pleaded with her to stay home. She smiled and assured me that she wouldn't be gone long, but it always ended the same...always. Mother returned in the middle of the night, her lipstick smeared, her hair a mess, her nylons torn, and scratches and bruises on her face. When I watched her stumble to the couch and pass out; she didn't look pretty anymore.

Late one night, my father decided our family should to for a drive. I suggested we go to Aunt Anne's so I could visit my cousin Lisa. Dad and mom were very drunk and dad thought I said Alexandria instead of Aunt Anne. Se we drove in the middle of the night to Grandma Elma's home about 150 miles away. She cooked us a meal and put us all to bed. I don't know if we missed school, but it didn't matter. My parents made drunken decisions based on what they chose to do at the moment. Nothing and I mean nothing, interfered with what they decided to do when drunk.

MOTHER ENTERED CHEMICAL DEPENDENCY treatment and this time our Grandmother Stella took us in. She was not an affectionate person. She and her husband had bad tempers that flared up constantly. Adding four children into their lives didn't improve their dispositions one bit.

Grandmother wasn't much of a cook. One day I smelled something odd in the kitchen. I looked in the kettle on the stove and to my surprise and disgust; she was boiling a pig's tail! It had the skin and hair still on it. My brothers and I were used to eating ketchup sandwiches, peanut butter and jelly, and lots of canned soup. After seeing that pig's tail, a ketchup sandwich sure sounded good!

My mother's sister, Anne, lived about two blocks from Grandmother Stella's house. She had pictures on the wall of two children that I didn't know. Mother told me that Social Services had removed the children. Anne had four other children—Lisa, Joseph and two babies. I loved to hold the babies and rock them. Aunt Anne had a terrible temper; she was even meaner and nastier that my mom. I felt sorry for my older cousins. They always had new bruises or welts on them. When Anne was angry, she hit her children like my mother did; but, when she was feeling really mean, she would beat them with an electric cord.

While staying at my grandmother's, I walked to school with Lisa. Once when she came to pick me up, I was clowning around and touched her back. She winced. I asked her if she had received another beating, and she said yes. I asked to look at her back and when she pulled up her shirt, I saw open, bleeding wounds. Lisa started to cry. I gently pulled her shirt down and told her I was lucky that mom was in treatment again. Grandma mostly yelled, but she didn't hit me. I suggested that Lisa go to the school nurse. Lisa didn't want to. She was afraid they would call her mom, and she would get a worse beating when she got home. I argued that if we asked the nurse not to tell because it would make things worse, she wouldn't tell. Lisa reluctantly agreed. The nurse promised she wouldn't tell anyone. Afterwards, with the soothing ointment on her back, Lisa didn't look like she was in quite as much pain.

Lisa and I walked home from school together that day. I turned at my grandmother's and Lisa continued on home. My grandmother met me at the door. She was visibly upset and ordered me to stay inside because Anne would be calling me. "Anne is very angry!" grandma said. She shook her head and said she couldn't help me out of this one. I knew in an instant what had happened. The nurse had called Anne anyway, even after her promises.

Ann worked nights as a dishwasher at a restaurant. I knew she probably had been called at work. I figured both Lisa and I were in serious danger. Lisa was right; we should have kept her beating to ourselves. Instead, I should have snuck her medicine from Grandmother Stella's medicine cabinet. I had done this before. I was very worried for Lisa and also for myself. Dad didn't have a phone, and I didn't know how to find his apartment. Mother was in treatment, so she couldn't protect me. Anyway, I knew mother would be angry that I interfered with Lisa and Anne. I had no one to call and nowhere to go.

I nervously sat at the kitchen table waiting for Anne to call. Grandma sat at the other end of the table, but she didn't look at me or talk to me. She just shook her head as if to indicate how wrong I had been. My brothers who were playing in the other room didn't seem to sense that I was in deep trouble. I sat quietly. Any little noise startled me. Finally, the phone rang at 9:30 pm. Grandma answered it and handed me the receiver. It was Anne.

Reluctantly I took it from her. Anne yelled at me and said I was in deep trouble. She wanted to know who I thought I was taking Lisa to the nurse. She said when she came home I'd be punished severely. She went on and on, and I was so numb with fear that I could hardly understand what she was saying. She said when she came home she was going to "whup" so hard on me; she'd make sure I'd never walk again, and then maybe I'd learn to mind my own business.

Anne reminded me that my father wasn't around and couldn't help me. She then slammed the phone down. By this time, my legs were so weak I could barely stand. I desperately tried to think of a way to escape. I knew grandmother wouldn't allow me to leave but even if I could where could I go. I had no doubt that I would receive a terrible beating. I had seen what she had done to her own children, and I had never heard Anne so angry. I believed that I wouldn't be walking away and she was right, there was no one to help me.

After setting the receiver back in its cradle, I walked back to my chair like a robot and sat down more frightened than I had ever been. Grandmother said nothing, but continued to look at me with her cold stare. I knew she wouldn't help me.

After a while I started to doze off in the chair, but my head falling forward woke me up. Grandmother had not moved. I asked her if I could go lay by my brothers. I promised I would stay awake until Anne arrived. Grandmother agreed to let me join my brothers who were sleeping on the floor. I wished I was anywhere else. I wished I hadn't taken Lisa to the school nurse. So many wishes, but it was clear wishing wasn't going to change the situation now.

I lay down by my brothers and watched them sleep. I cried silent tears. When I heard grandma shuffle into the bathroom, I knew it was my only chance. I whispered to my brothers that I would be back for them, then quickly changed my clothes and snuck out the back door. It was winter and very cold, but I didn't take time to dress appropriately. I walked about six or eight blocks to the drugstore on the corner. I knew it was late, but I couldn't think of anything else to do or anywhere else to go. I went into the store to warm up and walked around for some time, keeping a close watch on the window.

The clerk startled me when he asked me if I was going to buy something because he wanted to close up. I lied and told him I was waiting for my mother but that I could wait outside because she would be coming soon. I went outside and remember feeling so cold and alone, without a coat, and no one to help me. After standing outside for a time, a police car drove up. The officer asked me why I was out so late. I lied again and said I was waiting for my mother. The policeman didn't buy my lie. He instructed me to climb into the car and tell him again why I was out so late and where my parents were. He seemed so big and the car looked so warm and inviting that I didn't argue. I crawled into the back seat, the metal mesh separating us. I began to cry and everything that had happened began to spill out. I shared with him that my mother was in treatment and that I didn't know where my father lived. He asked for grandmother's address and I gave it to him, but I cried and pleaded with him not to take me back there because of the danger that awaited me.

The police officer laughed. As he slowly drove past grandmother's house, I could see that all the lights were on. The officer said, "See, your grandmother and aunt are worried about you. Go in.

Everything will work out fine." He was certain my family was concerned about me and would be happy to have me back safely. Again I cried and pleaded with him not to make me go back there. I knew Anne would be even more livid now.

The police officer drove around the block and slowed down at the house again. I insisted that as soon as he opened the door, I would run and this time no one would find me. Finally, disgusted with my behavior, the police officer called the local orphanage. They were to contact Social Services in the morning to decide what to do with me. I was afraid of where I was going but more afraid to return to grandmother's home.

I arrived at the orphanage very late that night. The staff wasn't pleased with my late arrival. I heard the police officer tell a staff person that he didn't know what else to do with me.

The admitting clerk wanted to know if I had bugs. The police officer responded that he hadn't noticed any on me. The officer left and the woman in charge roughly grabbed my arm and led me away. She swung me around so fast I almost fell down. She practically dragged me to a bathroom, where she looked at me with disgust. She roughly stripped me of my dirty clothes and looked me over. She put me in a hot bath and scrubbed me with a rough brush so hard that my skin hurt all over. She scrubbed my head especially hard and angrily demanded to know if I had any bugs. I insisted I didn't, but she kept scrubbing my head till my scalp was numb. She grabbed my arm, pulled out of the bath, rubbed me down roughly and gave me a tattered nightgown to put on. Then she roughly steered me to a bed. My skin hurt all over and when I climbed into the sheets, they felt sharp against my skin. She slammed the door and left. I cried myself to sleep all the time praying that I would think of some way to get out of this mess and return to my brothers. I missed them something terrible.

The next morning, I sat at a large dining table with other children. Most were older than I was and many exhibited odd behaviors. In retrospect, I realize they were mentally handicapped and this was their home. None of us talked while the staff went about their business. I wasn't hungry, only very tired. One staff person said that she didn't care if I ate or not; I could go hungry for all she cared. I didn't like the staff members; their angry glares made it clear that I had disrupted their routine. The children on the other hand were warm and welcoming.

After breakfast, I was told to help clear off the table. Soon they announced that I had a visitor in the lobby. To my surprise it was Peter Brinda, the social worker who had visited me in the park. Mr. Brinda smiled when he saw me and asked me how I was. I said I was fine but expressed my worry about my brothers. He asked me how I came to be at the orphanage.

I started to cry and told him how afraid of Aunt Anne I was. I expressed my fear that if I was sent back, she would severely beat me. I talked about Lisa and how Anne had threatened me. Mr. Brinda hugged me and said I didn't have to return if I was afraid. He said he would talk with my parents but I would have to stay at the orphanage until a decision could be made about where to place me. For the first time I felt relieved. I hoped and prayed that he was right that I wouldn't be sent back. While the orphanage wasn't great, it was my safest option.

The first week I was there, Mother and Aunt Anne came to visit. Mother pleaded with me to return to grandmother's home. Mother wanted to return to treatment and her plan was to send me to grandmothers. She assured me that Aunt Anne wouldn't hurt me. All the while, Aunt Anne glared at me. Fearful for my life, I ran and hid behind a staff person's legs. The woman sternly asked the two of them to leave. Unless the social worker approved it, she told Mother I wasn't going anywhere. Mother exploded and grabbed for my arm but I dodged her. Again, she demanded I leave with her. Then she threatened me and said I best leave with her if I knew what was good for me. The staff person didn't budge and finally mother and Aunt Anne left.

The next day father came to see me. He was crying as he hugged me. Through his tears he explained that I couldn't stay with him because he didn't have room and besides he had to find work. We both cried and then he hugged me once more and left. My heart sunk because at that moment I felt totally abandoned. I didn't know what was going to happen to me or if I would ever see my brothers again.

I was at the orphanage a couple of weeks. I was visited weekly by Mr. Brinda. He said he was looking for safe housing and assured me I would see my brothers soon.

One day a staff person told me that Mr. Brinda was coming to pick me up. She didn't know where I was going, but I needed to pack all my belongings.

When he arrived, he seemed like he was in a hurry. He informed me that my step-grandfather, Stella's husband, had been killed in a car accident. I was to go to a safe place, but we had to leave immediately, while everyone was at the funeral. He was taking me to live with my dad's sister, Aunt Rita. My brother Duane was already there. I was happy to hear I would be with Duane because I hadn't seen him in a long time. I wondered what he would be like and if he remembered me. I would also be close to Grandmother Elma, which thrilled me.

I was very nervous because I didn't know Aunt Rita well. I hoped she would like me. I knew she didn't have any children of her own. I also knew that in the past, she drank at the bars with my parents whenever we visited her.

We stopped at a mall to pick out some new clothing. Mr. Brinda asked the clerk to find me a pretty dress to wear and to throw away the clothes I had on. I remember the dress, socks and shoes very vividly to this day. The dress was cotton, a soft pastel plaid with a wide bib-type collar. The sales lady took me to the dressing room and gave me the dress and a slip to try on. I stood there looking at the dress and the slip. I knew how to put the dress over my head, but I didn't know what to do with the slip. I didn't know if it was another dress, or how I was supposed to wear both of them at the same time and if so, why.

After a time, the sales lady came in to see what was taking me so long. I expressed my confusion about the two dresses. She explained the purpose of the slip to me. I put it on, but it didn't feel right. She assured me that this was the proper way to wear a dress. I felt sad that I didn't know how to wear a dress properly. My anklets and shoes were white. With the outfit, I almost looked like some of the girls at school. Studying my reflection in the mirror, I knew that my aunt would want me.

Mr. Brinda took a comb from his pocket and combed my hair. He said he hardly recognized me, that I looked like a princess. I felt like one too. He said he knew there was a little girl in there and smiled warmly at me.

When we arrived at Aunt Rita's, my brother Duane ran out and we hugged each other for a long time. My aunt gave me a hug and said she was glad to have me. After Mr. Brinda and Aunt Rita talked for a while, he asked me to walk him to the car. He said he had to leave but that he would check up on me to see how I was doing. I became very sad. I had come to trust him. I asked him to check on my brothers to make sure they were okay. He hugged me and promised to monitor them. A deep sense of sadness overtook me as he drove away.

Chapter Two
Separation

I CAN'T REMEMBER MUCH of my stay with Aunt Rita and Uncle Hank. My aunt was not a warm or affectionate person, and her husband Hank acted angry all the time. I don't think he wanted us in his home. Most nights they stopped off at the bar before coming home and then they continued drinking at home. Duane and I were given a list of chores to do every day. My chores consisted of ironing, dusting, vacuuming, helping with meals, and clean up. My aunt was a perfectionist. Duane and I were verbally reprimanded with abusive language if our chores were not done to her or Uncle Hank's standards. They were rough and impatient. I found it difficult to know what it was they wanted from me, which left me open to more verbal abuse. I cried myself to sleep many nights. I missed my brothers and worried that they were in danger at Aunt Anne's.

I WAS EXPECTED TO GO to school every day. Mr. Brinda suggested I enter the fourth grade. Social Services couldn't find any records of what grade I was in or if I had even gone to school. Because of this, I was held back a grade. Education had taken a distant backseat in the concerns of the adults in my life.

Duane and I rode a bus to school. I found it difficult to fit in with my classmates on the bus and in the classroom. I struggled with math. Uncle Hand and I sat at the table in the evening and he used flash cards to quiz me. When I answered incorrectly, as I often did, he yelled and banged his fist on the table and called me "dumb" or "stupid." He'd throw the cards on the floor and storm out. I cried after such explosions, still I sat there until he returned. Then we'd start the flash card routine again. The more he yelled and grew upset, the more nervous I became. I'd start to cry again, then my crying made him angry, which made me even more nervous and I made more mistakes. The result was always the same – angry outbursts, name calling and throwing the cards across the room. This scenario happened every evening. I often heard Aunt Rita and Uncle Hank yelling and cursing at one another during the night, and I assumed it was about Duane and me.

The painful ritual of homework was an everyday occurrence. Because my schooling up to this point was spotty, I struggled with most aspects of education. I had never been read to as a child and no one had ever encouraged me. I quickly fell behind my classmates. Learning was hard for me. I grew to think of myself as dumb as did most everyone else in my life. Those expectations didn't help.

I didn't have any friends at school. This was most likely due to a number of factors. I know I didn't work hard at making or maintaining friendships. I missed my brothers and worried about them constantly.

Aunt Rita had a small dog she took everywhere. Grandmother was very fond of this dog and spent a lot of time with her. When the dog died that summer, Aunt Rita asked me not to tell grandmother because it would make her sad.

During the summer, grandma watched me while Aunt Rita was at work. The love and respect she showed me was a welcome respite from life at my aunt and uncle's. One day, grandma asked me where the dog was. I said nothing. Grandma asked me if I heard the question. I said yes, but that I wasn't supposed to say anything. This was difficult because I shared everything with her. Grandma gently said I could confide in her. I broke down and told her the truth. Grandma was very sad, but she hugged me and thanked me.

When Aunt Rita came to pick me up, I played outside while she and grandmother talked. Aunt Rita came outside and angrily yelled for me to get in the car. She was livid. She slammed the car door, lit a cigarette and stared straight ahead. She said that when I arrived home, I better do my chores and they better be done right. That's all she said. I couldn't figure out what she was upset about, so I remained silent.

Once home, I walked from the kitchen to the living room, while Aunt Rita looked through the mail. Almost casually and without looking up, she asked me if I had told grandma about the dead dog. I lied and said I hadn't. As I walked by her, she swung and hit me in the face so hard I fell to the ground. She leaned down and yelled in my face that I was a liar and that I had no right telling grandma about the dog. She demanded to know why I was so ungrateful after all she had done for me. I smelled alcohol on her breath. She screamed that she disliked liars and I better get out of her sight. I was frightened and longed to be with my brothers. At least there I knew the rules and understood my world.

Duane struggled with our living arrangement. He snuck away every chance he could, and they were angry with him most of the time, but it didn't seem to bother him. Duane often told me not to worry about Rita or Hank. He wanted to live on his own. I often saw Hank roughly pushing Duane up against the wall or giving him difficult chores to do. I tried to help Duane with his chores but this made Rita and Hank angrier.

I kept to myself and didn't share any feelings or thoughts with my aunt or uncle. I learned not to ask questions. I did as I was told, and only as I was told. I wholeheartedly believed that by behaving in this manner I would reunite my family.

Duane and I were weeding the garden one afternoon when a car pulled into the yard. It was Peter Brinda. I was excited to see him and to hear information about my brothers. Much to my amazement, Jerry, Jesse, and Lenny leapt out of the car. We hugged each other for a long time. We were all so excited to see each other. I hoped that they were going to stay with us, but Mr. Brinda said they were to stay with Aunt Victoria, another of my father's sisters.

Aunt Victoria had two grown children of her own but was willing to take my brothers. I asked Mr. Brinda why he removed by brothers. He said mother hadn't been feeding them and they were in danger of starvation.

ONE MORNING AUNT RITA SAID SHE wasn't going to work and I was to go to grandma's house for the day. She insisted I iron clothes before I left. I did as I was told. Later in the morning, Rita called me into the kitchen where she was sitting having a cigarette and a cup of coffee. I told her I wasn't done with the ironing yet because I knew how she felt about me leaving tasks unfinished. She said it was okay and that she needed to talk to me. This seemed odd because she hadn't talked to me since the dog incident.

I cautiously walked towards her and she insisted I sit on her lap. I could sense that something wasn't right. She had never asked me to sit on her lap before. She wasn't a warm, cuddly person. I was scared. She said that a social worker was coming to pick Duane and me up because she couldn't keep us anymore. She began to cry.

I was confused. What had happened? Had I done something wrong? I hadn't lied, I'd done my chores, I didn't understand.

I wondered if my brothers would know where I was. I wondered if Peter Brinda was moving us or someone else. I wondered if Grandmother Elma knew I wouldn't be coming during the week to see her. She would be sad like me. Would I ever see her again?

I hadn't seen mother since the orphanage, and I worried about her. I hadn't heard from my dad either. Maybe they were still angry with me for not returning to Grandma Stella's home. Maybe they didn't want to see my anymore because I had run away. My mind was spinning with so many unanswered questions. I hoped that all of us would be going home to mother soon.

Duane and I rode silently in the car as the social worker, someone I'd never met, described the foster home we were going to. She was very informative and said this would be a good home. The family had housed many foster children over the years. Duane and I said nothing. It worried me that Mr. Brinda didn't come.

SEVERAL LARGE, BARKING DOGS followed our car up the driveway to the Johnson home. There were cows in the pasture and a large barn. We followed the social worker into the house. Betsy and her young daughter greeted us. She welcomed us and offered us homemade coffee cake. Betsy and her daughter were dressed simply. While their home wasn't fancy, it smelled good.

Betsy and the social worker talked briefly of our history with our parents. I disliked having strangers talk about my mother and what went on in our house. I felt my anger rise. However, Betsy glanced warmly at Duane and me while she talked. Her smile seemed sincere and her eyes were kind. Shortly, Betsy's husband Elroy and her two boys, Sean, thirteen, and John, nine, came in from outside. Elroy smiled a big smile and took his hat off and wiped his brow. He requested something to drink from Betsy. Betsy asked if we would like something. Duane and I declined. Elroy had a loud voice, and he smiled as he spoke to us. He asked Duane and me if we would be staying for a while. We looked at the social worker for guidance and she responded that we were. But she didn't know for how long. Elroy asked if we were city folk or if we knew how to milk cows. We didn't of course, and he gave us a big grin. The social worker assured him that we were both good workers.

The sons looked at Duane and me with angry eyes, while they followed their father outside. I strongly sensed that the boys didn't want us there. I knew I best keep to myself during our stay. I wasn't interested in having their parents be my parents. I had parents and I was certain we would be reunited soon.

At this point, I didn't know if my brothers were okay or even where they were. I presumed they were still with Aunt Victoria but

I didn't know for sure. I knew my parents and Peter Brinda wouldn't approve of us living in this foster home. The only reason I ran away was because I didn't want to be around Aunt Anne. Fear drove me away. That was the only reason I left. As soon as mother returned home from treatment, I was certain we'd all be together again.

I devised a plan. I'd be patient, do as I was told, be good, and then they'd return me to my mother. I reasoned that my running away from Aunt Anne was the cause of all these placements. If only I could speak with Peter Brinda, I knew I could convince him that I belonged home. Besides, I knew how to take care of my brothers and cook and clean so mother wouldn't have to do so much. Mother would be glad to have us back; she must be missing us terribly. I was worried about her, worried about who she could talk to when she was sad, as she so often was. Who was protecting her from all of her abusive boyfriends? Who was helping her to bed, checking up on her in the morning? Who was making sure she didn't fall asleep with a lit cigarette? In my mind, I was convinced that she needed her children to help care for her. I knew mother had to be working with Peter Brinda to bring us home. I was certain of it.

I never saw Peter Brinda again. I don't know why he never came back. I trusted him. He helped and cared about us and promised he would return. Had he forgotten us too?

The new social worker had us bring in our clothes, and then she left. Duane and I were with strangers.

Betsy showed us to our room and gave us a tour of the house. She brought out a photo album and showed us all the foster children she had taken care of over the years. She pointed out some that were grown and still came back to visit. She spoke fondly of these children and said she was happy to be a part of their lives. Betsy was a very kind person. She walked us outside and showed us the farm.

Elroy motioned for Duane to join him and his sons. Betsy walked with me back to the house. She asked me if I would help her make supper. While she cooked I played with the baby. This made me miss my own brothers even more. I hoped they were being loved and cared for by Aunt Victoria. My eyes filled with tears, but

I had learned not to show anyone when I was sad or tearful. To the outside world, I felt I needed to appear okay.

After a while she turned to me and said I was an answer to her prayers. She had always wanted a daughter and now God had brought me. Startled, I reminded her that she already had a daughter, the baby I was playing with. Betsy told me that she had prayed for a long time before she had her daughter, and sometimes it takes God a little while to answer prayers because he has so many to answer. I knew she was trying to make me feel better but I really didn't think I was the answer to her prayers. I wasn't sure I wanted to be. I had prayed too, prayed to be with Grandmother Elma. Was this His answer? I didn't think God would just drop me out in the country where no one knew me or could find me. Grandmother Elma talked with God a lot too and she knew how to pray since she was a little girls. I was convinced God listened to my grandmother's prayers first.

Soon the family and Duane came in the house to eat. Duane didn't say much. He looked at me and then looked down. I knew he was unhappy and didn't want to be with this family. I wanted to go back home with mother while Duane longed to be on his own. He struggled with people trying to parent him. He had taken care of himself most of his life. So had I. Looking at him I could tell that trying to be a part of a family that was already a family felt as awkward to him as it did to me. And seeing the sad looks directed at me stirred up my anger. I didn't need people to feel sorry for me. These people didn't know anything about me. How could they? They never asked me about myself. I hated seeing pity in people's eyes; how I hated to be looked at like that.

Betsy was a good seamstress and while we were there, she sewed many outfits for me. Slowly, I began to look like other children. Betsy and Elroy gave us allowances for the chores we did. The money was kept in baby food jars on a shelf in the cupboard. After I earned a certain amount, Betsy asked me if I wanted to learn how to pay the piano like her son John. John complained about practicing, but they insisted he take lessons. I agreed, and soon I was playing the piano. I didn't mind practicing which was good because I needed to practice a lot. Eventually, I was entered in a recital where I played a short selection by Bach. Afterwards, I was given a small statue of Bach's head. Betsy had sewn me a very pretty dress for the recital and afterwards she told me how proud she was of me.

I went to a small country school and rode the bus. I realized even though I looked more like other kids, I still didn't fit in. I had difficulty making friends. I didn't have much in common with them. Besides, I was living on hold, patiently waiting for mom, dad, or Peter Brinda to pick me up. I usually sat on the playground during recess and watched everyone play. I had taken my brothers to the park to play but I wasn't very good at knowing how to play myself. I didn't know the games children played or their simple rhymes while they jumped rope. Plus, I reasoned that if I made friends, they would want to know why I wasn't living with my parents and I didn't want to talk about that. Since I'd be returning home soon, there wasn't any point in making friends.

I soon learned the extent of Sean and John's anger. When Betsy and Elroy went to town and left us alone, the boys taunted me. They swore and called me names. I tried to stay out of their way. I didn't want to be moved again, so I tolerated their behavior. One night, Sean stabbed me with a pencil in my right arm between my wrist and elbow. The wound was deep enough that the lead stayed in my arm. I think this scared him and he avoided me for a while, waiting to see if I would tell on him. I didn't, but to this day, I have a small bluish scar from the lead.

I found it difficult to stay quiet and not tell the boys what I thought of them. I think they mistook my silence for fear. Because of this, they continued with their verbal and physical attacks. My shoulders were sore most of the time because they found delight in slamming me against the walls. Though I hurt, I never let them see my cry. They also tripped me and pulled my hair and often trashed my personal belongings. I didn't tell their parents because I knew the boys would deny it and would inflict greater pain on me later. The boys were clever enough only to bully us when their parents weren't at home. One time Duane saw Sean push me into a wall. Duane grabbed Sean and told him to leave me alone if he knew what was good for him. The boys became careful not to push me around if Duane could see it. I kept my focus on waiting to return to live with mother. I knew it wouldn't be much longer before we were sent home.

I don't remember Christmas with the Johnson's but there is a picture of Duane and me standing next to a Christmas tree. The picture is ripped in half showing only Duane and me, so I must have torn off the portion of the picture with the boys on it.

Eventually, I received news about Jesse and Lenny. They were now residing at the Alters foster home. When we arrived, they were playing on tricycles and laughing. They promptly ran to me. After a long hug they showed me their bikes. I told them that we would be going home to mother soon and the toys probably wouldn't come with us. They seemed sad at this news, so I changed the subject and no more was said about going home to mother.

After a short while, Duane and I received news that we were being placed in a new home. I don't really know why we left Betsy and Elroy's foster home. Betsy told me they kept foster children until they were adults, so I don't know why the decision was made to move us to another foster home. I believe the intent may have been so we all could be together. I don't know if the Johnson's or Alters understood that our placement was only temporary. We were never given a reason for the change. We were powerless over the decisions made by adults. Jerry came to live with Duane and me for a short time at Johnson home. Then Duane returned to Aunt Rita and uncle Hank's home, while I joined Jerry, Lenny and Jesse in our new foster home, the Flynn's.

PAULA FLYNN WAS TWENTY-TWO AND CARL WAS TWENTY-SIX when they took the four of us into their home. Jesse and Lenny moved in first. Jerry and I joined them later. One day before we moved in, Jerry and were taken to the Flynn's to meet them. Carl was giving Jesse and Lenny a ride on a riding lawn mower when we drove up. They hopped off and ran over to hug us. I missed them terribly. I resented the fact that strangers were caring for them. My brothers were little and needed caregivers yet my trust in adults was almost non-existent, except for my grandmother.

The social worker visited with the Flynn's while I played with the boys. I was anxious to ask her when we would be returned to our mother. I prayed this would be a very short placement. I overheard her speak my parents' names and our names. During the car ride home, the social worker asked Jerry and me if we liked the Flynn's and offered to let us visit with our brothers for an entire weekend in the near future. I was excited about seeing my brothers again soon but I was sad at the same time because I suspected this meant we weren't going home anytime soon.

True to her word, the visit with Jesse and Lenny was set up. On that drive to the Flynn's, the social worker said that we needed be on our best behavior because this was our chance to live with our brothers. The Flynn's wanted a test weekend and if it went well, then there might be a chance they would agree to take all of us.

After the weekend visit, the Flynn's had three days to decide. They had been married for five years and didn't have any children of their own.

My mind was whirling. The social worker didn't say anything about returning to mom, only that we could all live together at this foster home if we behaved and the Flynn's liked us. I was devastated. This was not what I wanted to hear or what I anticipated. I didn't want to move into another foster home. I wanted to go home. I quit listening to the social worker and looked out the car window as tears ran down my cheeks. My brothers and I didn't belong in foster homes. They didn't understand us. These were not our homes.

We always had to act the way the adults thought we should and always be grateful and appreciative of what they did for us. I rarely felt grateful or appreciative. Either they had their own children or they wanted to make my younger brothers their children. My brothers were not their children. We belonged to our parents. We had a family; we had parents, and they needed us. The foster families didn't need us. I believed they took in foster children to look good to others and for the money the county paid them. At different times I overheard some of the foster parents' family members caution them about us with statements like: "You don't know what you're getting yourself into," or "Did you think it over carefully because these children will be a handful. They come from a troubled background." I was aware that mother didn't follow through the way the social workers wanted her to, and that she cussed and swore at them when they made her angry, but we knew who we were with her. Plus, I knew she needed us back. This was all wrong.

There was a court hearing regarding our custody. The Flynn's were not there, but Grandmother Elma and Aunt Victoria were. We sat in a room with them at the courthouse, which was large with big chairs and wide halls that echoed when you walked down them. I stayed close to Grandmother Elma. I was told the hearing would determine if we could live with mother again. We all sat and waited for mother to arrive.

I was extremely hopeful that we would be going home soon. We had been separated from mother for a long time. Mother was expected to stay sober for six weeks, and then she could regain custody. With great anticipation, I watched for her out of one of the windows, while my younger brothers sat on my grandmother's and aunt's lap, hopeful of our future back with mother. Grandma and Aunt Victoria hugged and kissed us and said how much they missed us. Suddenly, I saw mother at a distance. She had come! I was so excited to see her. I knew she couldn't see me in the window, but I watched her as she slowly came closer to the building. She was smoking and I was about to tell my brothers that she had arrived, when I saw her stagger. Mother was drunk.

My heart fell while tears swelled in my eyes. How could she do this to us? She could have come sober today, this one day, and lied that she had been sober all along. Why hadn't she tried? I couldn't look at my grandmother or my brothers. I knew today was not the day I would be going home, and I didn't know how to hope anymore. Didn't she know we wanted to be with her? Didn't she like us anymore? Didn't she miss us? Didn't she know how much we despised our foster homes? Didn't she know that we belonged with her?

Eventually, mother appeared. My brothers ran to her and hugged her. I watched her, our eyes met, and she looked away. We were called into court and the Judge's decision was for us to stay in foster care.

I was numb. Everybody was crying. I had no more ideas or hope. I wanted to be alone. I went into the bathroom, found a stall, closed the door and sat on the floor hugging my knees, rocking back and forth, crying. Eventually, Grandmother Elma found me and held me. Through her tears, she told me she loved me.

The decision was made for Jerry, Jesse, Lenny and me to live with the Flynn's. Everyone through we should be grateful that a home was found for all four of us to live together. For that I was happy because I didn't think I would have fared very well emotionally without my brothers. So, in August of 1970 when I was eleven years old, I entered the Flynn foster home. All of these changes meant I had to repeat fifth grade.

THE SCHOOL WAS THE SAME ONE I attended when I lived with Aunt Rita and Uncle Frank. My former classmates were now a grade ahead of me. I felt deeply embarrassed about this and hoped they'd forgotten me. I asked my foster parents if I could call them Mom and Dad. They seemed quite pleased about the request and said they would be honored, but I only asked this so the other kids in school wouldn't ask questions about my biological parents. I behaved the way the social worker and foster parents wanted me to. I still held onto the hope that mother would miss us enough to fight for our return. If she really wanted us back, which I believed she did, she would work on her sobriety.

Mother called a few times in the beginning of our stay at the Flynn's. She'd be drunk and call late. Because we cried and became upset after talking with her, the phone calls came less and less often. I don't know if mother stopped calling or we weren't allowed to talk to her. I overheard a phone conversation between Paula and Social Services asking for permission to screen out the calls mother made to us. She said it wasn't good for us to speak with our mother when she was drunk.

I was angry, but I had become accustomed to stuffing my anger deep inside. I needed to talk to mother even if she was drunk or sad. I needed to know she still cared about us. Later I discovered that our visits with our grandmother and other relatives were extremely limited by Social Services and our foster parents because they believed those visits prevented us from getting on with our new lives and brought back too many memories for us. Supposedly, these decisions were made with our best interest in mind and that, when we matured, we would understand. I didn't understand then, and I don't understand now. I suspect the real motive was that our emotions were easier to manage for the foster family with less involvement from our biological family. But that didn't make our emotions go away. I felt unlovable and unimportant to those I cared about.

We slowly adjusted to our life at Carl and Paula's home. I was able to connect emotionally with Carl's dad. He was elderly and lived on a farm run by his older children. He was very kind to me and was especially good at talking me out of my stubborn moods. He could make me laugh. He loved to play cards and taught me many card games. He told me I could call him grandpa because he liked that. I looked forward to visiting the farm. They had cows, pigs, and acres of farmland. I enjoyed being away from people. Carl had a brother who had ten children, and one of his daughters was my age and was in the same grade. Her name was Denise. She was kind and simple, not uppity or fancy like many of the school kids. Denise's family was financially poor because of all the children in her family. She never asked why I was in foster care, and we enjoyed each other's company when we were together. Denise had a physically handicapped sister so I think she knew what it felt like to be teased by kids. She didn't wear fancy clothes or fancy hairstyles, like me, and she didn't seem to fit in with other kids. We became instant friends. Denise visited the farm most weekends. We enjoyed spending time together playing or doing chores. It was peaceful at the farm because I felt like I fit in. I enjoyed the animals, especially the cows and pigs.

I was verbal and often spoke without thinking. I was argumentative and very stubborn. I was regularly sent to my room for talking back to my foster parents. I wasn't allowed to come out until I apologized for my words. That's where the stubborn came in. I sat in my room all day and all night if I didn't believe what I said was wrong. I wouldn't apologize. This frustrated Carl and Paula to no end.

One Sunday when we were going to the farm, I had back-talked to Paula and I was told to sit in the car until I apologized. This was hurtful because I liked being at the farm. I sat in the car for a long time. Pretty soon the grandfather came out and asked me if I would like to play cards. He said he had been looking forward to my visit all week. I tearfully told him what I had done. He kindly asked if I would apologize which I did. I spent the rest of the day with him. With a twinkle in his eye, he said I was the best card player he knew. At the end of every game, he folded his hands over mine and thanked me for spending time with an old man. He gave me food for the kittens in the barn. He knew I loved tending to them in the barn. He was a blessing for me during this difficult time.

Although my relationship with Carl's dad was very good, I did not bond well with Carl or Paula. They represented a barrier between my mother and me. Plus, I harbored anger for their limiting my time with my grandmother and hindering my reunification with my mother. I also think Paula and I were too close in age. She didn't know how to parent me. Truthfully, I wasn't very easy to parent. I believe their parenting skills were quite limited plus they lacked the ability to handle children with special needs. I didn't trust them. I knew they mostly wanted Lenny and Jesse to be their children, not Jerry and me. Jerry seemed to be adjusting okay in school and made friends with some kids who were also outcasts. Jerry and I both did what we were supposed to do but in our hearts our loyalty was to our biological family. Jesse and Lenny were easier to distract and could be pleased with toys. Jerry and I had spent more time with our biological family and we still maintained hope that we would be living with mother soon.

Jesse had several medical problems. He had wandering eyes, an enlarged chest cavity and a heart murmur. He also had difficulty learning in school and had been held back a grade. He was a bed-wetter, and for this he was constantly shamed and humiliated by Carl and Paula. They scolded him in front of others, which made him sad. I did my best to shield him from their hurtful comments, but it affected him. Jesse was quite active. When he became over-excited, the Flynn's placed him in the corner even if people were over. Jesse didn't realize it, but his actions showed how ashamed he felt. I was angry at his treatment. If I spoke up and questioned their behavior, I was sent to my room. While his shame and hurt were obvious to me, they were oblivious to it. He tried so hard to please them.

We had many pets. I had a black female rabbit. She was very gentle and soft. Carl purchased a couple of Shetland ponies and a donkey. My brothers and I enjoyed the animals and spent a great deal of time outside with them.

Jerry had a special raccoon that he played with all the time. He always liked odd animals. When we lived with mother, Jerry haunted the pet shop. Odd animals that didn't sell, they'd give to Jerry. He had an alligator that he stayed up all night petting with a wire coat hanger until the alligator allowed Jerry to pick him up. He also had an opossum that lodged itself under the sink and dad couldn't get him out. One afternoon Jerry went to play with his raccoon but she was gone. I remember him being very sad over the loss. He was especially excited when Carl brought home a donkey. When Jerry would pet him, he would lay down like he was sick. He didn't want Jerry to ride him. As soon as the donkey believed it was safe, he would jump up and take off before Jerry could catch him. The donkey was fun and playful and made us laugh.

Carl purchased a Welsh pony for me to ride because I had become so attached to the Shetland ponies. However, I didn't bond with it. He was skittish and didn't mind commands. I had to be on guard because he would take off at the slightest noise.

Lenny and I spent a lot of time together playing with the animals. These memories I hold deep in my heart. We had raccoons that one day escaped from their cages. The raccoons sat in the rafters of the garage and when Jesse and Lenny entered, they attacked them. They had swollen eyes and cheeks from being scratched and bitten. It was a miracle they weren't seriously hurt. I don't remember them going to the doctor or Social Services being notified of this accident. Again, I felt anger towards my foster parents and the system for the total lack of attention they showed us.

Carla and Paula liked to drink with Paula's family. On occasion, they drank at home on weekends. This made me very moody and angry. I couldn't live with my mother because she drank, but it didn't seem to matter that our foster parents did. I didn't understand why we couldn't live with mother instead. Nothing made sense to me. The adults around me seemed to be able to make up their own rules. Why did everyone think my mother was such a terrible person? Life didn't make sense. It frustrated me that no one seemed interested in our feelings or thoughts.

Carl read about a Morgan horse for sale in the paper and wanted to buy it for Paula. We all went to look at Trigger. With his soft brown eyes and gentle demeanor, he immediately found a place in my heart. Trigger and I bonded instantly. This did not please Carl or Paula because I was supposed to ride the Welsh pony. However, Paula didn't like riding so I was allowed to take him out on long trail rides. I loved being outdoors with Trigger. I spent hours petting, grooming and talking to him. I liked him more than people. Trigger provided a much needed emotional release for me. My fondest memories of foster care were the times spent with Trigger. He listened when I told him about how much I missed Grandmother Elma and how I didn't understand why mother hadn't come for us. He was truly my best friend.

Paula and Carl bought baby rabbits for us to play with. I was excited until I discovered that the male rabbit was mean to the female. He tugged on her until he pulled her fur out. Carl and Paula explained that this was how rabbits mated. Because it reminded me of my mother and what happened to her when she returned home with her boyfriends, I pleaded with them to take them away, which he did.

We also owned goats. I milked them as part of my morning and evening chores. I learned that with goat's milk you didn't need to use any eggs in baking because the milk was so rich. Over time, our hobby farm had a dog, horses, a donkey, rabbits, goats, raccoons, baby bear cubs, and fawns.

I quickly became aware that adults said polite words to our faces, but looked at us with pity and whispered about us. I heard words: "Isn't it a shame," and then a more judgmental discussion of my parents. Anger remained a constant in my body language, my eyes, and in my heart. Sometimes I remember being so angry that I became emotionally exhausted, but I knew it wasn't safe to show others I was vulnerable. Adults thought they knew what was best for me, but they knew nothing. They didn't talk to me, so how could they know? I continued to hope that we might return to our parents. I was certain I would figure out a way to make that happen.

Jerry loved country music. When we lived with mother, she found some money and bought him a guitar. When mother had friends over, she asked him to play and sing. The combination of alcohol and country music made her laugh or cry. The songs brought out strong emotions in both my parents. Songs about relationships, cheating, divorce, drinking and fighting seemed to mirror their lives. My parents emotionally related to them. After hearing a song, mother might start crying or become angry; depending upon what memory was triggered. My dad liked the son "Ole Shep," about a boy and his dog. The dog dies in the song and this made him cry every time. Other songs stirred up anger in him. Certain songs triggered his need to show his strength by breaking something or being belligerent with mother.

Even today, country music can emotionally affect me like it did my parents. When I listen to country music, it stirs up many memories of my parents and my childhood.

We were visited by a male social worker a few months after we moved in with the Flynn's. I was with the animals when he arrived. He had his briefcase and didn't look much older than Duane. He pulled out some papers and asked if I was Karen. He asked me if I could tell him why I was in foster care because he hadn't had time to read my file. Just the sight of him made me angry. I told him my mother had some problems with drinking but she was working on being sober, and we were to join her soon. The social worker said okay and left. I don't know who else in the family he talked to, but I never saw him again. It would be years before I saw a social worker again. Whether they were in contact with our foster parents, I don't know. I was never told.

Chapter Three
A Roof Over Our Heads

I REMEMBER ONE VISIT WITH MOTHER in Minneapolis the first year I lived at the Flynn's. Mother met Jerry, Jesse, Lenny and me at the bus station. At the time, she was living with an elderly man she called gramps. Mother must have been in her late thirties or early forties, while he was in his sixties. The attraction most likely was because he owned a bar. Mother's apartment was small with one bedroom. She said she was his waitress at the bar. Mother and gramps drank almost the whole weekend we were there. They argued loudly. The sound of broken bottles disturbed our sleep. I sat behind a door hugging my knees and crying. I felt confused. I wanted to be with mother, but I didn't want this. She swore at us and slapped at us just like before. She still talked to herself and looked at the ceiling. Life had not changed for her in any way.

She seemed older now. She wore glasses and didn't smile very much. It was clear to me that mother no longer needed us and purposefully was not making any efforts for us to return to her. I was angry and disgusted with her. Jesse and Lenny slept on a tattered love seat. I slept in a rocking chair, and Jerry slept on the floor. Gramps and mother slept in the small bedroom.

Mother had no idea what it was like for us being away from her, and she didn't ask. She was very belligerent about Social Services and our foster parents. After the visit, I was glad to return to the foster home, but this confused me too. I didn't know where I fit in anymore. I didn't fit at the foster home and it was clear none of us fit with mother. When it was time for us to leave, mother seemed sad, but she didn't ask us to visit again. I don't recall any more visits to see her while at Flynn's. My yearning to return to her was no longer an intense emotion or deeply felt goal. I made the decision to be compliant with my situation. I no longer had anything to pray or hope for.

I did okay in school. On one outing, my class took a field trip to the fire station. Our teacher requested that we all write a thank you note to the fire chief, and she would pick the best one to send to him. My thank you note was picked. For one of the few times in my life, I felt proud.

I was apprehensive to start sixth grade. Students were tested on all the states and their capitals and a failing grade meant being held back. In preparation, I frequented the school library to gather information. I was afraid I might fail, afraid I couldn't learn as well as my classmates. My hard work paid off. I not only passed the test, I answered every question correctly.

I was friendly with all my classmates but still kept to myself. My best friend was still Denise. I received an S- in conduct because I talked too much. One time, the teacher moved my desk next to hers to eliminate my incessant visiting with other students. Her solution didn't work because she found herself visiting with me instead. Eventually, she moved me back to my regular spot in the classroom.

We rode a bus to school. When the bus picked us up, it was at the end of its route, so it was already full of students. There were unspoken rules on the bus. Older kids sat in the back, while the younger kids sat up front. Usually most every seat was taken; still the bus driver insisted we all find a spot.

There was one particular boy who was a grade younger than I was but quite a bit bigger. No matter where we sat on the bus to or from school, he moved from his seat and sat near us in order to call us names. I instructed my brothers to ignore him. I was worried that we would be moved to another foster home if we caused trouble on the bus.

One day, the bully started his name calling. When it was time for us to get off the bus at school, I had my brothers go in front of me. I then turned around and punched him in the nose. He was surprised, lost his balance, and fell to the ground. He yelled that I gave him a nose bleed – he had a small trickle of blood on the side of his nose. The bus driver ushered us all off the bus and requested that I wait. I looked over at my brothers standing on the sidewalk waiting for me. I was worried that I had ruined everything.

There was a strict rule of no fighting on the bus, but I couldn't take it anymore. When the last student exited, the bus driver came over to me. I looked down at the ground, worried about what would happen to us. I had reacted without thinking. Then he did the most amazing thing. He leaned down and asked me what had taken me so long. Startled, I looked up at him, and he winked! Then he became serious and said that as punishment, my brothers and I were to sit directly behind his seat for two weeks. A great sense of relief flooded over me.

I started menstruating in sixth grade. I was outside playing softball when I sensed the change. I had seen films on menstruation, but I wasn't emotionally prepared for it. I noticed the discoloration on my pants and asked my teacher if I could go to the nurse. I was extremely frightened and embarrassed. I asked the nurse if she would call Paula because I wanted to go home. I told Paula that I didn't feel well.

I waited outside for her to pick me up. I didn't say much, but the school nurse told her what happened. Paula matter-of-factly stated that this happened to all girls as they developed into women. She said it was a fact of life and necessary in order for women to have children.

I said nothing. My mind was whirling about what kind of woman I would be. Would I be like mother? Would I want children because I was like my mother? Would I drink too much and not care for them like she did? Would I hurt them? I decided I didn't want any children because I didn't want to be like her. I didn't want to treat my children the way she had treated us. I didn't want my children to be afraid of me.

Tears came to my eyes as I imagined myself as my mother. My thoughts were interrupted as we pulled into the driveway. Paula told me to change my clothes and come downstairs. She said she'd show me the necessary supplies that women used. I didn't want to come downstairs. I wanted to stay in my room and be by myself. Fear of what the future held filled my mind. Eventually, I went downstairs and Paula met me in the bathroom. She explained about tampons, but I was not hearing her. She told me to try one and if I needed help to let her know. She left the bathroom. I held the Tampax and sat on the stool, crying. After a period of time, Paula yelled from the kitchen to inquire as to how it was going? I didn't want to talk about it with her. She came into the bathroom and told me to take of my pants so she could help me. I didn't want her to touch me or to see me naked. I felt vulnerable because I couldn't control the situation.

She tried different ways to help me, but none of them worked. Finally, she became frustrated and threw the tampon in the garbage. I was in tears. She angrily said I would have to figure it out myself and she stormed out the door. I felt deep sadness because knew I wasn't like other girls. I felt different.

I left the bathroom and went upstairs to my room. After a while Paula came in. I could sense her anger and disappointment. She said she was taking me to the drugstore to buy sanitary napkins since I couldn't figure out how to use tampons. I didn't want to be seen buying them, but she insisted I go with her so I would know how to buy them in the future. Either that or I had to make a serious effort to use tampons. I apologized and suggested that maybe there was something wrong with me. She sighed and drove me to the drugstore. I was embarrassed and ashamed. I begged her to please not to tell anyone what happened. She curtly said this was the day I became a woman and I should be happy about it. I didn't see anything to be happy about. I wondered if my mother would be glad I was turning into a woman.

When my brothers came home from school, they wondered what was wrong. I lied and said I was ill, which really wasn't a lie. I was doing homework at the table when Carl approached me and said: "I hear you're a woman now." He patted my shoulder and walked away. I didn't look up because I was so ashamed that Paula had told him. This was no one's business but mine. I was very angry with her and knew I couldn't trust her. Our relationship basically stalled from that point on. I was nothing more than a child placed by Social Services. I never talked with her about my feelings, about school, or anything important to me. I sensed she didn't really care anyway.

Like most students entering seventh grade, I worried all summer about the changes about to occur. I worried I'd look foolish and not be able to find my classrooms. In particular, I obsessed about gym class. I knew that students had to take showers after class. This bothered me. I didn't undress in front of anyone because I was certain I was different than other girls. Jerry was going into the ninth grade and he told me he to ignore him. He didn't want his friends to know I was his sister. I knew he was trying to act smart, but I lost a lot of sleep over the transition into junior high.

We had to line up to receive lunch tickets. I hadn't paid any attention to lunch tickets before until one of my classmates pointed out that my ticket was a different color than everyone else's. I tried to blow off this discovery by saying it must be because I was special. The comment by my classmate bothered me. I went to the school office and asked why my lunch ticket was different from the other students and why mine was free. I was told my ticket was a different color because I was a foster child and thus eligible for a free lunch.

I felt so ashamed. Why was I different from everyone else? I began skipping lunch, so I wouldn't be reminded daily how different I was.

I met a girl who was shy and appeared awkward around other students. One day we ended up walking side by side and she offered me a piece of gum. Some male classmates walked by and teased her because she was so shy. She ran off. I became angry and verbally taunted the boys about their appearance. Eventually, Jan and I became friends. I was more social than she was, but we both preferred to stay away from large crowds.

Jan and I talked mostly about school, horses, and generic things. I didn't share personal information about my mother or foster parents, and she didn't ask.

I'm certain we celebrated every Christmas at the Flynn's, but only one stands out in my memory. I received a pair of white fashion boots, similar to the ones that all the girls wore. They were too small but I didn't mind if they flopped about. I finally owned something that made me fit in. I was extremely excited to where them but because I was so worried that they would be stolen during gym class, I wrote my name on the inside of the leg portion in big blue letters. The next morning when I went to put them on, I discovered the marker had bled through the material. They were ruined. I cried about those silly boots for a long time. I wore them at home all the time, even though I couldn't wear them to school.

I don't ever recall believing in Santa, but my younger brothers did, so I was happy for them when they received presents. To me they don't hold many special memories at all.

We took a few short family trips in the summer. I believe we went to the Black Hills and another time we traveled to Colorado. Once on a trip to Iowa, a friend of mine came along. That is a fond memory.

Jerry became restless at the Flynn's'. The Flynn's did not attend church regularly. They were Catholic, while we were baptized Lutherans. We attended the Catholic Church with them on holidays. I believed that it didn't matter what church you went to as long as one tried to do what was right. God knew everyone's heart. Jerry had stronger feelings about his religion and he wanted to attend the Lutheran church and be confirmed.

In June of 1974, Jerry left partly for this reason. He was sixteen, and I was fifteen. When he left the Flynn's, he was placed in a different foster home for a couple of weeks. He was then allowed to go to Minneapolis to stay with mom. He worked at McDonalds while there; but, he found mother's drinking too hard to live with. Eventually he returned to the same town we lived in and moved into a foster home that was more like apartment living for older foster children.

I worried when he left us. I liked us being together. He and I were close, even if we had our sibling squabbles. I wasn't sure how I would do with him gone. Would the Flynn's want us all to leave? Would we be split up again and moved to another foster home? I never told Jerry that I didn't want him to leave because he needed to do what was important to him. But I wondered and worried how Jesse, Lenny, and I would fare without him

Carl and Paula were upset with his decision to leave. They barely spoke to any of us during this time. Jesse and Lenny didn't seem to understand the full meaning of his leaving. I wanted more than anything for Jesse and Lenny to have a home, someplace to come back to when they grew up, someplace they fit in. I tried extra hard to please the Flynn's by talking back less. I tried to make an effort to let them know that we wanted to stay. This additional effort was solely for my brothers' benefit. The Flynn's would never feel like home to me. By this time, my brothers had adjusted and it would be difficult to split us up or move again. They needed stability if nothing else. I was angry at Jerry at first for not considering what his decision meant to the rest of us. But I knew he didn't move to be insensitive; he wanted to do something he believed in. This transitional time was very difficult for everyone.

I tried to help Carl with jobs that Jerry had usually done. I was something of a tomboy anyway, and I liked to be outdoors. I felt that the Flynn's would keep us if I was able to pick up the slack. I did my best to ease the stress and bring back some balance to the family, but I missed Jerry very much. One time I walked down to the pasture and found Carl leaning up against the fence. I was going to ask him if I could go riding when I noticed he was crying. I asked him why he was so sad and he said he missed Jerry. I tried to console him by saying that Jerry needed his own church, and that he wasn't trying to hurt anyone. Carl thanked me, walked over and gave me a hug and kissed me on the mouth.

I backed up and looked at him in disbelief. He said, "I'm sorry," then he gave me permission to go and ride. I didn't take time to saddle my horse. I was confused by what had happened. I thought he must have acted impulsively because he was so sad about Jerry leaving. I tried to put the incident out of my mind.

If we had done something to upset Paula during the day, Carl disciplined us after he came home from work. He would scold us and take away privileges and/or assign extra chores. My crime was generally for back-talking to Paula. Carl might send me to my room, which didn't bother me, or take away my horseback riding privileges, which hurt something awful. Many times he tried to reason with me and asked me to curb my sharp tongue.

I didn't see Jerry the rest of the summer. When school started, the Flynn's forbade us from visiting with him. They had contacted the school and informed them that Jerry was not allowed to see us. Jerry was no longer welcome in their home and could not come to the house to visit us. This made me really angry. They continued to try to control who we cared about and who we could see just as they had done with our other relatives. Jerry was my brother; no one was going to tell me I couldn't see my own brother. I kept my thoughts to myself, however, and made my own decisions concerning him. I didn't want to jeopardize my status with Carl and Paula. However, Jerry was still my brother, and nothing and no one was going to change that.

One day, the school nurse asked me if I wanted to earn some extra money. She said the nursing home was looking for a student to do odd jobs. I was excited about the opportunity, applied for the position and was hired.

The nursing home staff and residents were very kind to me. I immediately loved the job. I especially enjoyed conversations with the residents. I missed Grandmother Elma so it felt good to be around elderly people. Most of them had soft, warm smiles and twinkles in their eyes. After I had worked there about nine months, the nursing home staff suggested I become a CNA. I signed up for classes and after two weeks of training I was put on to the regular schedule.

The other way I made money was babysitting – fifty cents per hour, no matter how many children. I loved taking care of children, especially babies, and it provided money for school clothes and other items. I liked paying for my own things. Having the Flynn's pay made me feel as if I owed them. I also worked in the school cafeteria so I could earn a free lunch. I no longer had to present tickets that were a different color from everyone else's.

Many of the cafeteria women were elderly. They regularly sent me home with carrots, celery, and apples for my horse. He waited in the pasture near the bus stop because he knew I carried treats. He looked forward to seeing me and I looked forward to seeing him. Hardly a day went by when I didn't ride him before or after school.

I did my best to make the transition easier without Jerry. When Paula and I went school shopping, she insisted I buy a dress. She said I needed to wear more dresses to present myself as more feminine. Dresses were uncomfortable to me. Plus, I saw how boys at school looked and talked about girls in dresses. I tried to avoid any attention from males. I was quite plain, with straight hair with bangs. I was five feet, four inches tall, weighed about 100 pounds and was barely developed. I looked more like a small boy than an adolescent girl. I didn't wear any makeup; Carl and Paula forbid it anyway. I was allowed to wear mascara when I turned sixteen, but I didn't really see the point of putting on something I couldn't see.

When Carl came home from work, Paula requested that I put the dress on and show him how it looked on me. I had an uneasy sense about how he looked at me. However, he agreed with Paula that I was growing into a beautiful young woman. His comment made me extremely uncomfortable.

One September night, I was home alone with Carl. He had fallen asleep on the couch while watching TV. I gently woke him and told him I had finished the house chores and wanted to go riding. He slowly sat up. After a little while, he stood up and walked over to my chair and knelt down in front of me. He said he was growing to care about me more and more every day. I was uncomfortable and sensed things weren't right. I responded that it was good we all cared about one another. Then I changed the subject and asked if I could I go riding. He gently touched my arm and said he cared about me more than a daughter. I wanted to leave, but I didn't know what to do or what to say. I just nodded. He then leaned over and kissed me on the mouth and said, "That isn't so bad, is it?" Startled, I stood up and said I was going riding.

Time passed and nothing more was said. I tried to put the whole incident out of my mind and stayed busy with my activities. I tried to avoid Carl because I was very confused about what his intentions were. I felt uneasy around him. It wasn't long before he started rubbing my shoulders or kissing my neck when I stood at the sink doing dishes. He said I looked pretty and asked me about my day in school. I had the urge to bolt out of the room when he did this, but how would I explain to Paula why I didn't finish washing the dishes?

I hoped Carl's behavior would stop, but it didn't. One day he visited me in the small barn while I was with my horse. He hugged me and kissed me and told me how attractive I was and said he knew I cared about him too. He asked me why I never expressed my appreciation to him for all he had done for me. As I pulled away, my knees trembling, I reminded him that he was married and this wasn't right. He said he couldn't help it because he thought of me all the time and wanted to spend time with me. He tried to reassure me by saying he still loved Paula, but he loved me too and that he wanted to show me how much he loved me. When I resisted, he said I should be thankful he considered me a special person, especially considering my childhood.

The angered immediately swelled up in me. With a trembling voice I told him I didn't think it was necessary to have to prove how much one cared about someone else. The conversation made me sick to my stomach. Carl shrugged it off and suggested I take a long ride and think about what he had said. He hugged and kissed me again and left. I knew what he was suggesting and I was afraid of what was going to happen next.

Over the past couple of weeks, I was aware he had defended me to Paula on numerous occasions when I had argued with her. He begged her to be more understanding. It didn't appear that she noticed the special attention he was giving me or how I avoided any room he was in.

Carl and his brothers loved deer hunting. It was a major family event each fall. Carl approached me a couple of days before the opening weekend to tell me I'd be going with him. He was very excited and said this would provide the opportunity for us to show each other how much we cared about one another. He said, "You do care about me, don't you?"

I became tearful as I told him I did care about him but this wasn't right. He said there was nothing wrong with showing someone you cared about them. I pleaded with him to reconsider. I told him that I had never been with a man before and if Social Services found out, they would remove me from the home. Despite my many protestations, he calmly assured me there was no reason to be afraid. But I was afraid; the most afraid I had ever been in my life. He said he knew a secluded place where he could take me. No one would need to know.

From that moment on, I found it difficult to focus no school or anything else. I became very moody. The days raced by, and I grew more fearful as deer hunting weekend approached.

When the day came, the entire hunting party met at the predetermined spot in the woods. The children were placed strategically and instructed to watch for the signal to being banging their coffee cans. Carl told the group that he was taking me to his deer stand because he wanted to give me an opportunity to shoot a deer. He was anxious to put my gun training to the test. Everyone teased me about my first hunt. We split from the group and my heart was heavy. I prayed as we walked that he would change his mind. But he didn't. When he heard the children bang their coffee cans, he took off his outer jacket and placed it on the ground. We had lots of time he said. I was emotionally numb and found it difficult to stand. As he lowered my pants, my y mind raced, desperately trying to think of an escape. I tried to think where could I run and who I could tell, but who would believe me? I felt like a robot.

As the assault began, I felt a sharp pain. I winced. He said he would try to be more careful but it was difficult because he was so excited to be with me. I'm certain he didn't notice the tears falling down my cheeks. When he finished, he stood up and noticed blood. He appeared shocked. He said, "I would never have guessed you were a virgin considering where from where you came from." This made me very angry. He pulled me up and said I needed to dress quickly. I was very sore and felt very dirty. After I dressed, I sat on a tree stump for a while. He was very quiet. He said we had to rejoin the group before the others became suspicious. He kissed me and thanked me for showing him how much I cared about him.

I was numb as we walked back towards camp. When we met up with the group to eat lunch, I told them I wasn't feeling well. Carl offered to take me home.

We were silent on the drive home. He reached over and squeezed my hand and said I would be fine and that he would talk with me later. I said nothing. Paula questioned why I came home when I loved being in the woods. Carl said I didn't feel well. I went up to my room and lay down. I had no thoughts and no emotions. Later I went downstairs and took a shower and tried to wash off the dirty feeling. I scrubbed as hard as I could, but I couldn't get the feeling to go away. I returned to my room and went to bed. This was the beginning of an emotional nightmare that lasted four and one half years.

Carl didn't make any advances toward me for about three weeks. I tried to convince myself that the one incident was the end of it. I tried my hardest to put it out of my mind but it was always lurking just below the surface. I said nothing but remained moody and rode my horse every chance I could. Carl allowed me to ride anytime I wanted to now. Many days I dismounted, sat by a tree and cried. I cried for what seemed like hours. Trigger stood close by me, my best friend in the world.

Paula didn't share my love of horses, which meant I could ride alone. Jesse and Lenny were more interested in big trucks and spent their time constructing semi rigs out of cardboard boxes. Time alone was a welcome respite during this painful and difficult time.

About four weeks after the incident in the woods, Carl approached me in the barn. He asked me how I felt and if I realized that our relationship was a special one. He said no one else would understand how we felt about one another and that it was important that we didn't talk about it to anyone else. If people found out, they might remove us from his home and split our family. Tears welled in my eyes I was so angry. I pushed him aside and rode off. Due to the flood of tears, I struggled to see where Trigger was going. He took me to our favorite spot in the woods where we often rested. I leaned down and hugged his neck and continued sobbing. My fear was true – I could be split up from my brothers over this. How had this happened? Why had it happened? What had I done wrong this time? I stayed out until dark. When I returned home, Paula was angry. She didn't care that I had missed supper. She ordered me to finish the dishes and go to bed.

I wasn't hungry. I didn't care about supper. I went to the kitchen and she followed me, ranting about how disrespectful I was and how I never appreciated anything and how I never thought of anyone else but myself. I pleaded with her to leave me alone. She threatened to tell Carl about my behavior plus she took my riding privileges away for two weeks. I threw the dish I had in my hand into the sink and ran to my room and slammed the door. I had never felt such intense anger. I didn't care if I couldn't ride. I still could go out to the small pasture and be with Trigger, but I knew he would miss our rides as much as I would. I cursed this place; I hated everything. I hated my mother! If she had come for us, I wouldn't be here. Life was becoming more confused and chaotic. I couldn't make sense of anything. *Pretend, pretend, and pretend some more to always make everyone happy!* I couldn't do it anymore.

I was exhausted and quickly fell asleep. Jesse and Lenny snuck upstairs and gently knocked on my bedroom door. They came in and asked if I was okay. I lied and said I was fine. I promised them I would try not to argue so much. They were scared that I was going to be sent away. I assured them that wouldn't happen. They'd overheard Paula informing Carl that she was tired of my behavior. I promised them I would apologize in the morning. They gave me a hug and snuck back downstairs.

Shortly after my brothers left, Carl entered. He said that Paula was very angry with me and that it took a lot of talking by him to calm her down. She suggested that I move out. I made it clear I wasn't leaving without Jesse and Lenny because she treated them poorly. While she didn't physically abuse them, she was verbally abusive, often because she was angry with me. She mocked them and expected too much from a ten and eleven. Her expectations were unrealistic considering that no one had ever taught or guided them in so many areas.

Carl suggested to Paula that I was argumentative because I missed Jerry. He reasoned that it might be a good idea if he spent more time with me. Paul agreed. He strongly suggested I apologize to her in the morning. He then brought up the subject of driver's training. He was certain he could convince Paula that I needed a car for my job at the nursing home.

I liked the idea of having a car and spending less time with both of them. I wanted to be out of the home as much as possible. He said we'd go riding together the next day when he came home from work. When I said I'd lost my riding privileges, he said it wasn't a problem. He gently squeezed my hand and left. I became nauseous and lay down on the bed. I knew what he meant when he said he'd be spending extra time with me. I felt trapped, exhausted.

The next day while riding, Carl forced himself on me. Afterwards, he talked about his deep feelings for me and how others wouldn't understand our relationship. If others knew, they would make something to beautiful seem wrong. I didn't say anything, I was too numb. He mentioned the car again. He encouraged me not to disagree with Paula if I didn't want to jeopardize the living arrangement. As time went on, the sexual incidents became more frequent. At first it was once a month but then it became weekly. He liked to compliment me on my appearance, tell me how mature I was and allow me to smoke with him after sex.

I began to accept this as normal. It became a regular part of my life, much like going to school, washing dishes or riding a horse. I was able to detach my emotions from the physical part of me and accept this as a part of life. This is how I had coped living with my mother. Emotional detachment was how I survived in a life of emotional pain and confusion when I had no available adult or peer to trust.

Carl asked me to put notes in his lunch bag because he wanted to know I was thinking of him. Sometimes I wrote what he wanted; other times I suggested our relationship had to end. He disliked those notes and told me they upset him the whole time he was at work. He said he saved the loving notes and threw away the ones that bothered him. He scolded me if I failed to acknowledge how special our relationship was. He constantly pestered me about whether the boys in school were interested in me.

One day, Jerry showed up at school and stood outside my classroom. I told him that Carl and Paula had contacted the school to block our contact. He said no one was going to tell him he couldn't see his sister and brothers.

I desperately wanted to tell him about the sexual abuse, but I knew how angry he would become. It would only make it worse for all of us if he found out. He promised I'd see him again soon although he didn't know when.

I felt strong emotions when he walked away. I felt so alone and empty. I knew it would be difficult for Jerry to convince Social Services about altering visitation. I knew he'd try, but I didn't hold out much hope.

The sexual abuse continued until I was almost twenty years old. It became more frequent and routine. I did my best not to argue with Paula, and considering the strange, horrible circumstances, life seemed tolerable. Life goes on. At times I was confused enough that I looked forward to his company. It didn't occur to me until later that I had very little contact with anyone else during this period. Carl was angry if I spent too much time riding my horse or if I decided to baby-sit on a night he was home alone. Other times I irked him if I stayed at my girlfriend's house on a Friday night. I asked for these privileges from Paula because she wanted me out of the house. I knew she would say yes to any request. The time away from him gave me a mental and physical break.

Early in 1975, when I was sixteen, Carl told me he thought Jesse and Lenny needed a permanent home. He wanted to adopt them if it would make me happy. He didn't want to adopt me because of our special relationship. I was very excited about the possibility of a permanent home for them. He suggested I ask to have my parents' rights terminated. I didn't understand what he was asking but after he explained it to me it didn't seem like such a big deal. After all, my parents had been out of my life for a long time. What he said next cut me deep to the heart. He said my Grandmother Elma's rights would be terminated as well.

I hadn't seen Grandma Elma for a long time although she was always in my heart. Every day I tried to behave like I knew she wanted me to. I became very sad and began to cry. Carl asked me to send her a letter informing her of my wish. He also suggested that I write a letter to the court and explain why I wanted my parents' rights terminated. He was certain the court would grant my wish now that I was sixteen years old. He felt the court would agree that I was too old to be adopted. I was conflicted and didn't know what to say. He asked me to think about it. He said Paula agreed with this plan.

I seriously pondered the decision for a week. I ultimately agreed to write a letter to the courts. I also wrote a letter to Grandma Elma. That letter I will always regret, knowing the pain it must have caused her. I didn't believe in my heart what I wrote. The letter contained all the anger I felt inside against mother. I incorporated the rage I felt about having to choose between a permanent home for my brothers and accepting the relationship I had with Carl. I was very angry and confused. In the letter, I accused her of not caring about me and forgetting me. I wrote about our new family and how there wasn't room in it for her. I claimed we were happy with the Flynn's and were tired of waiting for someone to want us. I finished it with the most painful statement of all. I said I didn't care about her or want to see her anymore. Tears flooded down my cheeks as I wrote the last line.

I showed Carl and Paula the letter. They said I should hold it for a week to see how I felt at that time. I felt I had to prove I was willing to give up everything, even though I didn't have much, to secure my brothers some type of future. Writing the letter was extremely painful and stirred up old anger in my heart. I decided if Jesse and Lenny were going to have a permanent home, we should start the process and be done with it. I was convinced that if the courts thought I was too old to be adopted, it wouldn't be long before they reasoned that the boys were too.

A female social worker came to the house that summer. I hadn't seen a social worker in years. I didn't know her or have much to say to her. We all sat around the table and she asked questions like, "How is it going? Or, "how do you like school?" They were generic questions that required generic answers and little thought. After a short time the conversation moved towards the termination of my parents' rights and what was going to happen in court. The social worker didn't think my parents would object because they hadn't made any attempts to regain custody. She said that the chances of us returning to live with them were slim.

I didn't feel or think anything. Nothing seemed to matter. The social worker asked me if I understood that at my age, the likelihood of adoption was slim to none. My concern was with my brothers. I wanted them to have a home to call their own. She said she would let us know the court date and she left. Soon after, I went riding. I was gone a long time.

My parents' rights were terminated in December of 1975. There was never any more discussion about adopting Jesse and Lenny. As I look back now, I realize it was Carl's ploy to isolate me even more. I had nowhere to go or anyone to talk to. The court action cut me off from my family and any small sense of belonging I felt.

Carl no longer had to worry about me leaving and he showered me with favors. He helped me secure a loan on my first car – a white Vega hatchback with a red and blue pinstripe. It's obvious now that these were tokens to maintain my compliance and silence regarding the intimate relationship we shared. He never failed to remind me how he was taking such good care of my brothers. Without his approval, he stressed that Paula would never have agreed to let me purchase a car. Again, I was expected to be grateful. Carl wanted me to show my appreciation for all that he had done and continued to do on behalf of my brothers and me. Carl taught me how to drive the clutch, another excuse to be alone with me. I wanted the car to gain independence to free myself from him. However, he made it very clear that I had to have his permission to drive the car anywhere other than work. If he caught me lying about where I was, he took the keys.

I didn't date. My only outings were work, volleyball, school and horseback riding. When I was invited by classmates to go to a movie or other event I wasn't permitted to go. Soon they stopped asking. It was a relief not to be asked. Then I didn't have to think up lies why I couldn't go. I never bothered to ask permission to date because I knew how Carl would react. He was becoming increasingly jealous, and his conversations usually centered on my interest in boys at school. This made me angry, even though no boys were interested in me. But he didn't believe me. I asked him: Did he see me going anywhere with my classmates? Did anyone call me other than an occasional girlfriend?

I kept to myself at school to insure no boy noticed me. If they pursued me, I knew this would cause problems at home. I kept to myself at home too, other than spending time with Jesse and Lenny. This kept life as simple as possible with less tension from Carl and Paula.

Paula occasionally commented on my lack of dating, but Carl assured her that, due to being a foster child, I couldn't be expected to behave like other children. She agreed that I was a bit odd. He seemed to know how to make my behavior understandable to her.

I usually took Jesse and Lenny out to eat when I was paid. One evening I came home from work and yelled for them when I walked in the door. I thought we could go to the Dairy Queen. Oddly, they didn't respond. Paula emerged from the kitchen and said they wouldn't be going to the Dairy Queen. They had misbehaved and had been sent to their room without supper. I demanded to know what her problem was. Sometimes I felt she was mean to them just because she knew they were important to me. "How dare you send my brothers to bed without supper," I demanded to know. "We're in foster care because we didn't have food and other necessities like other children. How dare you punish them this way?"

I pushed past her, and went up to their room. I marched them right past her as we left for the Dairy Queen. I don't recall them being sent to their room without a meal after that. However, she continued to punish them by limiting the time I spent with them. This only fueled my anger with her, and conversations took place only if they had to. I worried about how she treated them when I wasn't home, because she verbally and emotionally abused them when I was home. She might mimic them by disfiguring her hands in front of her face, crossing her eyes, tilting her head or talking, and acting like she was mentally retarded. Other times, she asked them if they deserved to stay at a friend's house because Jesse still wet the bed. They had to plead with her for everything. I did my best to keep them away from her.

They were children and didn't deserve to be treated with such disrespect. They shouldn't have to beg or tolerate her rudeness for simple requests. I didn't see any parenting or nurturing. The very sight of Paula made me angry.

I worked the afternoon shift, 2:00 to 10:00 p.m., at the nursing home. It was about a mile from home. I worked weekends and occasionally before and after school. It was during this time that Carl went to work for the police department. He was referred to as a "posse" member. He assisted the police several evenings a month. Sometimes he had the officer pull me over on my way home from work and acted like it was funny. I could tell the officer felt uncomfortable about it. Carl liked to walk up to my car window and insist I go straight home. Sometimes he woke me in the middle of the night after he was off duty. These actions appeared to make him feel more powerful. It also gave him a reason to be out at night and watch me. He was obsessed with the notion that I had male friends, which I didn't.

His stalking unnerved me, but I couldn't think of a solution. Once I threatened to call Paula or a social worker about our relationship, but he laughed. He smiled and said, "If my wife finds out, you'll be separated from your brothers because she'll throw you out." Besides he added, "who in social services would take a foster child's word over his?" He had never been in trouble with the law and said community members looked upon him as charitable because he provided foster children a home. Then he produced the notes he forced me to write him—the notes claiming I cared for him. He was certain if anyone read them, they would blame me for trying to break up his marriage.

I knew he was right. Who would believe me? Who could I tell? He asked me how I thought my brothers would feel towards me after they found out about our illicit relationship. It was hopeless. I realized I was trapped in the relationship with Carl with no way out.

Jerry showed up unexpectedly one day with his girlfriend. He announced he was getting married. He and I went to the barn to talk. He said his fiancée was pregnant. Jerry had just enlisted in the army but he would be allowed to return for his wedding.

I attended Jerry's wedding, but only because I lied to Carl and Paula. Since they had forbidden any contact with Jerry, I had to fib and say I was going to work early.

Carl and Paula forbid Jesse and Lenny from attending, and they were very disappointed. I couldn't think of a way to sneak them out of the house without Carl and Paula finding out. Duane was the best man. I hadn't seen him in a long time. Jerry told me later that Duane asked who I was. I felt very sad that we had lost touch for so long that he didn't recognize his own sister. Sadly, I couldn't stay for the reception because I had to go into work. I had pushed my luck as it was.

THAT WINTER JERRY CALLED TO SAY that mother's boyfriend, Gramps, had died. Jerry asked me to go with him to see mother. He came from Alaska and we met at the bus station. I had mixed feelings because I hadn't seen mother in a long time. In one respect, I was curious and wanted to know if I was like her. Deep down I hoped she had changed and wanted to know me. Mother supposedly told Jerry that she wanted to see me. I'm not sure if mother actually said that, or if Jerry made it up to encourage me. I suspected the latter. When I met Jerry at the bus station, he pleaded with me not to be argumentative with mother.

The house looked the same. Mother sat at the table, numerous empty beer and liquor bottles surrounding her. She was very intoxicated and flew into a rage the instant she saw me. She cursed and swore at me and demanded to know why I thought I was better than everyone else. The same old scenario, the same language, the same drunken woman I remembered, only older and more fragile. Jerry, under the influence himself tried to soften her statements. "She doesn't mean what she's saying. Just ignore it. She needs us now."

Her eyes couldn't focus, her speech was slurred, and her stomach was bloated – she looked like she was about eight months pregnant. I discovered later that she needed surgery, but the surgeons wouldn't perform it until she quit drinking. The sight of her nauseated me.

I excused myself and found a quiet place to sit. I kept asking myself why I had come. She didn't need me. She didn't need anybody. All she cared about were the bottles sitting in front of her. I leaned my head back and wished she would sober up so our conversation could at least be civil. It was difficult to stuff my anger with her, especially when she acted belligerent towards me.

Jerry prepared food for her. She criticized everything he made. I wasn't sure why Jerry bothered to fix her anything at all. Later, after I had dozed off in the chair, I sensed her presence. I opened my eyes to see her coming towards me with her arms outstretched, going for my hair, all the while cussing and yelling.

I jumped up. She was only a foot away from me. I planted myself in front of her and our eyes locked. "I am no longer a small child," I said, the anger rising in my voice. "You will never drag me around by my hair or hurt me in any way again." She stood there, motionless. After a few seconds she put her hand down by her side, turned and staggered back to the table. She sat down, looked up at the ceiling and mumbled. It was the last time she ever raised her fist to me.

I couldn't sleep the rest of the night because I was too angry. The next night, Duane stopped by. I hadn't seen him since Jerry's wedding. Mother was drunk and passed out at the table. He tried to wake her, but it was hopeless. Duane appeared high and gave me a big hug. He offered to take me to a party and while I didn't really want to go it sounded better than babysitting my drunken mother.

It was a big party. Duane introduced me to his friends, many of whom were sitting around smoking pot or snorting cocaine. Duane quickly left me and went off to party. I knew this wasn't where I wanted to be either. I took a cab back to mother's apartment. She was still passed out. The next day, Jerry left for Alaska and I returned to my foster home. I left without saying anything to mother.

I TOLD CARL THAT I WANTED to attend prom with a friend, Grant. Carl was furious. I assured him that Grant was strictly a friend and wasn't interested in dating me. I reasoned with Carl that Paula would grow suspicious if she thought I wasn't interested in boys. He finally consented. Carl warned me that he'd be riding with the police that evening and he'd be watching me.

Paula insisted on helping me pick out a dress. I didn't want her help, but I needed to keep her on my side so Carl wouldn't change his mind. She said that all fathers are overprotective of their daughters, but a time comes when they grow up and leave home. She sounded relieved about the possibility of my moving out. I wanted to leave as much as she wanted me to. I realized at that moment she could be an ally of mine. I quickly hatched a plan where I would move out, rent my own place and then come back for Jesse and Lenny. I knew this would be difficult because Carl was becoming more possessive all the time – wanting to know where I was, checking to see if my car was at work, questioning me about meeting boys at volleyball. I made sure I came home early after the prom. My prom experience was tainted by the fact that I was so tense I could hardly enjoy it.

I graduated in February of 1978. I was not an exceptional student, a B average, but I had finished school and felt proud of my accomplishment.

Carl threw me a graduation party. A few of my friends and some of Carl's family attended. Carl signed one whole page in my school annual, emphasizing how much he cared about me and signed it "with love," but he only put X's for his name. I didn't care to look at my school annual after that. My one close girlfriend came to the party. Carl drank heavily, and I saw him talking to her in the corner. She glanced over at me, her eyes huge in disbelief. I froze, realizing he must be telling her about our relationship. I had told no one, and now he was telling my best friend. I hated him.

A few weeks after the party, she brought up the conversation she had with Carl. She said she understood why I didn't date in school. I was angry and tried to explain that our relationship was sick and I desperately wanted out of it. Somehow he had persuaded her that he cared for me. I'm certain he neglected to tell her how young I was when he first assaulted me. We never talked about him again.

After graduation, I worked full time as a nursing assistant. I enrolled at the technical school in the medical secretary program and began classes that fall.

Carl felt I should commute to school but I wanted to move out. This discussion created a great deal of tension in the household. Paula agreed that I should move out and experience the real world. Carl pleaded with me to stay, saying he had come to care for me as a partner and did not have the same feelings for his wife that he used to have.

Carl suggested I work at his firm during the summer. I didn't want to leave my job because I enjoyed it but he made life so miserable for all of us I finally consented. I dreaded having to go to work with him every day, knowing he was watching my every move. I grew anxious, worried that I would never break free of his control. My desperation and anger were just below the surface all the time.

ONE SPRING DAY, I came home from school and Paula and all her belongings were gone. She had moved out. I don't know what happened between Carl and her, and Carl didn't say, other than she left a note stating she was unhappy. I never saw her again. With Paula gone, I presumed Social Services would remove us, but that didn't happen. Social Services had disappeared from our lives.

One afternoon I came home from work and found Carl loading up my horse into someone else's horse trailer. I flew into a rage. With Paula gone, he no longer wanted Trigger. I was devastated. I'd lost my best friend. My mood quickly became sullen and moody. In that instant I made up my mind that the abuse was going to stop. Carl would no longer control me.

In addition to working at Carl's place of business that summer, I returned to the nursing home as well. One evening, I worked a little later than usual because I had to cover part of a shift for a co-worker who had car trouble. When I arrived home, Carl was waiting for me. He smelled of alcohol. He raised a pistol to my temple as I walked through the door and said, "I told you not to be late!"

I stopped in the doorway, terrified, but told him to shoot me if he had to. I looked him square in the eye and said I was tired and going to bed. Then I walked away. I no longer cared if he shot me; I felt dead already. He pulled the gun away, called me a few filthy names and I left.

Moments later, I heard gunshots. I cautiously walked back downstairs. I felt my heart pounding in my head. I walked towards the back of the house and found him sitting on the steps shooting at blackbirds. I remember walking back towards the steps to go back to my room, and the next thing I knew I was waking up in the hospital emergency room. The doctors told me a cyst had burst on my ovary. I knew different. I knew I had passed out, unable to handle the emotional trauma that night, but I didn't say anything. Carl never mentioned the incident again.

CARL AND I RODE TO WORK TOGETHER. I was becoming more distant and no longer hid my distaste for him and his behavior. A co-worker, AJ, had taken an interest in me. He teased me about how overprotective Carl was. He said Carl advised him to stay away from me, but he laughed about it and didn't take his threats seriously. AJ asked me to go on a motorcycle ride. I was excited about the prospect while at the same time nervous and scared. Carl warned me daily not to talk to AJ or he would have to teach him a lesson. I tried to discourage AJ, but to no avail.

AJ suggested we sneak away without Carl knowing, and I agreed. We dated, but I was leery of becoming involved. Carl had a terrible temper and I didn't want AJ to find out about my relationship with him. I felt very ashamed and dirty.

That summer, I asked Carl to transport me to Minneapolis to see my cousin Lisa. She was Anne's daughter, the cousin whose abuse I had reported to the school nurse. I had Anne's address and hoped she could tell me where Lisa was living. Carl agreed but only if I would go to the movie *Deep Throat* with him. This sickened me but I was so anxious to see Linda that I consented to his terms.

Anne was living in the same residence. The house was condemned. All the windows were broken, and I heard critters scurrying about. I yelled upstairs and a woman's voice answered. She told us to come up. I carefully climbed the steps as they weaved and creaked. There were big holes in the steps and the walls were filthy, with plaster falling off them. When I reached the top, ahead of me was a small room that was dark except for a small light. I walked towards the light. I peered in the room before entering tentatively. The room was in shambles, with a tiny bed, one chair, and a lamp with no shade. Anne sat in the chair. She looked the same, only older. She was unkempt and dirty, and there was a fragile man of color lying on the bed with his eyes shut. Anne demanded to know who I was. I told her I was Doris' daughter and that I wanted Lisa's address.

Anne looked at me like she had seen a ghost. "I'll be damned," she said. Anne gave me Lisa's address and said Lisa was married and had three children. The entire time she stared at me. I told her it was good to see her after all these years, and I was looking forward to seeing Lisa. I quietly left, carefully watching my step as I exited. Oddly, considering our past, I felt sad for Anne. She lived in a condemned house that was literally falling down around her. She looked old and fragile and unable to hurt anyone anymore.

It took a while, but we finally located Lisa's residence. I hoped Lisa had somehow risen above the despair of her mother's home. I went up to the door and knocked. A large black man answered the door and with a booming voice, demanded to know what the hell I wanted. I said I was looking for my cousin, Lisa. Two small children about the ages of two and three ran past the door. The man said he didn't know any Lisa. He grabbed the slip of paper from my hand. While he was looking at it, a rather large woman came to the door. I recognized her as Lisa. She looked the same, only older. The man threw the paper on the floor and walked away. Lisa held a baby about six months old. She quickly hugged me and said she couldn't believe it was me after all these years. I asked her if she wanted to go out for a bite to eat. Her face became sad; much like I remembered it from when she was a child. Her eyes filled with tears. In a hushed tone she whispered that her husband wouldn't like it. She introduced her three children and said she was very happy. I noticed fresh bruises on her cheekbone and around her neck. She wore a dirty bathrobe and she looked tired. Still, her eyes sparkled as we talked briefly. I could see the shadow of her husband lurking behind her. She quickly hugged me again and thanked me for stopping by. She said she couldn't ask me in. I understood her meaning all too well. I didn't want to put her in any danger, so sadly I left.

I left Lisa with a heavy heart and tears in my own eyes. She was still mired in the cycle of poverty and abuse. Her mother no longer abused her; but now it was her husband. I recognized the small child I had known years ago. It made me sad to think she knew no other lifestyle.

I have not seen Lisa since then, though I pray she will find relief from the abuse she has suffered unnecessarily. The memory of my last visit with her still brings tears to my eyes.

Carl waited impatiently in the truck while I visited Linda. He was eager to take me to *Deep Throat*. The rundown theatre was in a decaying neighborhood populated with street people toting brown paper bags. There were only a handful of people in attendance. I didn't pay much attention to the movie, my mind remained fixed on Lisa. As we drove home, Carl asked me if I had learned anything new from the movie. When I responded that the repetitive sex scenes did nothing for me, he expressed disdain. He was disgusted with my response and didn't talk to me the rest of the way home. My mind had returned to my childhood so I was grateful for his silence.

CARL WAS BECOMING INCREASINGLY POSSESSIVE AND JEALOUS. I became more distant and moody. I disliked the fact that he had control over everything in my life. I knew I only had one option left and that was to move out. I told him that I would be gone before school started and only visit on weekends. He became extremely angry and threatened to tell my brothers about our relationship. In turn I threatened him by saying I would never come back if he revealed anything to my brothers. I had tried to keep the peace with Carl for my brothers' sakes, but it was becoming more and more difficult.

Out of desperation and fear for Lenny and Jesse's safety, I made the decision to speak with Carl's police partner. I shared with him only small details of the relationship with Carl. I asked if he could help us leave Carl's house. I could tell he was uncomfortable. I made him promise not to say anything to Carl about what I had shared with him. The police officer said he didn't know what to do so he suggested I talk with the sheriff.

After work the next week, I stopped by the law enforcement center. The sheriff said he wasn't the appropriate person and referred me to Social Services. I called the director of Social Services and left him numerous messages, saying I needed to talk with him. In my message I informed him that my brothers were in danger. The director never returned my calls. After a couple of weeks of no response, I visited Social Services. I asked to see the director. The secretary said he was not taking any appointments. Desperate, I walked past the secretary and into his office. He was standing at his desk, the anger painted on his face. I told him that I wasn't trying to cause trouble for Carl, but I was concerned about my brothers' safety. I attempted to explain the sexual abuse but he didn't want to hear it. The director looked at me with cold eyes and said, "You were promised a roof over your head. That's what you got, now get the hell out of my office!"

I was in shock. There was nowhere else to turn. I went numb. I couldn't help myself much less my brothers. No one was willing to help us. I slowly walked out of the building and wept in my car for a long time. I thought about suicide because I saw no way out. Eventually, I rejected that idea. If I hurt myself, who would protect my brothers from Carl's anger? I knew I had to stay.

Chapter Four
From Carl to AJ

AJ ASKED IF I WANTED TO MEET HIS FAMILY. He said that he was beginning to care about me very much. I decided to be honest with him about my relationship with Carl, believing he would break our friendship off after hearing the truth. I felt so ashamed and damaged. AJ gave me a ride on his motorcycle and we went to a wooded area to talk.

I cried through my explanation of the sexual relationship with Carl. AJ felt sad for me and promised to help me move out of Carl's house. I was surprised by his reaction. I cried, amazed that he didn't think badly of me. To keep our relationship a secret, AJ stopped talking to me at work, but we passed notes back and forth. Carl stopped ranting about AJ because he believed he was no longer interested in me.

I suggested to Carl that I should rent an apartment near school. This would save me gas money. I promised I would come home every weekend to see him and my brothers. I raised this subject over and over. He must have tired of my begging be he eventually agreed.

The first six weeks of school were hell. Carl continually called my apartment and the school to make sure I was there. He left desperate messages for me to call him back. On weekends, he insisted that I return home, even giving me money for gas. I started a job as a cashier at a department store which meant I couldn't travel home on weekends. He was becoming more agitated because he couldn't force me to return to him.

It became a little easier to see AJ, but Carl made me account for all my time away from home, especially if he called and I wasn't there. I became exhausted trying to juggle school, work, Carl, my brothers, and AJ. I was sure if Carl found out about AJ, he would hurt him or try and punish me by hurting Lenny and Jesse. I urged AJ to break off the relationship with me. I was emotionally exhausted and losing hope of ever freeing myself from Carl.

Carl worked in the town where I attended school. He stopped by the apartment frequently. AJ and I exercised extreme caution during this period.

Once I was called out of class. The messenger said it was a family emergency. I immediately thought of Jesse and Lenny. I answered the phone in the school office and it was Carl. He said Lenny and Jesse were holding hands and he was holding Jesse's other hand. In Carl's other hand, he held a scissors. He said he would cut the extension cord and electrocute all three of them if I wasn't home in twenty minutes. Then all I'd have to worry about would be where to bury them. He hung up; I looked at my watch and bolted out of the building.

It usually took me thirty-five minutes to drive home, but it didn't that day. I cried and shook all the way, worried that he would hurt my brothers. I felt tremendous guilt about not being able to keep them safe. When I arrived, my legs were so weak I could barely stand. I ran into the house. Lenny and Jesse were safe and Carl was crying on the couch. He sobbed, saying he couldn't stand it if I didn't come home every night. Through tears he cried that my schoolwork and job didn't allow me enough time to spend with him. He admitted his behavior wasn't right but he said he loved and needed me ant that he couldn't help himself. He promised to marry me if I returned home.

I could sense that something was wrong with him, more than usual. I tried to pacify him by saying I cared for him. I had no intention of returning to his house permanently ever again. If I did, I'd never escape. I resolved at that moment to devise a plan to find an apartment so the boys could live with me.

While I tried to comfort him, my mind raced, trying to think of a way to escape this craziness. I felt trapped, burdened with constant anxiety. I felt hopeless and helpless and saw no way out.

During a weekend visit, Carl claimed he had told Lenny and Jesse about our relationship. I flew into an instant rage. He had promised never to tell the boys about us. Shame filled every crevice of my body.

That he involved my brothers infuriated me. They were young and didn't understand the nature of our one-sided relationship. I told Carl that I would not marry him. In fact, I blurted out that I had met someone and was moving out and taking the boys with me.

Carl flew into a rage and ordered me to leave. He called me a lying slut and told me never to enter his house again. I said I was leaving but not without Jesse and Lenny. He pushed me out the door and locked it. I heard him yelling that I better leave or he was going to fetch his gun. I ran to my car, tears filling my eyes. What would happen to Lenny and Jesse? I couldn't check on them on weekends and as disturbed as he was he might try to hunt me down. I was an emotional wreck. I contacted AJ. We decided that some evening when Carl was working, we'd go to the house so I could retrieve my belongings.

It was a rainy night when I returned. My brothers let me in and told me to hurry because they were concerned that Carl might catch me. They said they had never seen him so angry as the last time I was there. Lenny promised to take care of my poodle. Lenny and Jesse said that Carl wasn't angry with them, only me. They weren't afraid of him, but they had promised him they wouldn't have anything to do with me. I promised them I would find a place for us to be together. They hugged me, and I left with some of my belongings, mainly clothing. If Carl somehow determined I had been to the house, we decided the boys would say they never saw me.

Those were the only belongings I ever retrieved. I took only the most necessary items, falsely believing I might be able to gather the rest later. I left behind pictures, which I greatly regretted. Later, I would feel as if my life at the Flynn foster home had been erased. It was like all those years never existed. I just left.

Grandmother Elma lived in the same town where I attended school. I often thought of visiting her and apologizing for the letter and the words I had written three years earlier. I wanted her to know that I didn't mean the terrible things I said. I wondered if she had disowned me. After a few weeks of worrying about it, I decided to visit.

I knocked on her door and said, "Grandma, it's me, Karen." I was very nervous and anxious about how she would respond. I interrupted her prayer time but when she saw it was me, she rushed to over to me. She cried as she hugged and kissed me. She kept saying over and over that she knew I would return, that her prayers had been answered. I cried too and told her how sorry I was for the letter and hurting her. Grandma said she hadn't believed a word of it, that she forgave me and kept saying over and over how her prayers had been answered by my return.

Grandmother's house seemed so small compared to what I remembered. She seemed smaller too. I was quite young the last time I saw her. It was a wonderful reunion for both of us. Grandmother still loved me after all these years. She even thought I was an answer to her prayers! I felt special being in her presence again. I looked behind her entrance door for the small box of toys she always kept for me when I was a little girl, and they were still there. If felt so warm to walk into her home, so full of good memories. It smelled of chocolate and mints.

Grandmother's eyes sparkled as she sat by me and held my hand. She prepared jelly bread and coffee with milk. I told her I was attending technical school and asked if I could come to visit her. She was delighted. She said she missed me all the years we were separated and prayed for my safe return. I shared much with her but purposely omitted the relationship trauma with Carl. I didn't want her to be ashamed of me. I felt safe again. I had missed her deeply. She truly was one of the beautiful women in my life, and her beauty was not only on the outside, because her soul was pure and honest. I knew God held a special place in his heart for Grandmother and others like her. I felt special just knowing her and knowing she loved me. From that day forward, we resumed our relationship.

I quit school shortly after I started. It was difficult for me to focus. I was always on the lookout for Carl, no matter where I went or what I did. I never slept well because I knew I needed to remain alert. I called Lenny and Jesse when I knew Carl was at work to make sure they were okay. Before long, my brothers began calling me nasty names. Then they quit taking my calls altogether. I eventually quit calling. I was certain Carl had poisoned them against me.

One evening when I was cashiering at the store, a woman approached me and asked if I was Karen. She said she had some important information concerning Carl. He had been admitted to a mental health facility. She asked if I'd be willing to meet with his mental health professionals. His doctor felt facing me might be his only hope for recovery.

While I was skeptical about this request, I didn't want to feel responsible for his illness. I talked it over with AJ and although he didn't like the idea, he supported my choice. I contacted the facility and said I'd meet with them.

I was escorted into a large meeting room. There were six or seven men in white coats sitting around the table. I was placed at one end of the table and soon Carl walked in accompanied by a man in a white coat. He sat at the opposite end of the table from me. The room was silent, and I sensed Carl's anger. No one said anything at first. The doctor said, "We requested your presence, Karen, because your foster father is having a difficult time emotionally in trying to get over the relationship he had with you." He went on to say, "We think it would be helpful if your foster father was able to speak to you about his feelings directly and in person.

Suddenly, Carl stood up and began shaking his fist at me. He swore at me and called me filthy names. I ran out of the room and found a restroom, where I threw up. My legs were weak. I cleaned myself up and was putting cool water on my face when one of the staff people came in. He spoke gently and said, "I understand you're engaged to be married. Best of luck and thank you for coming." Then he left. I ran out of the building crying. I had terrible nightmares that lasted for weeks. I dreamt of Carl hunting me down and shooting me.

The same fall I received a call in the middle of the night from my aunt Victoria. She had heard on her police scanner the names of Lenny and Jesse, and it sounded like they were hurt. I quickly dressed and drove to Carl's house. When I arrived, I was met by Carl at the door. Lenny and Jesse stood behind him. He opened the door a small crack.

I remember it being very cold with a little snow on the ground. Carl answered the door with a gun, and he shouted for me to leave his property. I yelled to my brothers, asking if they were all right. He again ordered me off his property. Lenny and Jesse yelled and shouted obscenities at me. Lenny was in a cast and I could tell by his slurred speech that he was on medication. Frustrated, I left. Later, I discovered they had both been injured in a sledding accident, but their injuries were minor.

It was difficult to hear my brothers call me hurtful names. I hated Carl for what he had done to my family. My brothers were the most important thing in my life and now he had damaged our relationship.

AJ asked me to marry him and I accepted. I was so alone and he seemed to offer a safe refuge. He was the only man I had been involved with other than Carl. His parents lived on a large farm where they had raised Carl and his twelve siblings. They all expressed happiness about or upcoming wedding. I wanted Duane to be a part of my special day but I didn't know where he was. Jerry was stationed in Alaska so I wasn't sure he could come home. I wanted a big wedding so I could invite all my relatives, many of whom I hadn't seen for many years. I especially wanted my parents to attend. AJ and I went to each of their apartments and told them how much it would mean to me if they attended. I offered to pay for their wedding expenses.

Our visit with mother ended abruptly with her cussing and swearing at me. She said she wasn't interested in attending "my damn wedding." Dad said, "No thanks." I was devastated. I left crying. Naively I thought they would want to be part of my life, but they didn't. I knew it would be a long time before I made the effort to see either of them again. My wedding was to be a special day, and my parents had missed so many of my special days.

Grandmother Elma was happy that I was taking religion classes with AJ. I was to be confirmed in the Lutheran faith prior to our marriage. Grandmother explained that confirmation meant I was responsible for my own sins. Until a child was confirmed, their sins were on their parents. I agreed with her that my parents had enough of their own troubles to contend with without having my sins too. My confirmation made her very happy and it felt good to please her. My spirituality remains with me today, however, I still struggle with organized religion.

Jesse and Lenny did not attend the wedding. On occasion I saw Carl's truck, which caused instant nausea and lightheadedness. I did my best to avoid him. My brothers appeared loyal to him. I had not had any contact with Jesse and Lenny for quite some time, and missed them very much. While Carl was in the mental institution, Lenny and Jesse had been left at the foster home to care for themselves. Social Services did not intervene or remove them at that time, even though they were still minors. We had to fend for ourselves our entire childhood while adults remained out of control and uncaring.

I was married in a beautiful ceremony in May of 1979 when I was twenty years old. The relatives who attended were from my father's side of the family. I think they were as curious about me as I was about them. AJ and I paid for most of the cost. I wore a beautiful white dress and felt very special. That day will always remain a special memory in my mind and in my heart.

The hard portion of the reception was the seating arrangement at the wedding table. AJ's parents sat next to us while mine were absent. Nobody questioned why I wanted Grandmother Elma to sit with us but sadly she couldn't attend due to illness. After the meal, I drove to grandmother's home in my wedding dress and had afternoon lunch with her at her kitchen table. She didn't say anything at first. She just smiled at me. I was glad she could share my special day with me; it wouldn't have been as special without her. She hugged me close and whispered in my ear to be happy.

While my day was tainted a bit by not having Jesse and Lenny with me, it warmed my heart to at least have my grandmother.

AJ and I purchased a trailer house while we saved money for a house. I loved thinking about "someday." I sounded like other people with plans and dreams. I didn't even care if they came true; it just felt so good to have something positive to talk about like other people.

A few weeks later after I was married, Grandmother Elma became ill and was admitted to the hospital. She appeared to be near death. I worried that if she died, she would never see Lenny and Jesse again. I made an attempt to contact my brothers to tell them how ill she was. I reached Lenny by phone, and he seemed happy I called. He loved grandmother very much and wanted to see her. I was surprised at his tone and how happy he seemed to be to hear from me. He expressed a desire to leave Carl and apologized for his previous outbursts. He felt he had to feign anger at me to appease Carl.

I cried with relief at hearing this news. He related that on my wedding day, Carl had driven around with them looking for the church where I was to be married. He had brought along his gun. However, Carl had been drinking heavily that day and Jesse and Lenny were able to mislead him. Carl bragged that he was going to shoot me as I walked out of the church.

When I brought up the subject of Lenny and Jesse moving in with us, AJ became furious. This caught me by surprise because we had discussed it prior to our marriage and he hadn't expressed opposition. He complained it would be too costly. He didn't seem as concerned about their welfare as I was.

We picked an evening when Carl wasn't home to pick Lenny and Jesse up. Lenny was willing, but Jesse was undecided. I was relieved when I arrived at our designated meeting spot to see both of them. We hugged and cried for a long time. Finally, they were safe. We talked and talked all the way back to the trailer. Jesse kept saying how much trouble and danger we were in for doing this. But he also knew how angry Carl would be when he discovered their disappearance, so he didn't want to stay behind.

My relationship with AJ began to deteriorate shortly after Jesse and Lenny came to live with us. He was moody and disliked all the attention I showered on them. He felt the boys were old enough to work and take care of themselves.

I immediately reported to Social Services that my brothers were living with me so that they would stop foster care payments. I was not eligible for any financial assistance for my brothers because there were no such provisions then. This didn't bother me, but it certainly bothered AJ. He complained incessantly about the cost of feeding two extra people. It angered me that he was more concerned about money than my brothers' safety. Life was quite tense during this time. My brothers had picked up some bad habits. They cussed a great deal; they smoked, drank alcohol, and skipped a lot of school. They said no one at school cared if they were truant, and they weren't sure how many credits they still needed to graduate from high school. I was flabbergasted to learn that they had had no guidance regarding school or their reckless behavior. They said they spent most of the school year out in a fish house with buddies drinking and smoking.

I was enraged by the fact that Social Services was in charge of children, but they never bothered to monitor their progress. Social Services didn't do anything when our foster mother moved out or when I told them about the sexual abuse. They didn't do anything to care for my brothers while Carl was in the mental institution; and they didn't care that my brothers were left alone most of the time and not attending high school. What a mess our lives had become while in the custody of Social Services.

A few months after Lenny and Jesse moved in, I received a phone call from Paula. The boys said they had seen her in town a few weeks earlier and had spoken with her. I had mixed feelings regarding Paula and was surprised to hear her voice on the other end of the line. She asked me if I had been sleeping with Carl. The memories her question produced in my mind left me feeling numb and speechless, so I hung up the phone. I never heard from her again.

AJ complained constantly about my brother's presence. I also disliked aspects of their behavior and disrespectful attitude towards others, but I felt, given time, they would improve.

However, time was something I had little of. The situation was deteriorating quickly and I knew that I had to fix the situation and soon. I felt torn between my brothers and AJ. Emotionally exhausted, I contacted Social Services and requested services for them. It was suggested that they live where Jerry had lived a few years earlier, in an assisted-living foster home. The home offered guidance, but the rules weren't too rigid. This turned out to be a good solution for them. They could still live in the same town I did, but I wouldn't feel the pressure from AJ.

In 1979, Jerry came home from the service with his wife and two young sons. Jerry's wife, Sally, and I became friends quickly. The only friends I had were the wives of AJ's friends, and for the most part, we had little in common.

That fall I found out I was pregnant. We were elated; however, I worried that I wasn't at all certain how to take care of a baby. I tried talking to my mother-in-law about my fears, but she provided little insight. Child bearing was extremely easy for her. She merely jumped off her tractor, delivered, then jumped back on. Or at least that was how she described it. She made light of my questions and concerns. I didn't share my feelings with her after that. She gave the impression that I had asked silly questions. I felt ashamed, felt that I should know this information somehow. Again, I felt inadequate and worried constantly.

I was two weeks overdue with Shawna. I overheard AJ saying that, if the baby didn't come soon, he was going to hook a chain up to me like they did the cows and pull the baby out with a tractor. He and his friends laughed at his comments. I didn't think they were funny and this only added to my worry. I didn't talk to AJ about my fears. He only made fun of my feelings and laughed about them with his family.

Sally was very helpful and she often shared her thoughts and ideas about pregnancy. She liked to crochet and make potholders. Although I wasn't crafty, I asked AJ if I could buy yarn and crochet books and teach myself. He was reluctant but eventually agreed. I wanted to make something for the baby. Sally and I went to garage sales, but I bought little. AJ didn't give me much money, so we mainly looked.

Sally shared that her marriage was not going well. The relationship had been on shaky ground for some time. Part of the turbulence was due to Jerry's drinking. He was often verbally and physically abusive when he drank.

I was deeply saddened by this. I knew Jerry drank excessively, but I hoped he would be cautious, knowing how drinking had affected our family.

Most of the time I felt torn between my loyalty for Jerry and my deep friendship with Sally; she was my only friend. They were both good people with a deep love for their children; however, his unstable childhood ill prepared him for marriage or parenthood. They divorced a short time later and Jerry sank deeper into the depths of alcoholism. He became someone I no longer knew or liked when he drank. His life was spinning out of control and he was slowly losing his family. I felt at a loss as how to help him or Sally. I worried that I would lose him after his divorce. I tried to talk with him about his drinking but it was futile. He denied that here was any problem and continued in his destructive lifestyle.

AJ WAS OFTEN CRITICAL OF MY FAMILY. I overheard him talking to his family, criticizing my parents and my brothers. This hurt me a great deal and we slowly became more distant in our relationship.

During my pregnancy and doctors visits, I was asked a lot of questions about my parents' health, my mother's pregnancies and miscarriages, family health history, and what childhood illnesses I had. I was overwhelmed by these questions and became very anxious about doctors' visits. I couldn't answer the questions, and I didn't want to tell them why. I was ashamed to divulge that my mother had lost four babies due to alcoholism and violence. I didn't remember what childhood illness I had had or at what ages I had them. The doctor made it sound as if this information was extremely important to the health of my baby, and it was a problem that I didn't have any answers. I often cried for a long time after my appointments and worried constantly about my unborn child.

Tests discovered that I was Rh-negative. It was explained to me that Rh-negative women's bodies sometimes rejected their babies. I thought, *my goodness, what have I done in wanting to have a child of my own?* Now even my blood was different from everyone else's and it could harm my child! I felt extremely guilty for not knowing more about myself. My mother was likely Rh-negative as well, and this may have been a contributing factor to her four miscarriages.

Despite all my worries, I delivered a healthy baby. Shawna was born after thirteen hours of labor. She weighed seven pounds, fifteen ounces. She had lots of hair and was perfect. She had all her fingers and toes and very bright eyes for a newborn. I cried for joy. The nurses insisted that I rest, but all I wanted to do was look at her and hold her. The first night as I held Shawna while she slept, I prayed. I prayed deep and hard. I thanked God for blessing me with such a beautiful miracle, and I promised him that I would always do my best for her. I was elated. She thrived despite my ignorance.

Once home, I called mother to let her know about her granddaughter. I thought she would be excited about the baby and want to know all about her. Distantly, I even hoped she might want to come and visit. I was so excited at this prospect; I didn't stop and think what other reaction she might have. Mother had no phone. There was a phone in the hall all the residents used. I called and a man answered and agreed to go find her. I heard mother's voice faintly as she approached the phone. She yelled, "Hello? Who is it?"

I could tell by her slurred speech that she was intoxicated. Plus, she sounded angry. I didn't care. I excitedly informed her that I had delivered her a granddaughter. I prattled on about how beautiful Shawna was and how much she weighed when she loudly interrupted me with loud cursing. She yelled, "Who do you think you are? Do you think having a baby makes you a woman?" She swore and cursed and told me I was a no good slut and that's all I would ever be.

I slammed the phone down and sat on the floor and cried. I regained my sense of balance and took Shawna out of her crib and held her close to me. I told her how sorry I was that her grandmother didn't love her, but it didn't matter. I would love her always. Later that day, Jerry stopped over to see Shawna.

When I conveyed mother's reaction, he made me promise that I wouldn't call her again about the baby. He felt she had nothing to offer in terms of parenting, and I knew he was right.

AJ felt that I should quit work and stay home with Shawna. He suggested I do child care for one of his friend's babies as well. AJ didn't want a childcare bill. I didn't question this decision because I liked staying at home. Life was more peaceful than it had been in a long time. I was not good at socializing with others anyway so I found the idea of being a stay-at-home mom to be restful emotionally. AJ preferred to take care of everything, including the finances, and I didn't mind because I wasn't adept at managing money. I never really had any to manage.

AJ stayed busy with work, house, and vehicle maintenance. On weekends he went to his family's farm and helped with fieldwork and chores. In the beginning I accompanied him to the farm, but because everybody worked outside I eventually quit going because it didn't make sense for me to sit in the house by myself.

We spent holidays with his family. I was awed by the amount of food. Sometimes there were two kinds of meat, two vegetables, potatoes, different beverages, and two or three different choices of desserts. AJ's mother was a very good cook. She cooked and did chores outside as well – a very hard worker. AJ's grandmother lived in town so we took her with us when we went. She was quite elderly, but she also was a wonderful cook and would begin the meal before my mother-in-law came in from chores. I observed how they prepared food and learned a great deal. AJ's grandmother was very kind and fun to be around. She loved playing with Shawna. I often played cards with her when Shawna slept. I bonded with her quickly and easily, but not so much with the others. They were kind and we got along, but their way of life and language was unfamiliar. I felt uncomfortable if we stayed too long. After a couple of hours, I was ready to return to the familiar surroundings of our home.

I asked AJ if on occasion we could go out to eat, but he claimed we were broke. I knew what broke meant, and we certainly weren't broke, but, nonetheless, I never asked for anything that cost money. AJ cashed my childcare checks and paid the bills. I felt guilty much of the time because my checks were small.

In the fall of 1981 I discovered I was pregnant again. I was extremely excited. I wasn't as nervous or scared this time. I worried, but it wasn't as emotionally intense as with Shawna. I longed to get out of the house. After six weeks of being housebound, I pleaded with AJ to take me out. Again he refused and said we didn't have money. I felt guilty for asking but I felt so cooped up. AJ did the grocery shopping because he said he didn't want me buying frivolous items such as pop or magazines. He said we had to save our money if we wanted a house.

One time I asked him why we didn't have beer in the house. He said that because of the addiction in my family, it wasn't a good idea to have alcohol available to me. I was aware of what he was implying and it infuriated me.

One day AJ said he was going to buy land for us to put a house on. "How can we afford to buy land when we can't afford to go out for fast food?" I asked. He opened his wallet to show me $5,000 in cash. I shouted at him, "How could you have $5,000 and yet refuse to take your family out to eat even once?" He said he didn't tell me because I would have wanted to frivolously spend his money. I was very hurt that he couldn't spare $20 for his family and that he felt he had to keep the cash a secret. I never had any money in my purse unless I asked him for some. Even then he had to know why I needed the money. When I asked if I could keep my baby-sitting money, he said no. He said there wasn't anything I needed to buy – he put the gas in the car, bought the groceries and picked up necessities like diapers and laundry soap. If anything was needed, he bought it. He insisted I would make wasteful choices and that's why he couldn't trust me with money. We didn't save money together. It was his savings he said and it would stay that way because he felt I was incompetent. While I wanted to be a part of the decision making process, he chose to exclude me. There were no shared goals. He did what he wanted, and I had no say.

AJ put money down on the land, borrowed money from his mother and took out a loan from the bank. He quickly paid his mother back. We traded our mobile home for a modular home.

Sandy was born in June of 1982. She weighed seven pounds, seven ounces and had long legs and arms. Another miracle! I was truly blessed. Again I cried and promised God that I would always do my best for her.

We moved into our home when Sandy was six weeks old. It was the most beautiful home I had ever seen. Each of the girls had their own bedroom plus we had a microwave, a washer and dryer, and a yard. I envisioned the children having a sandbox and swing set in the backyard. My relationship with AJ was strained. I was good at avoiding painful situations, so I chose not to notice or acknowledge the deterioration of our relationship. I stayed busy with our children and asked very little of him. He seemed content and preoccupied with all the necessary projects around the house. The rest of the time he spent at the farm. He picked up extra shifts at work whenever he could. I was restless and wanted more from my day. I longed for some adult company. I felt very isolated and alone.

At Thanksgiving time, Jerry called to say that father was in a hospital in Minneapolis. He had suffered a serious seizure. Dad had been drinking vast amounts of rubbing alcohol and water because alcohol had become too expensive to purchase. I informed AJ that I wanted to accompany Jerry to the hospital.

AJ and I had a huge argument. He scoffed at my request and said I couldn't be running off to see my parents every time they were sick. I objected, saying that father could be dying. He allowed me to go, but he refused to give me any money so I was unable to help Jerry with gas or food. AJ didn't talk to me for a long time after I returned. He didn't even ask how my father was. He felt that I should feel lucky that he even permitted me to go.

Jerry was very angry with our parents and their inability to care for themselves. The reality of our childhood continued to haunt us. No matter how hard we tried to pretend we were like everyone else, it was quite obvious we weren't. Now our dad might die and for such a senseless reason. When Jerry and I arrived at the hospital, it was a sight I will never forget. Dad was strapped down in a bed with a hospital gown on. He had IV's in his arm. Dad was flailing about in the bed, and his wrists looked raw from struggling against the straps to keep him from pulling them out. He couldn't speak, but he kept making grunting noises, and he was foaming at the mouth. His eyes were rolled up into his head. Jerry and I became tearful. We were told that he had had numerous seizures brought on by alcohol so they put him on large doses of Valium to try to stabilize him.

He had been treated for over 100 seizures in the past year and the medical staff encouraged us to look into a nursing home. He was in his early fifties and possibly needed a nursing home. This was a sad reality. We had a couple of weeks to make arrangements before he was released from the hospital.

Jerry and I went to dad's apartment to pack up his belongings. It was clear he wouldn't be returning. Jerry was angry and vented about our childhood, father's present condition, and mother and her alcoholism.

The apartment was in a troubled part of town where people who are alone, forgotten or estranged from their families live and barely eke out an existence. We asked the manager for a key to the apartment. The manager wore a black stocking cap pulled down over his eyes and nose, with two holes cut in the cap so he could see out. How strange. We followed him upstairs, and he opened the apartment door. The manager watched us suspiciously, which made me uncomfortable.

It was a one-room apartment. There was a stained mattress with a small, dirty, tattered army blanket draped across it, a rickety and mostly unused dresser, two stained shirts and a pair of dirty jeans. The apartment had a distinct odor of must, dust, and stale alcohol. I was so angered and saddened by the conditions; I excused myself and walked to the bathroom located in the hall.

At the end of the hall I found a large room with stalls in it. I shouted out before entering. There were no doors on any of the bathroom stalls. There was cockroach powder everywhere, including on the seats of the toilets. Afterwards, I noticed the cockroach powder in the apartment. Our father's day-do-day reality was deeply painful to my mind and my heart. No human being should live this way and be so alone. Why didn't my parents see how their lives were deteriorating?

We stopped and talked with mother before we left town. Not surprisingly she was drunk. We updated her on dad's condition. She didn't know what she could do for him and was unwilling and unable to check on him. Mother had difficulty caring for herself and her current boyfriend, who was an alcoholic and ex-convict. Jerry and I left, feeling even more disgusted and angry with both of our parents and their inability to care for themselves after all these years.

Strangely, our parents remained in contact with each other over the years. I think they had a deep love for one another, although their drinking took precedence over anything or anyone else. Their relationship endured until their deaths, much to my amazement. They shared a past, children and alcoholism. The ties that bind us!

On the way home, Jerry shared that his wife was angry that he had to make this trip and I agreed that AJ wasn't happy about it either. He thought it was because other people didn't have our histories; he wished we didn't either. We both agreed it was hard to describe our lives and harder for others to understand. He felt he'd have to make up a story as to why he missed work and why our father was in the hospital. He didn't feel he could be honest with others about the situation. He was ashamed of our parent's behavior and lifestyle. I agreed there was no one I could talk to either, not even my husband. He said he could talk with his wife, and she understood, but they couldn't afford the additional expenses.

Dad stayed in the hospital for several weeks. Jerry asked me to go with him to pick him up. Our only hope was to convince dad to put himself into a chemical dependency treatment center. Jerry offered to cash his work check and buy dad all new clothing. I asked AJ for money but he refused. He was upset I even asked. He reminded me how my family continued to interfere in our marriage. By now I was immune to his nasty comments and ignored him. Again I went with no money, and Jerry paid for all of dad's expenses. He could scarcely afford it with a wife and two small children. Jerry lectured dad the whole way to the treatment center. Dad looked out the car window and said nothing. Jerry had been working on his own sobriety and had his own personal struggles trying to rebuild his relationship with his family.

When we dropped dad at the center he was quiet, and Jerry and I both cried at the choice we were forced to make. During his stay in treatment, Jerry returned to drinking, and when dad received a home pass for a weekend, they drank together. Jerry and I had a strong argument regarding their sobriety. I don't believe dad had made a commitment to sobriety and would have returned to drinking with or without Jerry's involvement. Alcoholism was as much a part of father as his height, hair color and eye color until his death at the age of fifty-nine. Jerry blamed himself but in reality, I believe his years of sobriety had shown him that our father was ultimately responsible for his own sobriety. No one could do it for him. Dad remained in the town where Jerry and I lived and never returned to Minneapolis or the horrific lifestyle he led. Jerry and I made sure of that. However, he continued to drink and to have seizures.

Father's mental health was not good due to his seizures and the destructive lifestyle. I pursued SSI for him. I was happy he lived close by; it gave me hope that his grandchildren could get to know him. Due to his alcoholism however, I decided that the time he spent with us would be limited. We tried to see him when he was sober, which was very early in the morning and even then, there was no guarantee. When he completed the SSI testing, the psychologist asked me how many children were in the family. I told him there were five of us. The psychologist said that was interesting because my father could only remember three. This was not a big surprise, but the truth was extremely painful. After our visits, I oftentimes cried all the way home.

Lenny and Jesse graduated from high school and signed up for the Army. Lenny had so many physical difficulties he was required to have open-heart surgery for his heart murmur before he could join the service. I wanted to give my brothers a small going away party. AJ was opposed and didn't participate in the celebration. Plus, he refused to contribute any money for the party. Embarrassed, I asked the guests to bring a food dish. Everyone generously contributed. It was awkward making the day work. The party was held in our garage, but AJ remained in the house. I told people he wasn't feeling well. I developed a life-size picture of Jesse and Lenny with their arms around each other. I had the picture pinned up with Christmas lights around it.

My brothers appreciated the party. I could sense their fear of the unknown and our impending separation. They assured me they would stay in contact and asked me to write often. After most everyone left, Lenny and I sat up and drank and acted silly. I didn't want the night to end. I was worried about his leaving. Plus, I didn't want to go into the house and have to endure AJ's complaints.

When the party ended, AJ complained the moment I walked in. I stopped him and in my drunkenness, told him I didn't want to hear it and that I was going to bed. I could deal with him more courageously when I drank.

ON RARE OCCASIONS, we went with another couple to a bar and had a few drinks. By the end of the night, I was not afraid to tell AJ what I thought of his money, his personal possessions, and our relationship. I always felt sad about what I had said to him, but the next day he pretended it had never happened, so I never discussed it either. Our relationship remained rocky at best.

I became friends with the family next door. They had a young son. The wife was about ten years younger than her husband and she didn't work. I found them to be very pleasant when we chatted outside. On the other side of our home was a small church. We didn't have many neighbors, so I valued this family enormously.

The family I did childcare for had another baby, a boy. My days were filled with children while my nights were filled with cooking, baking, laundry and cleaning. AJ disliked toys lying around inside or outside. With four small children wanting to play, this was a challenge. He complained that I never had the house picked up or that I washed the clothes on the wrong day. If I washed clothes on Wednesday, he would say I should have washed them on Tuesday. It never seemed to matter when I did; I could never do it right, no matter how hard I tried. Our home didn't feel like a home to me. It wasn't comfortable to be in, always having to be neat and clean. It felt sterile. I couldn't put my feet on the couch. AJ carried the children to the vehicles because he didn't want sand or dirt in the car or truck. He disliked the children playing in the yard because it flattened the grass. He built a sandbox for the children and put it on the far end of the yard, but constantly cleaned around it and complained of how much the sand ruined his yard. The children didn't play outside much – it was less stressful for me to have them play in the house where I could easily pick up their toys before AJ came home from work. Normal, day-to-day routines caused me a great deal of stress, due to AJ's obsessive nature.

On occasion, Sally asked me to go clothes shopping with her. I had to beg AJ for a long time before he would consent. He only gave me fifty dollars with orders to plan ahead for the children because he wouldn't give me any more for the year, and he didn't. I did my best to anticipate how much they might grow over the next few months. We didn't eat out because there wasn't any extra money. Instead, we grabbed a pop and chips. Sally never asked me to assist with gas because she knew AJ never gave me money for extras. This made me angry. I always felt like a moocher. I was grateful that Sally asked me but felt sadness over how little I was able to financially contribute to the day. AJ dictated what time I had to be home, but Sally never complained and continued to ask me to go with her.

AJ always cashed and kept my childcare money. I didn't mind, but I felt he should understand it wasn't fair for others to have to pay my way. I felt ashamed that I couldn't contribute or treat anyone that had treated me. I think he hoped that no one would ask me. I felt isolated.

I held small birthday parties for my daughters, something my mother had never done. I invited Grandmother Elma and several other relatives. AJ always grumbled about the cost. A few weeks before Shawna's birthday, I told AJ that I wanted to buy our daughter a special gift from us. I suggested a charm bracelet. He said nothing, but later I overheard him on the phone requesting that his mother buy it for her. I began talking to AJ less and less.

AJ didn't want to spend money on his own children. I began to despise his presence. I slowly quit communicating with him. We didn't believe in the same values. His idea of what a family was and mine were totally different. I disliked how AJ's older siblings talked to their parents; they were loud and disrespectful. This made me uncomfortable because I was never sure if a fight would break out. I couldn't understand why they spoke this way to their parents. I found it difficult to figure out the rules of family dynamics.

One of our serious arguments was about a small boat he wanted to buy and then sell to make money. Again, it was about the money. He purchased the boat. I overheard him talking on the phone to his younger brother, who was sixteen or seventeen years old. I was aware that he had purchased the boat for $200. He told his brother he would sell it to him for $400. When he hung up the phone, I confronted him. I told him I didn't understand how he could cheat his brother. I asked him why he didn't give his brother the boat, or at the very least, sell him the boat for what he paid for it. I found his behavior disgusting and dishonest. I reminded him that when we built our home, his brother had helped with no compensation. We couldn't he take this opportunity to repay his brother for the kindness he had shown us? I lost respect for AJ because he cared about money more than family. I didn't understand this. If I had anything my brothers wanted or needed, I gave it to them or bought it for them. It was obvious that his children and wife lacked importance to him.

I disliked having to ask him for money so the girls and I could buy him a Father's Day gift. He said he didn't need anything and we shouldn't waste the money. Occasionally he grew tired of my asking and gave me $15 or $20 and drove us to the store to purchase a gift. It was difficult because he never seemed to like what we found – such a small amount of money made for few choices. We usually picked out a new shirt. It should have been a fun family experience, but it wasn't. Because I had to beg for the money for weeks in advance and because he would constantly complain about it, I found the whole experience distasteful. It completely ruined the spirit of wanting to buy him something. AJ's idea of taking me out for Mother's Day was to go to a store selling brats and a pop in the parking lot. Then he'd brag to his friends and family how he took me out on Mother's Day. I continued to distance myself from him emotionally and stayed focused on my children. I was isolated and alone.

Money grew to be a large barrier between us. I often asked him about taking a family trip, like going to the Black Hills. He said we didn't have money for such foolishness, and needed to stay home to maintain the house and vehicles. He claimed that was why most families never got ahead. Instead of spending money, they should be saving it. Again, I thought maybe I didn't understand money or how much it took to keep our home going. I felt sad inside that I was being selfish when I should be grateful for all I had. This was, after all, the most I had ever had. I did childcare but compared to his paychecks, mine must have paled in comparison. If this was how normal people lived, I didn't like it any better than my previous lifestyle. It felt like I didn't fit in anywhere. I didn't fit with my mother, my foster parents, and now as a wife and mother.

One day while I was sitting outside on the edge of the neighbor's lawn sun tanning, she came over to say hi. Alison introduced herself and we talked about her family and the area. I apologized for sitting on her yard. I explained that AJ didn't like me to sit on the grass because I flattened it. Alison said she noticed he was extremely particular about everything; and, before she left, she said I should stop over sometime and visit. She gave me her phone number. Alison was pleasant and I was grateful for adult company.

I told AJ about my visit with Alison and how I enjoyed talking with her. He told me I should mind my own business and stay in the house. I disliked his response and made up my mind that I would visit her without telling him. AJ worked two shifts, one was days from 6:00 a.m. to 3:00 p.m. and the following week he would work 3:00 p.m. to 11:00 p.m. One day before he left for work at 2:30, he complained about how I packed his lunch. I had cut his sandwich the wrong way – instead of side-to-side; I should have cut it from top to bottom. He said something about too much crust on one side if I cut the sandwich from side-to-side. We had an argument over this. I said, "You do the grocery shopping, you do the laundry, you do the yard, all because I can't do it right, so now you can add packing your own lunch to your list." He grumbled about how worthless I was and left for work. After calming down, I decided to call Alison to see if she wanted to visit. She said she did and to bring the girls. I was ecstatic. I packed the girls a bag of toys and treats, and we walked over. Her husband Ron had just returned home from work, so the three of us sat and drank coffee while the kids played. Her husband was very likeable and he said it was enjoyable to have young ones around. They shared special events of their family life and how they met and became a couple. I mostly listened, but it was fascinating to hear about other people and how they lived. They had wanted to meet us earlier, but because AJ and I always looked busy, they hadn't intruded. The time flew by and soon it was suppertime. I mentioned that AJ always called around 7:00 to make sure I was home. Alison jokingly said, "Your husband sure keeps close check on you." They asked me to stop over again. It felt good to make friends.

Later that night, I thought more about what Alison had said. She seemed right. AJ did keep a close check on me at all times. I couldn't go anywhere during the day because it was too difficult to load up four children. Besides, where would I go? I didn't leave the house in the evening. Grandmother Elma went to bed early so AJ permitted me to visit her on Saturdays. Anywhere I went, he drove me. Why did he keep me so isolated and control all my actions?

One Saturday, AJ dropped the kids and me off at Grandmother Elma's. She was older and slower so I tried to visit her more often. The girls played while I sat holding her hand. We didn't talk much; it just felt good to be close to her. Her eyes twinkled as she looked at me. I didn't share with her my struggles as a wife and mother. She inspired me just by her presence. Aunt Victoria stopped occasionally and joined the conversation. I always felt relaxed after being with grandmother. I wanted so badly for her to be proud of me. I longed to share with her my difficulties with AJ, but I didn't know how. I disliked him most of the time. I worried constantly about whether I was a good mother because I didn't really know what a good mother was.

I remember one time when Shawna was three years old. She came to me while I was cleaning the kitchen. She asked me if I would make her a special dress with flowers on it. I was stunned. I told her I would talk to her about it later and encouraged her to go and play. As I watched her leave, I sat on the floor with my back up against a cupboard and wept. I thought about all the things my daughters might want from me. I didn't know how to do most of the things other mothers knew how to do. I desperately wanted to be a good mother, but there was so much I didn't know. The hard part was that I didn't have anyone I trusted to share my fears with. Our home felt sterile and our children weren't allowed to play in the yard without permission from their father. I even had to suntan in the neighbor's yard. I disliked our home and my daily routine. At times I thought of suicide but I dismissed those thoughts because I didn't want my children to grow up without a mother. I knew they would be teased and treated differently. I didn't want them to blame themselves for my actions. I decided not to take the easy way out and to mother my children to the best of my ability, which I knew wasn't much. I worried that my girls would be ashamed of me once they went to school and met other kids who talked about all the special talents their mothers possessed. I was all too familiar with my limitations and weaknesses, and AJ never failed to point out a few I wasn't aware of.

Karen Wussow

Duane started calling me regularly. He lived in Michigan with a girlfriend. He usually called when he was very intoxicated. The conversations were repetitive and often didn't make sense. I worried about him and asked him to visit, but he declined. He liked to talk about our parents. Duane was upset that mother didn't have a phone and he couldn't get in touch with her. Mother never had a phone, so I wasn't sure why he expected her to have one now. Duane was more emotionally bonded to mother than the rest of us; although I can't say mother had any attachments to any of her children.

One day Duane's girlfriend called. She said their relationship was strained due to his abuse of drugs and alcohol. Duane was experiencing occasional seizures, and she was worried about him. He would disappear for days and she had no idea where he was or if he was safe. She cried off and on throughout our phone conversation. She asked about our family because Duane provided her with inconsistent information. Duane had informed her that our parents were very rich and lived on a large farm with hired hands. When I revealed the truth, she became silent. She asked if Duane was a twin. I said no, our younger brothers were nine months apart in age. She cried on the phone and apologized for calling. I understood why Duane made up a fairytale life. The reality was too painful. It's difficult to share our history with someone for fear of rejection, which we all knew too well. I shared with her that I didn't know Duane very well, but I welcomed his efforts to make contact with me. I wanted him to be a part of my life and that of my daughters.

Before our phone conversation ended, she said she wasn't sure how long they would continue as a couple. He seemed so confused at times. He would have bouts of extreme anger and behave abusively; or, he would be vulnerable and tearful. She said she loved Duane very much, but their relationship was very strained. Later I learned that their relationship ended soon after our conversation.

102

Chapter Five
Five-Dollar-a-Week Allowance

MY SIBLINGS AND I HAVE DEALT with our chaotic childhood in different ways at different times in our lives. At times we choose not to acknowledge who we truly are. Society appears more accepting of us if we make up information that is more the norm. In an environment with other individuals like ourselves, we aren't expected to explain. Unfortunately, many of these people are mired in unhealthy relationships and are struggling in one way or another. Because we had few positive role models or mentors, it is difficult to make appropriate choices because we don't know what the choices are or what steps it takes to arrive there. As adults, our emotional battles continue in a world we are not comfortable in and don't fully understand. My brothers and I are emotionally close as this provides safety from the outside world. It also provides security much like what we had as children. We understand each other's limitations and fears and accept them without question. The outside world is less understanding or our faults and lack of knowledge.

One evening I received a phone call from Jerry. He said mother had called him from the Anoka emergency room. Her boyfriend had beaten her up and left her at the hospital. She was intoxicated on arrival so after treating her for her injuries they placed her in the detoxification unit. Jerry asked if I would visit her and help her with clothing and cigarette money. AJ wasn't happy but begrudgingly transported me to the center. He waited in the car.

The majority of the women were young. Mother wasn't in her room. I asked a woman in the hall if she had seen her. The woman said, "You must be looking for Ma. She's in the break room," and she pointed me in the right direction.

I felt my anger bubbling. Virtual strangers were calling her "Ma," while ironically she had never been a mother to me. I found her in the break room. Only a few bruises remained and she looked and sounded good. A staff member was conversing with her about housing. Our visit was interrupted several times by young women stopping by to greet "Ma." She introduced me as her daughter, and the women shared how much they enjoyed mother in their groups. They especially appreciated her wonderful sense of humor was.

I found little in common with mother that day. I thought I would offer support towards her sobriety, but it appeared that she had all the support she needed from others. I had foolishly hoped we could start over – commence a mother/daughter relationship. Instead, I felt like an outsider. I left knowing that a relationship with mother was never going to happen. I hugged her, wished her well and encouraged her to keep in contact. I walked away tearful, realizing the reality of my relationship with her. I stopped at a bathroom to regain my composure before returning to the car. AJ didn't ask about mother, just like mother hadn't asked about my children or my husband. AJ remained silent all the way home. My thoughts drifted back to painful memories from my childhood.

ONE EVENING I RECEIVED a collect call. I was glad I picked up the phone because AJ didn't accept collect calls. For some time my mother had been calling me collect. AJ forbid me from taking them if he was around. Mother was usually intoxicated and they came very late. Her calls left me emotionally drained, but I worried about her when I couldn't speak with her.

This time however, the collect call was from Lenny and I was thrilled to hear from him. When the operator asked if I would accept charges, I excitedly said yes! At first I was a little taken aback when he said, "Mom, how are you and the girls?" He went on to talk about basic training and how well he was doing.

We laughed and talked for half an hour. He was fine but lonesome. His former foster mother had sent him homemade cookies and breads. We were both tearful when we had to say good-bye, but he promised to call and let me know where he would be stationed next. Then he said, "I hope you don't mind that I called you mom. We all stand in line to call home and everyone called their mother, so I didn't want the guys to hear that I wasn't calling mine."

I assured him that I didn't mind. After the call ended, I sat quietly in my rocking chair and thought about our conversation. My heart went out to him for feeling the need to call me mom when his army friends were nearby. Mother had no idea how she still affected our lives as adults. My solitude didn't last long because AJ came into the room and angrily asked if the phone call was from my brother. I said it was and he erupted. He said there wouldn't be any more collect calls. When I argued that it was unlikely Lenny had much money to call, he said: "I guess he won't be calling then, will he?"

I slept in a chair that night, hating my life and not knowing how to change it. I felt so trapped. Someone always ruined what few good memories I had. The only thing that kept me going was my daughters. A body and mind can withstand many painful experiences when the heart is committed to a loved one. AJ was verbally abusive but I often thought it would be less painful if he just hit me. Scars of the heart don't heal like bruises on the skin.

AJ was a workaholic. When he came home from his forty-hour a week factory job, he spent the rest of the day working on vehicles or our home. On weekends he worked at the farm. Our relationship became non-existent. The children kept me busy and confined to the home. I enjoyed my time with the girls; we rocked and read books and colored. I wasn't very good at these activities, but they were happy to have my company, as I was to have theirs.

I visited my neighbor Alison more frequently. We initially drank coffee but soon switched to beer. I was having three to four beers a night. Ron and Alison were good to me and I enjoyed my time with them. Sometimes I didn't go home even though I knew AJ would call at 7:00 p.m. This angered him and he ordered me to stay home. He called them alcoholics and said I was becoming one as well. He reiterated that I was worthless and didn't know anything. He called me damaged and said I should be grateful he had married me because no one else would have.

I decided that if we truly needed additional income like AJ claimed, I would look for work. I know he didn't want me to work, but what could he do if I found a job? I wasn't sure what I could do because my work history was limited.

I contacted a single-parent agency. I met with a representative who said I was employable. My preference was clerical work so he promised to contact me if he had any job leads. I gave him times to call me when AJ wasn't at home.

That evening, AJ noticed the car had been moved and the mileage was different. He angrily asked where I had been. I lied and said I had visited my grandmother. He didn't talk to me for a long time. He scolded me and reminded me that my place was in the home.

The agency called me a few weeks later. They had a secretarial job opportunity that paid $6.00 an hour. At the time, this was more than minimum wage. I was in heaven. I was sure AJ would be pleased with the additional income and this might improve our marriage. At first, the agency suggested a night job, but I rejected that notion, certain that AJ would object. Instead they suggested I interview for a secretarial position with the chemical dependency counselor at the high school. We agreed on a time and date for the interview. He suggested I dress appropriately.

Now I was worried! What did he mean, "Dress appropriately for the interview?" I figured this was something that everyone must know, but I didn't. After I hung up the phone, I looked in my closet. Casual clothing was all I owned, so I'd have to wear that.

My sister-in-law watched the children while I went to the interview. I was very nervous and wasn't sure if my legs would carry me through the school doors. My self-talk was negative. I couldn't imagine why they would consider hiring someone who hadn't worked in four years. I desperately wanted a better relationship with AJ and I naively believed finding a job would help. I was very early for my appointment and sat in the car a long time.

I finally worked up enough courage to go inside. I sat down with three other women waiting to be interviewed. They wore pretty dresses with matching shoes. They were all smartly attired and had their hair and nails done. They sat looking forward, not acknowledging each other. In comparison, I was dressed very casually with my sweater, corduroy pants and loafers. I was not like these women. I did not look like a career woman or a woman who worked regularly. I didn't own clothing like they wore. I thought to myself, *I must be silly thinking I could get a job at the school considering who I am.* I was so busy with negative self-thoughts; I nearly missed my name being called.

During the interview, I was honest about my lack of secretarial skills. I said I was a quick learner, enjoyed children and that I possessed very good typing and spelling skills. I was relieved when the interview ended. With the other qualified candidates, I knew I didn't have a chance. I made a mental note to call the agency and let them know that I'd take a cashier or nursing home position.

Much to my surprise, a week later I was offered the job as the school. Why would they select me when they had the well-dressed, professional looking women to choose from? Apparently, they were impressed with my honesty and they preferred someone who could fit in with children. I would be less intimidating. She asked when I could start. *Oh my goodness*, I hadn't even told AJ I was *looking* for a job, and now I had one. I agreed to start in two weeks.

I was stunned beyond belief that I was chosen. I was determined to make my boss proud of me. How to tell AJ? When I finally worked up the courage, he was furious. In fact, he was angrier than I had ever seen him before. He called me a liar and asked what kind of wife I was sneaking around behind his back. He called me names and carried on for a long time. He demanded I call the agency and tell them I wasn't taking the job.

Angrily, I made it clear that I was going to work because it was important to me. When I mentioned the extra money for the household, he grew more irate. Over the years I had become skilled at shutting out areas of my life that were not functional and focusing on what was. My marriage was no different. AJ seemed comfortable with the lack of physical and emotional contact between us. I was determined to work regardless of his objections so I turned my energy to finding childcare.

Eventually I found a provider, but I felt a twinge of oddness in my stomach when I met her. I blew it off, attributing it to nervousness about childcare and the job. Several weeks later, Shawna told me she disliked it when the sitter put her in the basement as punishment for not picking up her toys.

I was very upset and called the provider to see if this was true. She defended her disciplinary approach and was angry when I said my children deserved better and would not be coming back. I hugged my daughter a long time, telling her that it wasn't right to be put in the basement, and I was sorry. I was thankful Shawna felt comfortable confiding in me, or I may have never known. I had concerns about Sandy because she was too young to verbalize how she was treated. I located another provider who I felt more comfortable with.

The job was emotionally challenging. I felt uncomfortable being around a lot of people, so adjusting to the school setting was difficult. The staff and students were supportive so it wasn't long before I felt welcome. My boss, John, was very relaxed, so everyone felt comfortable around him. My job duties consisted of scheduling appointments, typing letters and organizing staff time. John facilitated chemical dependency support groups in all the schools plus he counseled children with troubled backgrounds. If John had a conflict in his schedule, he'd ask me to show a film or facilitate one of the support groups. Grant writing took a lot of his time, so I felt honored to assist him in any way I could. John was a wonderful mentor who taught and trusted me. He treated me with respect and dignity. He remains an exquisite person and role model for me today. He was one of the first people to believe in my abilities and in me.

One time I ordered a check in the amount of $3,000 to pay a speaker but it never arrived. I called accounting to see about the delay. They said it had been sent to our office the week before. I felt so ashamed. How could I have lost it? I looked everywhere, but to no avail. I worried that John would think I had stolen it and I'd be fired. I began to imagine all kinds of horrible repercussions. Imagine my dread when John asked me into his office. He said, "Karen, you haven't acted like yourself lately. Are you doing okay?" I began to cry and told him about the check. I swore to him that I hadn't taken it. He said he wished I'd come and talked to him sooner. He knew I didn't take the check and said he had no intention of firing me. "These things always turn up," he assured me. He gave me a hug and suggested I look in the inner school mail envelopes. After a quick look, I found the check. I was so relieved I cried. He hugged me and made me promise to talk with him the next time I had a major concern.

John didn't know my history, but he trusted me, treated me respectfully and believed in me. For this man, I would have worked for free. He was truly a blessing. He taught me about honesty and integrity.

I usually took my breaks away from other staff because I preferred to be alone. Occasionally, a coworker joined me. I enjoyed her company and I thought we were becoming friends. After about a month, I asked her how her family celebrated their holidays. She looked at me oddly and said, "Why do you ask?" I told her briefly about growing up in foster homes and that I didn't know how families celebrated holidays. In reply, she said, "But you seem so nice." I never saw her again in the break room. I learned a valuable lesson about sharing who I was with potential friends. This realization made me sad. I missed her company and our visits and wished I hadn't asked. I would be more careful in the future.

I took home approximately $800 per month, definitely more than I earned doing childcare. My hours were spaced for me to work full-time in the winter when school was in session and only part-time in the summer. John had a large library of books on chemical dependency, depression, youth, and related topics. I asked him if I could borrow books to become more familiar with the students we worked with. I didn't share that I wanted this information to learn more about my situation as well. I learned a great deal about family dynamics and how alcoholism played a part in my parents' lives and their parenting abilities.

When payday arrived, I was very excited. However, like usual, AJ showed up to pick up my check. That would be the last I saw of it. I didn't question what he did with the money. I assumed it was needed for bills and I was happy to contribute to the household. The job did wonders for my self-esteem. AJ gave me a $5.00 a week allowance, which I used to purchase cigarettes.

One time the secretaries asked me to join them for lunch. This sounded like fun, so I asked AJ for a little extra money to buy lunch. He refused, saying I had $5.00 and it was my decision how to spend it – cigarettes or lunch. I skipped lunch. I figured I wouldn't fit in too well with the women anyway.

My job was subsidized employment and scheduled to last six months. John liked me and wanted to keep me. I connected well with the students and they often sought me out if John was out of the office. Fortunately, John secured a grant and hired me part-time. I also worked part-time for the Special Education Director. The combination of both jobs made me a full-time employee.

AJ wanted me to quit, but I refused. I kept my job for five years. The only time he came to the office was to pick up my paycheck. I noticed other husbands and wives went out to lunch, but AJ said we couldn't afford it, so I quit asking.

I started to take my breaks in the janitor's room. It was usually quiet and I could be alone. Occasionally, one or two of the janitors came in but not often. The janitors sometimes complained about the uppity secretaries and how they made demands. They didn't feel appreciated by the secretarial staff. They often teased me that I was the best looking janitor in their crew.

Often before work I stopped to see my father and have a cup of coffee with him. He usually was sober in the morning. Father was no longer capable of holding a job. He almost seemed like a normal father.

When AJ discovered extra mileage on the car, he ordered me to stop visiting my relatives. I ignored him and decided to use my lunch break to visit Grandma Elma. I didn't have the children with me, so we could visit over jelly bread and peach sauce. Sometimes, my grandmother's sister, Aunt Helen, would stop over. I knew visiting grandmother made matters worse between AJ and me, but I had such a strong desire to see my family that the consequences didn't matter anymore.

I became friends with a secretary in the Special Education Department. She was in her early forties and we had daughters the same age. We shared an office that was quite isolated from the other offices. Over time, she became a mother figure to me as well as a friend. She was open, honest and knowledgeable. She had been a single parent and had recently married.

She had dated quite a bit and had many interesting jobs in her lifetime. Often she asked me what I thought about something. This made me nervous because I kept thinking there must be a right answer. She laughed gently at my naïveté and encouraged me to think and have thoughts and ideas of my own. She was very mentally stimulating and she taught me a great deal. She encouraged me to ask questions when I didn't understand. We laughed a lot. I came to trust her and shared with her my marital concerns and family history. She didn't laugh or ignore me. Instead, she said this helped her to understand me better. We talked about my parents which prompted her to share some of the regrets she had about parenting choices she had made. She stressed that we were all human beings and we make mistakes; that this was what life was about. I found this new way of thinking unusual but interesting.

She said she'd be angry if the only time her husband showed up at work was to pick up her paycheck. She'd put a halt to that behavior right away. I asked her what she meant, and she explained that most women kept part of their own paycheck. I was under the impression that all money earned needed to go toward the household. When I asked what other women did with their money, she said they shopped, bought birthday gifts or took trips.

Later I asked AJ why I had an allowance when other women didn't. As usual, he became angry and said this was the reason he didn't want me to work. He insisted that working wives break up families. He said it would be best for the family if I quit and stayed home where I belonged. I countered by saying that not working wasn't best for the family, it was best for him. By working and interacting with others, I had discovered how normal people lived. Other couples went out to eat, took in a movie or traveled. The extra money should have allowed us to do more activities as a family. I felt stupid and ashamed. Foolishly, I had believed that he cared about me and that we needed extra money to make ends meet. I felt used, knowing he was taking my money to pad his wallet.

He was in charge of the checkbook, however, he allowed me to help him write out bills monthly. I never thought to add them up to see how they compared with our dual income. I knew how much I made, but I never saw one of his paychecks. Suddenly, his motives had become clear to me. He wanted me hone where I'd never be exposed to normal people. The sight of him disgusted me because he was dishonest and deceitful. I no longer had any respect for him and I wasn't interested in making our marriage work. I couldn't understand how he could treat loved ones this way. I didn't know what to do, but I realized I needed a change. From now on I would question everything.

Through work, I became familiar with the Adult Children of Alcoholics support group. John encouraged me to join the group. He suggested it might help me understand why I thought and acted the way I did. Best of all, there were others who felt the same emotional isolation I did. He felt I would gain valuable insight and personal growth. I looked forward to meeting other individuals who were confused and struggling with their lives just like I was. It was a daily struggle when one felt inferior and continually doubted themselves. I was relieved to think I might fit in somewhere.

When I informed AJ that I intended to join, he said I couldn't. He didn't want me hanging out with freaks as he referred to group member and that I was needed at home. I said our girls weren't babies anymore and besides he worked the day shift so he should be able to watch them. He argued that he needed time to change the oil in the cars or do yard work. I stood my ground and said he would have to do his tasks on different nights.

On the first evening of group, AJ screamed at me as he stood in front of the door. For the first time in our relationship, he physically picked me up and threw me into our bedroom. He ordered me to stay inside because no wife of his was going to any freak show. He held the door closed. It was a terrible scene, with both of us yelling and me crying and banging on the door. I finally lay on the bed, exhausted. After a while, he walked away. I rushed out, grabbed my coat and left.

I was quiet during the meeting and listened. It was therapeutic to sit with people honestly discussing how difficult life is. At the second meeting, I was confronted by the facilitator of the group. She said that I was very attentive to those who were sharing their life stories, but I had not shared mine. She asked me how fair that was to the others in the group. They had taken a risk by sharing their story in my presence, but I had not been respectful by sharing mine in return.

I stated that I meant no disrespect, but I felt the need emotionally to absorb a place that felt safe for the first time in my life. I was cautious about what I shared. The facilitator concluded from this that trust was a strong issue for me. She suggested that trust was something I could work on with the group. She asked for suggestions from those in attendance on how I could do this. One member suggested that I share something that I hadn't shared with anyone else. It didn't have to be deep or painful, but it needed to be something that bothered me.

After pondering the suggestion for a minute, I revealed that I didn't have a library card. Therefore, I didn't know how to check out books for my children. I often wanted to ask someone how to obtain one, but I was afraid others would laugh at me because it seemed most people knew how to do this.

One member of the group offered to go with me to the library before our next meeting. She was a little order than I was, and she too had been fearful of the library. Afterwards, I shared the experience with everyone. The hard part for me wasn't obtaining the card; it was the uncertainty of how to actually do it. I will always be grateful to the woman who accompanied me. I began checking out books on my lunch hour for the girls. I felt so proud of myself. I didn't tell anyone else until much later what a huge fear this had been for me.

I came to trust the people in group and I was a regular member for almost two and one-half years. After every meeting, some of us would stop for coffee. Or on holidays, we might go for a meal. Most of our extended families still drank and practiced abusive behavior. Over coffee or a meal we talked about the sadness of our lost families. We ended these get-togethers with positive messages and encouragement. For once, I fit in. I facilitated the group for an additional year and a half after the facilitator left. During this time, I grew emotionally and became increasingly inquisitive about my relationship with AJ.

One day Duane called to say he was coming to visit. I hadn't seen him in years and was excited that he wanted to see us. Not surprisingly, AJ said he couldn't stay with us.

On the day Duane was supposed to arrive, he called to say he was stranded at a truck stop. He sounded drunk and asked if I could pick him up. When I informed AJ of the predicament, he said I wasn't going anywhere. It was an extremely cold winter night he said and he didn't want his vehicle out in it. I pleaded with him but to no avail.

It broke my heart to tell Duane I couldn't come to assist him. I encouraged him to stay at the truck stop until morning. Duane became angry and said he hadn't come this far to fail in his mission and hung up the phone.

I didn't sleep all night because of worry for Duane and my anger at AJ. Early the next morning, I received a collect call from Duane. A policeman had picked him up. When the officer discovered he had outstanding warrants, he arrested him. He was jailed for six weeks.

I look back now and know Duane's request was unreasonable. He could have found a safe place to sleep if he had chosen to, but he wasn't thinking clearly due to the intoxication. I was continuing the role I had assumed as a child. I had always tried to fix everything, but I was slowly beginning to learn that I couldn't fix other people.

In the spring of 1985, my father was involved in a hit and run accident. A teenage driver deliberately hit him, stopped, backed up and ran over him again. I received a call from one of his drinking friends who had witnessed the incident. Father had been walking home to his trailer when struck. Severely wounded, he crawled to his trailer. The gravel in his wounds actually prevented him from bleeding to death. His leg was broken and turned completely around from the knee down.

The doctor wouldn't discharge unless he could live someone. Jerry was working out of town and Duane was homeless, so I decided he could live with us. He protested because he didn't want to be a bother, but it felt good to assist him.

AJ disliked having father with us. Father made every attempt to be a thoughtful guest, but whatever he did, it bothered AJ. In the morning, father arose very early so he could be finished in the bathroom before the rest of us were up. AJ woke up early just so he could race him to the bathroom. With his crutches and bad leg, father always lost the race and would be forced to turn around and hobble back to his room. I confronted AJ about his rude behavior. He said it was his bathroom and he would use it any time he liked. If I didn't like it, I should tell my father to leave. Father never complained, but he was truly uncomfortable. When AJ decided to charge father for his accommodations, I contacted the county to see what other options were available.

He returned home after only a week. The county provided in-home services. It wasn't long before he reverted back to drinking. He was intoxicated by the time I stopped by to visit him after work. The county quickly pulled out due to his belligerent behavior toward the home visitors. I apologized and agreed that she didn't deserve to be treated so disrespectfully. From that point on, he was virtually alone.

JERRY AND SALLY DIVORCED, but she and I remained friends. I was terribly concerned about Jerry and his drinking. He was reckless and often found trouble at the bars he frequented. He was a totally different man when he drank. When sober, he would give you the shirt off his back, but when he drank, he would take the shirt off your back. Jerry was in a great deal of emotional pain due to his divorce. Many times he was angry with me because he said he couldn't provide a house for his family like AJ did for me. He felt like a failure. His children loved him and missed him very much while they were separated, but Jerry's parenting abilities were as limited as mine. We felt cheated by our parents for our lack of knowledge.

I attempted to talk with Jerry about my concerns but he was so intoxicated most of the time that it did little good. This created more tension between us. Jerry missed work and didn't eat. The times I did talk with him, he didn't make sense.

I received a phone call from Aunt Victoria late one afternoon. Jerry had been to her home and was extremely drunk. He told her he was driving to Minneapolis despite his condition. I decided to try and stop him. I looked all over for him but couldn't locate him. The next day I found him, still drunk, at a friend's home. He rushed out of the house wielding a baseball bat. He was delusional and mistook my vehicle for a police wagon. It took a lot of talking on my part to convince him I was his sister.

The fact that I lived in a house, was still married, and had a husband who wasn't an alcoholic remained a barrier between Jerry and me. I missed my brother, but he wouldn't let me get close to him. He was in extreme pain and angry at losing his family. He cried often about how he didn't want to put his children through what we had been through. Ironically, he thought my life was a success.

Shortly after Jesse and Lenny complete basic training, they asked to visit. AJ made it clear that they couldn't stay with us. Jesse and Lenny planned to stop at Jerry's first before joining me for dinner. When I didn't hear from them, I became worried. They had a habit of fighting when they drank.

Early the next morning, I drove to Jerry's. I looked through the screen door and saw his bloodied body sleeping in the kitchen chair. I stormed in and kicked the chair out from under him. He woke with a start. He was angry and raised his fist to me. I threatened that I'd knock him down again if he didn't tell me where Jesse and Lenny were. Jerry looked a bit dazed. One side of his face was swollen, while the top of one of his hands was bruised and had dried blood on it. I demanded to know where our brothers were. He started to cry and said he didn't know. They had a terrible fight, but he didn't know if the blood on him was theirs or his. He was sure he had hurt one of them, although he didn't know how badly. I grabbed Jerry and shook him hard. I had never been so afraid or angry. I demanded an explanation while I dragged him to my vehicle. When Jesse and Lenny arrived at his place, still in uniform, he was reminded of his own time in the service and how much he had enjoyed it. He became angry and resentful. He taunted them, saying they were worthless and that their uniforms didn't make them men. Then he suggested they kill themselves and do the world a favor.

Jerry's opinion of them was very important to Jesse and Lenny. Jerry hadn't meant to hurt them; however, the alcohol had turned him into a powder keg. He was so unhappy in his own life; he took out his anger on his brothers.

We searched and eventually found them at a friend's house. Both had bruises on their faces and knuckles and some small cuts around their eyebrows, but I was thankful they were both alive.

Before their leave ended, I had a picture of them in their uniforms taken with Grandma Elma. They both looked so handsome. I prayed that their lives would be less troubled than Jerry's and mine, but I had my doubts.

Eventually, Jesse received a medical discharge from the Army due to his heart problems. He fathered a child with a sixteen-year-old girl. They rented a trailer across the highway from me. It was in terrible condition and didn't have running water. I bought their groceries and washed their dishes for them when AJ wasn't home. I knew AJ would be furious if he discovered I was aiding them. Jesse smoked marijuana frequently, and I suspected his girlfriend did also. I kept in close contact with them after the baby arrived because I worried about their parenting capabilities. I babysat for them often.

Their relationship soured quickly, and she returned home to live with her family. He had little further contact with his daughter. His chemical use continued which led to numerous failed relationships.

That year, Jerry moved to Minneapolis. Shortly after he left, Aunt Helen was diagnosed with lung cancer. After surgery her prognosis was good. Later that day, Aunt Victoria called to say she had spoken to the doctor and there had been a misdiagnosis. The cancer had spread, and Helen's condition was terminal. In fact, she might not live through the night.

I knew Jerry would want to see Aunt Helen before she died. He had always been very close to her and Uncle Eddie. They thought of him as a son. Eddie drank heavily but; however, he was not mean or unkind.

Jerry lived in an apartment where the only phone was in the hallway. I called but with no success.

It was so painful for me to see Helen dying. I silently cried as I held her hand. I informed her I was trying to reach Jerry because I knew he would want to be there. Aunt Helen worried about Jerry. She knew her dying would be difficult for him. Aunt Victoria attempted to console Uncle Eddie, but he was struggling emotionally. He needed Jerry too.

I called AJ to inform him of the situation. When he arrived at the hospital, he asked to speak privately with me. He demanded to know how long I was going to be at the hospital and angrily reminded me that I belonged at home. I didn't understand his behavior. My aunt was dying. I made it clear that I would stay until Jerry arrived or Helen passed away. He abruptly turned and walked away. I ran after him and asked for money. He said no and left. I was furious but didn't make a scene. I had no money to buy snacks, pop or coffee. We all had been at the hospital for over five hours. We were emotionally exhausted and grieving. Some food or drink would have helped. Again AJ exercised his power and control. This time however, his actions affected others whom I cared about deeply while they were in an extremely vulnerable situation. I wouldn't make excuses for his behavior. This I could not forgive.

Aunt Helen's condition deteriorated rapidly. When I eventually contacted Jerry, he was drunk and couldn't comprehend what I was saying. Eventually, I convinced him to take the bus trip north.

When I went to the bus depot to meet Jerry, he wasn't there. I called him. He was confused and thought Aunt Helen had the flu. I repeated myself three or four times, "Helen's dying. You need to get here and soon!" He still sounded groggy but said he'd catch the next bus. I prayed that Jerry would see Helen before she died. I sat with Helen while she dozed off and on. I held her hand, closed my eyes and cried. She died an hour or so later. Her loss pained me, and I knew Jerry would feel it more than me.

When Jerry arrived, I gently explained that Helen had passed away. He didn't believe me. He was devastated and began to sob so hard his whole body shook. He raced into the hospital where Uncle Ralph and Aunt Victoria sat. Ralph looked relieved to see Jerry. Jerry insisted on going to see Helen and stayed with her a long time. When he came out of her room, he looked whipped; his eyes showing the extreme pain he was feeling. Jerry hugged Eddie long and fiercely. Those two men knew the feeling of pain only too well, but had no idea how to deal with it.

I gave Jerry and Eddie a ride home. Everyone was quiet. I was exhausted and feeling the pain of losing Helen. I cried all the way home. Once home, I sat in my rocking chair and rocked until the sun came up. AJ didn't talk to me. I knew the next few days were going to be difficult for Jerry. I checked on Jerry and Eddie on my way to work. They had sat up the rest of the night and attempted to drink away their grief.

The next night after dinner, I packed up the leftovers and made sandwiches for Jerry and Eddie. I was about to leave the house when AJ confronted me. When I told him I was taking the food to Eddie's, he glared at me. I stared him down and told him it was my money that purchased the groceries, and I left. He said nothing.

Jerry moved to Minneapolis after his divorce was final. I was afraid that I would lose him forever. I didn't think he would live long with his lifestyle. He promised to see his boys often and that he would work to make sure they didn't want for anything. Shortly after he arrived in Minneapolis, he hit rock bottom. One day he woke up in a beaten down building near a toilet stool. A cockroach was climbing out of the glass of beer he still held in his hand. He felt physically, emotionally, and spiritually dead. He said he never prayed so hard in his life to God. If he couldn't escape the despair in which he was mired, he prayed for God to take him. This was the turning point for Jerry, and he has been sober ever since.

WORKING REMAINED MY SALVATION. It was a safe place to be and I was treated with respect and kindness. Work energized me. My relationship with AJ, on the other hand, exhausted me. Gina suggested I try therapy. I asked John about it and he provided the name of a therapist he thought was good and honest. I scheduled an appointment during work hours so AJ wouldn't know.

My first session with Marie was enlightening. She asked why I was there and what I hoped to gain.

Marie was pregnant. When I became tearful, I attempted to direct the conversation to her baby. Her response was that I should take a friend to coffee if I wanted to visit. It would certainly be cheaper than paying her $75 an hour. I appreciated her honesty.

Marie asked about my childhood. This confused me. I didn't understand how the past could affect my marital situation. But I was desperate and trusted John's advice, so I opened up to her. It felt good to speak openly and honestly about my feelings.

Marie gave me permission to cry and be angry about all that had happened in my life. She was gentle with my feelings and encouraged me to be honest with myself about who I was. When I discussed my thoughts of suicide, she asked why I felt that death was the only solution to my marital woes. She suggested another option, divorce. I had never considered divorce. I was tired of living I pain and it seemed no matter what decisions I made with best intentions, I returned to live in pain. I was afraid the system wouldn't grant me custody of my children. The thought of being separated from them would feel like death. If I was awarded custody, how would I know how to raise them? I knew how to love them, but that was not enough. Parents were responsible to teach their children how to live; how to grow up and be responsible, honest, caring people. I didn't know how to teach my children these important lessons. Marie said we could work on all those issues. Life seemed so complex and painful. Nothing was simple or easy, and I was tired of trying. She said, "You do need to rest emotionally, however, suicide is more permanent than a rest." I smiled and agreed with her. I never wanted to be far from my children. I had promised God that I would do my best. I didn't want to give up on life, but I needed tools to progress. I didn't know why life seemed so hard. Could I be crazy?

Marie asked me if I took showers, brushed my teeth, and dressed every day. I laughed and said, "Of course, that's a silly question. What does that have to do with being a crazy person?" She said that for many people suffering from mental illness, daily tasks were difficult to accomplish. If that wasn't it, then why couldn't my own mother love me? Perhaps others can see it even if I can't. Mother must have seen it, but she didn't tell me what it was.

Marie asked about my mother, and I told her how much I missed her and the lack of emotional attachment. When she asked me about life in the foster home, I looked down, afraid she would see my tears. I shamefully shared with her the sexual abuse I suffered. I was startled by a loud noise. I looked up to see tears in Marie's eyes. She had thrown a notebook down. She said she was sad for me because I was a child deserving protection. This was the first time anyone had told me what had happened was wrong and cruel.

I was confused and dumbfounded by her reaction. I assured her I didn't mean to upset her but I was being open and honest like she requested. She said she wasn't upset with me; she was upset about the circumstances of my childhood. It was the first time anyone was upset or sad on my behalf.

My mother taught me what I didn't want to be, but I didn't know what else I could be. I was emotionally exhausted from trying to figure this out on my own. I constantly worried about my brothers. It was difficult to watch when I didn't know how to help them. I knew how to help them when we were children, but I didn't know how to help them now. I disliked my past and present life. If these were the predictors for my future, I wasn't sure I could go on. Marie said we could work on all these issues and concerns. It gave me enough hope to continue on with my life. Where there had only been darkness, now there was a glimmer of light.

We talked about realistic goal-setting. I learned about the difference between needs and wants. In counseling we talked about appropriateness, the definition of love, the different levels of love and friendship, and the definition of a mother. Marie defined privacy and secrecy. She gave me hope! She asked me to believe that life was worth living and that it didn't have to be all pain. I began to realize that I didn't have to look through the eyes of a victim. She not only told me I was a person of value, she treated me like I had value. She encouraged me to think and express my ideas. She treated me respectfully and gently. I looked forward to our appointments. I believe that God works through others to reach our hearts. She was truly an angel during one of the darkest periods of my life!

Chapter Six
Hinged on My Past

DESPITE MY ATTEMPTS TO PERSUADE THE MILITARY, Jesse and Lenny were not allowed to come home for Aunt Helen's funeral. Leaves were only granted for immediate family. It saddened all of us that we couldn't pay our respects to her as a family.

My relationship with AJ continued to deteriorate. We hardly talked and when we did, there was no willingness to compromise on his part. He picked up the girls from childcare after work, but when I came home, I found them sitting on the couch, totally bored. There was no television, no books and no toys. He ordered them to stay put and not move until I came home. When I confronted him about this, his response was always the same. If I'd stay home like he wanted, it wouldn't be a problem. He didn't want the girls playing on the grass and didn't want them to bother him when he changed oil. Everything was always about him and what he wanted. I suggested leaving the girls at childcare where I could pick them up. He rejected this solution as a waste of money. Our relationship exhausted and negatively impacted our daughters. What were my choices? I didn't know, but hoped and prayed therapy would provide some answers.

When I confided to Marie that my house didn't feel like a home, she suggested I try something different. One day when AJ left his checkbook home, I purchased paint. I reasoned that if our walls were painted colors other than white, they might not feel so sterile. I panted the kitchen canary and the living room mauve. When AJ came home and discovered my updates, he was furious.

Changing the colors didn't make the house feel any warmer. I realized I disliked living in my home regardless of what color the walls were.

Marie suggested family therapy. If I wanted AJ to join me in therapy, I would have to tell him I had been going to therapy in the first place. This was a difficult decision, but I decided to be honest. When I approached AJ about it, his response was that if I did what he ordered me to do, our relationship would be fine. He was extremely upset and said his friends might see my car at the therapist's office and assume I was some sort of nut. He felt embarrassed to call me his wife. I informed him that Marie's office was at the clinic. If people saw my car, they would think it was a medical appointment.

Again he reminded me of how stupid and gullible I was. He said it wasn't normal for anyone to go to a doctor twice a month, every month. I pointed out that I was trying to help our relationship, and if he felt it was important, he would agree to try it. He agreed that someone like me probably needed therapy. His opinion was that I should be grateful he married me because he damn well knew no one else would have!

I said nothing about individual counseling for a few months. He was able to silence me with his cruel reminders that I was not like everyone else. According to him, I was damaged, I was never grateful no matter how much he did for me, and I continued to be an embarrassment to him.

Marie asked me what I felt my options were. I said I couldn't take living like this any longer and that thoughts of suicide still surfaced. Life was so painful all the time. I loved my children and had promised God I would take care of them, and my promise was the only factor that made suicide a less viable option. All my choices seemed difficult. Marie said these were not my only two choices. Although she didn't promote divorce, she suggested that a separation might be helpful to our relationship. This would give us time to work on what was important to us and our relationship. "AJ will never agree to it," I responded. She said he didn't have to. "If you need an emotional break, then you need to take one," she said. I knew AJ would be extremely angry with me and would never consider compromise, but if I didn't figure out what was important to me, there was no hope anyway.

That evening I worked up the courage to tell him what I wanted. I offered three suggestions: couples therapy, physical separation or divorce. He was furious. He made it clear the discussion was over and I better never bring it up again. Then he stormed out to go change oil on one of his vehicles. Life wasn't supposed to be like this.

I made an appointment with a divorce attorney. This was my least desirable option. I didn't want my children to have divorced parents. Plus, I didn't want them to lose their home. Would they be better with their father because he made more money, or would they be able to thrive with a parent with no money and limited parenting skills? All I could provide for them was deep love. This did not feel like a good solution in my heart; but I truly needed information to make the right decision. My willingness to live was fading. Thoughts of my children being better off without me seemed to permeate my mind more frequently. They had no idea, at ages two and four, how damaged I was. They might be better off not knowing and starting fresh with their father.

I put the date and time of my appointment on the calendar. This appointment was six weeks off and I hoped I would be able to cancel it. I told AJ I had the appointment, but I offered to cancel it if he would try marital counseling. He said nothing and the tension remained. Finally a week before the appointment, AJ agreed to counseling.

On the way to the appointment, he asked if the therapist was male or female. When I responded female, he argued that a woman would be biased against him. To the contrary, I pointed out that she had many suggestions on how to improve our relationship, and she had never said anything bad about him and always encouraged me to try harder and communicate better. There was no living with me, he said. In his opinion, I was very difficult and damaged. After all he had done for me, I had made matters worse and was becoming more and more like my mother. He stated that he wasn't crazy, I was!

I felt very sad and had the sinking feeling this was not going to work. AJ had convinced all his friends and family that I was crazy and that he was a saint for marrying me. Feelings of shame and embarrassment began to flood my emotions. When we entered our appointment, I could tell that Marie was pleased AJ had come.

First Marie asked AJ if he knew why we were there. He said he knew why he was there and that he wasn't happy about it. Then he proceeded to explain all my problems to her. He said that I didn't listen to him, that I continued to visit my family when they were nothing but losers and drunks and damaged just like me. It was his opinion that no other man would have married a woman like me. He complained that I didn't accept his guidance but instead chose to argue with him. He further stated that I was unappreciative of his hard work and should be happy he put a roof over my head.

Marie listened but said little. AJ felt I should stay home with the children, instead of going to work where other women could fill my head with silly notions. He summed it up by stating that if I would simply listen to him and do as I was told, our relationship would be fine. Marie asked him if these were my thoughts as well. He said, "Of course not. That's why Karen thinks we should go this therapy stuff."

Marie asked if he had any other suggestion to improve our relationship. AJ said no, that it was quite simple - "Karen needs to quit her job and stay home, stop running around visiting her family and our neighbors, and quit thinking there are any problems. The only problems are the ones she creates!"

Marie ended our appointment a bit early and didn't say much. As I was leaving, she asked if I would be at our next appointment. I said yes, but felt very sad. All the way home, AJ said he was glad he had attended and set things straight; and, there certainly wasn't any need for any other family appointments. He demanded that I stop seeing Marie after my next appointment. He was convinced that Marie agreed with his assessment of our marriage. He concluded by saying that therapy wasn't difficult—was rather simple in fact—and he was glad the issue was settled. I was more confused about the whole situation than ever. Maybe AJ had convinced her, like everyone else, how crazy I really was.

At our next appointment, I asked Marie if she thought I was crazy like he claimed. She said, "First, your husband's not willing to look at his behavior and therefore, change will be most difficult for him. He does not feel he needs to change because he believes everything in the relationship is your fault, everything." She suggested individual counseling first for AJ and then additional family therapy.

I told her AJ said I should quit therapy. She asked me how I felt about our sessions. When I told her how much I looked forward to them and the progress I felt I was making, she encouraged me to continue. "The decision should be yours and not your husband's," she said. She asked if I planned to follow up with my plan to see a divorce lawyer, and I said yes. Marie asked what my response to AJ would be if I told him I wanted a separation and he said no. My plan was to ask him to move out, but if he refused, then I would keep my paycheck and rent an apartment. I wasn't knowledgeable about how to rent an apartment, but I was certain Jerry would assist me. I truly believed our marriage could be saved, and this was only a temporary situation. After all, there was no alcohol or physical abuse.

AJ visited my attorney prior to my first appointment and ordered him not to see me. The attorney told AJ that he had the appointment with me and that he best leave or he would call law enforcement. I was amazed that he had stood up for me to my husband.

I asked AJ for a separation. I suggested a six-week separation followed by family counseling. This would allow each of us time to decide if our marriage was worth saving.

AJ stated that the house was his so he wasn't going anywhere. He said he knew I didn't have any money and couldn't go anywhere, so I best start acting like his wife and quit having silly notions of counseling, separation and divorce. If I did leave, he said he'd be awarded custody of the kids, as no court would let a mother like me, a nut case, have custody. He challenged me to go live with my family, a family that never provided for me as a child. "They can't even take care of themselves. How are they going to take care of you?" If I kept pushing these topics, he thundered, he was going to contact my foster father and let the courts know exactly how damaged and crazy I was. I was emotionally defeated. I didn't want to be separated from my children, and I certainly didn't want any contact or involvement from Carl. It was clear that my options were limited and none were easy.

Again, I stated my intentions. I could keep my paycheck and rent an apartment, or he could move out. He reluctantly agreed to move out, saying he would return once I got my act together. AJ moved in with a coworker who lived across the street. He came home regularly to pack his lunch, mow the lawn and sometimes sleep over. I argued that this was not a separation. He stated this was his home and no one was going to tell him he couldn't come home!

My father-in-law came over during this "sorta" separation, stating that he wanted to see his grandchildren. This was unusual because he had rarely ever visited before. He arrived with AJ. While AJ took the children to the bedroom his father lit into me about our living situation. He asked me who I thought I was ordering his son to leave when it was his home. "A man's home is his castle, and this was his castle," he said. He called me names and said I was a poor excuse for a wife. He suggested I wise up or I wouldn't have anything. I went into the bedroom and asked AJ to take his father and leave. I knew at this point that the marriage was over. I couldn't tolerate the situation anymore.

I spoke with my father, on a day when he was sober, and asked him to help me look for an apartment. Father agreed but was teary-eyed as I suspected it reminded him of his own divorce and the unhappiness it brought to all of us. I felt sad I didn't have time to deal with his old memories, but my heart could not take on any more sadness.

My friend Gina assisted me with my move. I was starting to believe that I could parent my children because I was willing to learn how. I knew money would be an issue, however, I felt confident I could learn how to budget $800 per month. I applied for low-income housing and child care assistance, even though I found it difficult to ask for help. Based on my previous experience with foster care, it was emotionally draining.

On payday, AJ stopped in the office to pick up my check. For the first time I told him he couldn't have it because I needed it to pay rent. When I said I was moving out the next weekend, he was dumbfounded. It was clear from his reaction he never truly expected me to leave him or to stand up to him. I felt sad because it seemed that there was no compromise in our relationship. He treated me with little respect and I couldn't see that ever changing. He was not totally to blame because I had been treated disrespectfully for so long before I met him that I was accustomed to it, but it didn't feel very good in my heart. However painful, I viewed this as an opportunity to better my relationship and myself, so it was a step I had to take.

IN 1985 I MET CAL AT WORK. Cal had been hired to work on the computer systems. He had completed some legal obligations and was working on putting his life back on track. John wanted to help him out, so I did my best to assist him in any way I could. On his first day in the office, he seemed friendly.

As time went on, I found Cal to be cocky and somewhat arrogant. I began to dislike his presence in the office. One time I entered John's office and found him with his feet up on the desk and loud rock music blaring. He didn't attempt to move when I entered the office, nor when I turned the radio down. John favored classical music, so this was quite a shock. I thought Cal was disrespectful of John's good nature. He'd note my disgusted look and smile. That made me even angrier. I felt he should behave more appreciatively and respectfully in the boss' office.

It didn't take long for the teenage girls in the office to lavish him with attention. He enjoyed the attention; however, it angered me to see him take his work lightly. When I shot him disgusted looks, he smiled, which made me angrier.

One day I had to assist Cal with data entry training. This meant I had to spend the whole day with him. I found this difficult, as I had developed a strong dislike for him. As we trained together, he seemed to drop his arrogant attitude and became sincere about assisting me. During the day, AJ called and spoke very crudely to me. This made me tearful. Cal asked if I was okay. He was very sincere and kind. I shared with him that I was going through a divorce, and it was a very emotionally difficult time. He dropped his arrogant, cocky attitude and was genuinely pleasant and respectful after that. He asked if he could join me on my break. I told him I didn't think so because I took breaks in the janitor's room.

John asked if I'd give Cal a ride home. I truly didn't want to but I couldn't think of an excuse, so I half-heartedly agreed.

With the emotional trauma going on in my life, dealing with Cal was not something I wanted to add to my already hectic agenda. During our drive, I emphasized that I had other obligations to take care of when work was over, so this would be the one and only ride I'd give him. It was obvious I wasn't very happy about transporting him.

Cal was quiet, and when I dropped him off, he smiled and thanked me for the ride. Afterwards, I felt guilty. It was only a ten-minute drive and it was on my way home. I realized that he had quite a walk to work, especially if the weather was poor. Cal always made it to work on time and completed a full day. I never heard him complain. I promised myself that I wouldn't behave so selfishly or act so rudely from that point on.

A week later, he asked again if he could join me on break, and I reluctantly agreed. He asked about my divorce, my children, and if I had family support. I shared about the divorce and a little about my personal history. He said he felt sad for me and offered his support. I was very appreciative of his kindness. He talked a little about his history and how close he was to his mother and that he didn't know what he would do if he didn't have her love and support.

We became friends. He shared how his struggles with his own sobriety and his addictions to marijuana, street drugs and alcohol. He talked about night sweats and the jogging he did to eliminate the chemicals from his system. Sometimes he said he had sores on his hands and terrible nightmares. This left him exhausted. He had a brother who was not taking his sobriety seriously, and this made his struggle more difficult. I admired his strength and courage. Mostly I admired his honesty.

Cal had four sisters, and his mother was a single parent. He talked of his childhood and his wonderful relationship with his grandmother. He felt he had let his mother and grandmother down by breaking the law and spending time in jail. His mother and grandmother were both very emotionally supportive of him during his incarceration. He struggled daily with his sobriety. He was at a crossroads and needed to decide how much involvement chemicals would play in his life. John wanted him to work with the students who used chemicals so Cal agreed to run a group.

I admired all the struggles he had been through because I knew how chemicals ruined families. I shared more and more about my family and my anger at my parents. Like him, I didn't really fit in anywhere in society. I shared my fears about my own anxiety over alcohol. Although I only drank beer sporadically and never drank to excess, I worried about becoming like my mother. I worried that I could become abusive. These were huge fears in my heart. We talked about my brothers and their continued struggles with sobriety.

I found our conversations enlightening and enjoyed talking to someone who seemed to understand the negative impact of chemicals. His goal of sobriety was a huge one so I tried to encourage him the best as I could. As our relationship grew, he shared that he felt isolated from his family. We discovered we had a great deal in common and enjoyed each other's company. I appreciated his warm smile and easy laugh. Much to my amazement, we had become friends.

My father helped me look for housing. Fortunately, dad was sober and was able to accurately inspect the rental unit. The house was located only two blocks away from the girls' childcare, so it was very convenient.

My childcare provider was aware of my marital situation. She was very supportive and understanding. She offered to watch the girls for court dates or other appointments. I was grateful for her emotional support and kindness. I felt ashamed to have to tell her about my divorce. Also, it was difficult to accept childcare assistance, but my options were limited. I worried that AJ might talk to the provider and sabotage my childcare. I knew it was best to be open and honest from the start.

I went home to pick up a few personal items. I grabbed a few envelopes and surprisingly discovered money tucked in them. Also,

I found wads of bills stuffed in AJ's socks. There was money stashed all over the house. I was angry. Here I was, his wife, and he felt he had to hide money. I didn't want his money. The whole goal of my working was so we could afford to do family activities together. Finding this money made it clear he didn't trust me. I didn't want to live with someone I couldn't trust. If he couldn't trust me, why would he want to live with me? When he came home from work, I laid all the money I found on the table and said, "You keep your money, but you lose your family, is that what you want?" To look at him made me disgusted. I didn't understand his ways, and I wasn't sure I wanted to. I had come from nothing and I didn't need much. I knew how to get by on very little. He could keep his money. I walked away.

In September 1985, I moved into an apartment. AJ made an emotionally difficult experience even worse. He refused to let me take any of the girls' bedroom furniture.

Part of his anger could be attributed to his belief that I was cheating on him with Cal. Despite my assurance that we were just friends and coworkers, he didn't believe me. From others I discovered AJ was gossiping about me and making up horrific lies. He spread lies everywhere that I had multiple sex partners when in fact, I had only had two in my entire life, and one was my foster father. I couldn't understand how he could call me filthy names and spread vicious lies about while at the same time begging me to return to him. I was confused by his contradictory behavior. I felt insulted that he thought I'd cheat on him. I went to work and came home (aside from visiting my grandmother and father on occasion), and the children were always with me. When would I have an affair? I didn't even know any single men besides Cal, and I had just met him three weeks earlier.

AJ refused to let me take some of the toys. If I packed them, he unpacked them. He forbade me to take the girls' Slip-and-Slide, a $20 water summer toy. This was odd because he never let the girls play on it anyway for fear it would wreck the lawn. His action and behavior confused me. I still wanted to believe this was only a separation and I planned on returning, but I needed time and space away from him. AJ cried, swore and yelled out angry threats.

By the time we left, we were all emotionally exhausted. I was extremely frustrated because he knew this was imminent but had done nothing to prevent it. Maybe the separation would prompt him to work on our marriage. If not, at least I had my own place. I felt a deep sense of relief knowing I didn't have to return to the house ever again.

AJ's behavior worsened. He had his friends' wives call me and plead on his behalf. He had his mother ask me to lunch when she had never asked me to lunch before. Her main concern was that AJ's diet consisted of TV dinners.

One of his friends' wives worked as a bank teller. He started showing up at the bank begging her to talk some sense into me. She said his behavior was threatening her job so she suggested it would be easier for her if I returned to him. Friends stopped calling because of his behavior. They felt uncomfortable with it. I understood but felt even more isolated than ever.

I only met AJ in public places such as restaurants. Once he pinned me in the booth, threatening to hold me captive until I gave into his demands. I had to ask the waitress to help me leave. It was embarrassing and humiliating. When I didn't say what he wanted to hear, he became belligerent and called me filthy names. I became increasingly tired and weary of this non-stop emotional roller coaster I was on.

Separation wasn't my attempt to punish or manipulate AJ. I envisioned it as an opportunity to start our relationship anew and be respectful to each other. Instead, he became increasingly verbally abusive.

Cal offered to open up his home to my daughters and me should I need it. Also, John was supportive and assured me he would help me in any way he could.

Work offered a wonderful mental distraction from the emotional trauma I was experiencing. I had learned well as a child how to separate painful emotions from tasks I needed to do. Although I might be consumed with emotional pain, I could focus on what I needed to do. This is a skill that served me well then and continues to.

Chapter Seven
Cal

"You must be good in bed because you sure ain't much to look at." These were the first words my mother spoke to Cal.

IN SEPTEMBER 1985, DIVORCE proceedings began, though they would not be finalized for two more years. It was clear there was no hope to salvage our fractured relationship. The stress was taking its toll on Shawna and Sandy plus my own mental health was fragile.

I spent $50 on a suit to wear to court. I wanted the judge to see that I was not the victim I had been as a child. This was a large sum of money, but I knew I was in the fight of my life. I was aware that AJ would say terrible things about me so I wanted the judge to be able to look at me and know I was a good person. I was certain AJ would reveal my sexual abuse, the foster homes, the pervasive chemical dependency in my family and my therapy.

At our initial court hearing, AJ was awarded visitation with the children every other weekend and one evening during the week. My only outlet was work. I invited Cal over for supper on occasion. We played board games with my daughters or watched television. My favorite times though, were when we just talked. I felt sad for him sometimes because he was trying to maintain his sobriety and nobody seemed to recognize how difficult it can be to change one's lifestyle. I knew because I saw my parents and older brother try changing theirs many times.

Our society, in general, doesn't promote sobriety. Sobriety is talked about as a positive goal, but most people's behavior says something else. I shared with Cal my feelings of anger toward my parents and the confusion that gripped me. Cal was a good listener and encouraged my life changes. I didn't have to repeat my parent's mistakes. While I knew what I didn't want to be, it was difficult knowing what I could or should be.

I blame my parents for my brother's struggles in their personal lives and mine. We didn't know much about relationships. My brothers were never taught how to treat women, to be respectful, or even how to change oil or fix cars. My parents taught us how to sit at a bar and drink and that nothing else was important. Sometimes after I had verbally spouted off, I looked at Cal and saw tears in his eyes. He was sorry that life had been so hard for me. Sometimes this made me angry. I didn't like the feeling that someone felt sorry for me. I didn't need that. I was a competent adult and able-bodied. I knew how to work, I loved my children; yet I was just confused at times. The confusion scared me, but my anger kept me determined to manage whatever came my way. I was not someone to be pitied. We were misfits, but we were friends. I admired his courage and was proud of his efforts to make a change in his life.

Cal became active in the sobriety groups at work. John asked him to share his story with the students which he was happy to. John was wonderful that way. He was not judgmental. If any of us made a poor decision, he listened and offered suggestions. He never took it personally if someone rejected his advice. He incorporated healthy sober adults to offer support and guidance. The youth he worked with were often viewed as difficult members of the community. Most had barriers—truancy, legal issues, violence, foster children, abuse of chemicals, out-of-home placements or a combination. Many struggled due to lack of structure in the home, the result of chemically dependent parents or poor parenting skills. Is it any wonder I fit in well with the students and found it easy to talk with them and vice versa?

John struggled to balance the needs of the students while working within a community that was much more judgmental. He gently and positively touched many lives through his programs.

AJ'S BEHAVIOR WORSENED. HE threatened to ask Carl to come to our divorce hearing and tell the judge what kind of person I was. He monitored my actions day and night. He parked a short distance from my home and watched me. He left work early to witness my movements. His behavior resurrected old memories of Carl and his similar behavior. I was emotionally overwhelmed.

The day after I had the oil changed on the car, it wouldn't start. I cried because I couldn't afford another car bill. When my mechanic looked at it, he discovered that oil had been dumped over the engine. He said it was fortunate the car hadn't started because a spark could have caused a fire.

The malfunction seemed odd considering I had the car serviced the day before. I strongly suspected AJ was involved but had no proof. Didn't he realize he could have killed our children? I called the police and an officer was dispatched. He looked around the yard and discovered large-sized shoe tracks in the snow around the house and the garage. However disturbing this action was, his blatant attempt at intimidation did not deter me from moving forward with the divorce proceedings.

Cal expressed to me that he cared about me and wanted to be more than friends. I didn't know what to say. I felt close to him, but he was six years younger than I was and I was in the middle of a very difficult divorce. I hadn't emotionally adjusted to the fact that I was no longer separated but nearly divorced. I had two children. He had not been in a committed relationship, nor did he have children. He was a good friend but to be honest, I was afraid of emotions and men. I kept my feelings shutdown in order to function day-to-day. He said he understood and didn't pressure me.

My brothers disliked my participation in the Adult Children of Alcoholics class and also my pending divorce. I couldn't turn to them for support. I was changing, gaining some insights into our childhood, while my brothers preferred me the way I was before. They thought I should leave our past alone and move on with life. However, it seemed to me that my future hinged on my past—what I knew and, more importantly, what I didn't know.

I lost thirty pounds in six weeks. I was physically and emotionally ill. I went from a size 14 to a size 6. I couldn't swallow noodles. I tried to eat a cheeseburger and only managed a few mouthfuls before I began to feel nauseous. My monthly cycle stopped altogether.

Jerry was especially upset about my decision to divorce AJ. He felt I shouldn't see Cal due to my vulnerability. He encouraged me to reconcile with AJ because he worked, drank very little, and made a pleasant home for the girls and me. I respected Jerry's opinion; we had a strong history together, but he didn't know what it was like living with someone who didn't care. However, I temporarily put the divorce on hold to see if AJ would agree to some changes. Again he refused counseling, asked me to stop having contact with my family, including my grandmother, and ordered me to quit my ob. I truly tried to see things his way.

My life was improving through counseling, the support group and my supportive coworkers. Did I really want to give all this up? I waited for 30 days and made the decision that living with AJ was no longer an option. I was deeply hurt by his actions and words, so much so that I chose not to give up what I had worked so hard to accomplish.

In December of 1985, despite my hesitation, I expanded my relationship with Cal. My attorney advised me against it because AJ might use it against me in court. This angered me because in my quest to become a better person, I was still controlled by someone else. AJ began sending me flowers three times a week. He never gave me flowers the whole time we were married. His attempts at manipulation angered me more.

The wife of one of AJ's friends called me and asked me to lunch. During our meal, her husband showed up and demanded that she not see me anymore. He said I was a bad influence on his wife. He grabbed her arm and they left. She never spoke to me again. I felt deep shame.

I asked John what steps I would have to take to become a chemical dependency counselor. The training was short and I could work at a local CD treatment facility. John thought it was a good idea. I completed all the necessary paperwork and scheduled an interview. The interview was very difficult. One interviewer said he wouldn't recommend me for further training. When I asked why, he said because I was not chemically dependent, I'd have a difficult time relating and building rapport with the people who were chemically dependent. I countered by saying that I had been exposed to many people who were chemically dependent, but he said it didn't matter. The bottom line, I was not a chemically dependent person and due to my personal history, I should be attending co-dependent support groups, not facilitating them. I left crying. I felt angry that I had to be chemically dependent to work with people who might or might not be serious about their own recoveries.

John suggested I attend college. Surprised, I told him that college was for other people, not people like me. Besides, I didn't know the first thing about college. He said there was money available for single parents wanting to pursue a degree. At first I dismissed his suggestion, but the more I thought about it, the more the idea of building a better life for my family grew on me.

The thought of a four-year commitment with two children was scary. No one in my family had attended college; in fact, many hadn't even graduated from high school. I felt very proud that John thought I was smart enough; however, I wasn't sure how realistic a goal it was.

My life consisted of work and therapy. I felt very isolated and alone. My brothers were upset about the divorce and the support group. They were verbally abusive and tried to convince me to return to AJ. It pained me to be emotionally separated from them.

As my relationship with Cal grew more serious, we discussed our expectations of each other. I shared with him my history of sexual abuse and my fear of intimacy. I was much better with friendships. He was patient and said we could proceed very slowly. My main concern was that I didn't want to jeopardize my position in court regarding custody of my daughters. He understood that. One of his concerns was that I drank a beer occasionally. I made it clear that I wasn't going to have anyone tell me what to do. His sobriety was important to him so it bothered him to see beer in my refrigerator. This issue caused some friction between us.

The first time we were intimate, I shut the lights off and began to undress. He asked why I wanted it dark. I said I felt more comfortable if I wasn't seen. I began to cry. He held me for a long time and said I was beautiful. I confessed to him I felt so damaged and that I really didn't have anything to offer. He agreed to leave the lights off, but only because I wanted to, not because he did. He said that when one cares about someone, they care about that person's heart. We all have flaws, he said, and none of us is perfect. To him, intimacy was an expression of how one felt about someone, not about his or her flaws or scars.

Although I was certain not every man felt this way, I believed he truly looked past my perceived flaws and saw me for who I truly was. He wondered if I saw his flaws. I said I didn't which made us both laugh. Cal was very kind and gentle, and he told me I was beautiful inside and out. I didn't see a look of disgust in his eyes when he looked at me. He treated me kindly whenever we were together. I had never felt so at peace. Cal's actions matched what he said. I began to believe that, in his eyes, I was not damaged. My extreme anxiety and fear of vulnerability slowly subsided.

We spent extra time together on weekends when the girls were with their father; however, he never spent the night when they were home. He was very kind and respectful that way. He never was angry about having to go home at night or having limited time on weekends.

I looked forward to our time together. We laughed, ate out, took walks, fed ducks, rented movies or watched TV. It felt good to have something to look forward to and not be on my guard emotionally. My children weren't close to him. Cal was okay with this because he realized they had a father and he wasn't interested in trying to replace him. He understood that my daughters were struggling with the divorce as much as I was and consequently, they disliked having another man around their mom. Deep down I'm sure they hoped I might return to their father. For the girls' sake, we tried to see each other primarily when the children were with their father.

One winter night, Cal walked three miles to my home in a snowstorm to bring me smoked fish. When he arrived, he looked like a snowman. His moustache and eyebrows were frozen. At first I was confused about his behavior. He said he spotted the fish at the grocery store and remembered an earlier conversation with me when I had mentioned I hadn't had smoked fish since I was a child. I was deeply moved that he remembered such a conversation. I was touched that he walked that far for me. No one had ever done that. I was very tearful over his tender act. This endeared him more to my heart—we were friends.

AJ monitored my every move, but I didn't care what he or anyone thought about my relationship with Cal. I didn't care what my attorney or my brothers thought, and I certainly didn't care what AJ thought. I was tired of pleasing everyone. I wasn't doing anything wrong. I wanted to be myself for a change. Nobody seemed to know who that was, least of all me. But I knew it was time to find out.

I felt bad for Cal when AJ took his anger out on him. Cal walked or rode a bike. When he left my house, AJ would follow him in his truck. Cal said he wasn't scared of him, but he was cautious.

I discovered AJ was combing through my garbage. I became aware of this at the court hearing. He informed the judge how many beers I had consumed that week. He conveyed to the judge that it wouldn't be long and I'd be an alcoholic like my parents. Generally I only drank a beer after mowing the lawn. Having two or three beer cans in my garbage prompted him to bring this issue up in court. He equated my beer drinking and mothering as somehow related.

Eventually, I decided to quit drinking. One incident in particular prompted my decision. One evening I was paying bills after dropping the girls off at their father's for the weekend. My brother's girlfriend called me and asked if she could come over with a few wine coolers. A few other people saw her car and stopped in. Eventually, I had a houseful of people and I went to buy more beer. I had never purchased more than a six-pack before. We partied late and then I tired and went to bed. The next morning I came down and discovered people sleeping everywhere. I quickly realized I didn't know half of them. I was mortified that I allowed this to happen. I woke people up and sent them home. I vowed it would never happen again, and it didn't.

I haven't drunk since. This risk is too heavy. I scared myself with the one incident, afraid AJ might prove I was an unfit parent. Besides, Cal was trying to maintain his sobriety. Due to genetics and environment, I already had an 80% chance of becoming an alcoholic. I didn't like the odds.

Unbelievably, AJ asked Shawna and Sandy to spy on me. He wanted to know what went on in my home, who visited, and whether I went to work. He told them I took everything and left him with nothing. He wept in front of them which made the children feel sorry for him. Soon they became angry with me. He instructed them not to listen to me when they returned home from a visit. When he was angry with them, he compared them to me.

The war of emotions was very confusing for my girls. After all, they were only three and five years old. They were confused about not liking me, and when their father told them they were like me, this made them even more confused. Parenting during this period was very difficult, especially since I was not fully aware of what AJ said to them. It took them a few days to adjust to being home after a weekend with their father.

Cal and I had a good relationship built on respect and trust. We decided that neither of us would use chemicals of any kind, nor would we cheat on each other. If one felt he or she was interested in someone else, we agreed to talk about it instead of hiding it. That way, if either of us wanted out of the relationship, we had the choice without adding additional pain. We agreed not to lie to one another and to build on the strength of our relationship with trust and honesty. However, my fear was that I was older than he was. Plus, I had two children and was about to be divorced. I still felt different and incompetent compared to other women. I knew that I was not as smart as many, and with my insecurity, I felt certain he'd soon be attracted to a younger, more beautiful college student.

The divorce was granted with the stipulation that there would be a custody study. I knew I'd be devastated if I lost my children; they were my reason for living. I was certain AJ would keep them from me, although I believed his main reason for wanting them was to avoid paying child support. I worried that the people doing the study would interview my mother, father or brothers, and the chance of finding any of these relatives sober was remote. I worried this would reflect on my ability to parent my children. I worried that I didn't make as much money as AJ and that the courts would not grant me custody due to my childhood and limited income.

One day AJ blocked me in the driveway with his car. The girls raced in the house and as I stood at the door, AJ angrily said I best quit with the foolishness and return home where I belonged. He pulled open the screen door and grabbed my necklace and twisted it. I panicked because the harder I pulled away, the tighter he twisted. He threatened me, saying I better watch myself if I knew what was good for me. He angrily stated that if I thought I was going to be awarded custody of the girls, I had better think again. The courts wouldn't give them to a worthless mother like me.

After that, I decided I needed a safe place to meet and exchange the girls. When we went before the judge, he scolded both of us for our inability to behave like adults. He ordered me to continue dropping the children off at AJ's home. When I asked why we couldn't use a neutral site, he said that we needed to work together for the children. According to him, exchanging children in a public place was inappropriate. I looked at AJ and he smiled. I didn't understand why the judge ruled like he did. I didn't want to ask friends to accompany me because it would only make the judge angrier. I was truly fearful of further physical assaults.

Shawna was very upset about the divorce. She was protective of her father and didn't like feeling she had to choose. She wouldn't let me hug or kiss her. I tried each night before she went to bed, but without success. I finally asked John for advice. He referred me to the school social worker. The social worker suggested I hold her even if she initially fought me. Much to my relief, his recommendation worked. Shawna fought me for maybe half a minute before she went limp and put her arms around me and said she loved me. She hugged me very tight, and the two of us sat and cried. She still had her angry outbursts, but she accepted my hugs and kisses.

One time when the three of us were about to leave on a walk, Shawna lipped off to me. I scolded her and said she had to wait five minutes inside until we returned. She was extremely angry and stomped up the steps. When I returned, there was a police officer at my door. He asked my name and smelled the contents of my can of diet pop. He said that he had received a call that a little girl had been left home alone. I explained to the officer what had happened. He cautioned me that some people might want to make a case out of this.

While Sandy went into the house to watch TV, I sat out on the deck, tearful and angry. Shawna came to me and was crying. She said, "I'm so sorry, mommy." I assured her that it wasn't her fault and that I should have known better. She said she was so angry that she called her father. He gave her the police phone number and instructed her to call them. I learned a valuable lesson—AJ would use my children against me to make my life difficult in hopes that I would return to him.

AJ continuously brought child support issues to court. He hounded the public attorney about what services I was receiving (childcare assistance and low-income housing), so he could use this information to lower his obligations. Our divorce wasn't final six weeks before our first court appearance on child support. I had gone 18 months without child support when he brought me back into court to have the amount lowered. He was granted a reduction. However, the judge reprimanded both of us about our squabbling. I agreed, but this didn't seem likely unless I wanted to give up and return to his household.

When the divorce was finalized, I received my financial portion of the house. It was small because AJ convinced the court that I brought nothing into the household, and all the savings were his. During the court hearing, his mother testified on his behalf. I didn't really care anymore about the house or money. I just wanted out of the marriage and the opportunity to parent my daughters alone. With my settlement I paid my attorney, purchased a waterbed and bought new bikes for the three of us.

After the girls returned from a weekend visit with their father, Shawna refused to ride her bike. She said all she did was fall down anyway. I explained to her this was how we all learned to ride. I let the subject drop until the next night, when again she refused to ride her bike. She started to cry. I told her everybody who rides falls sometime. She said, "No, mommy. The bruises I get when I ride my bike and fall, dad says you caused them." I said this was silly, that she should tell her father the truth about where the bruises came from. She said she tried to tell him the truth, but he wouldn't listen. He insisted they would sit at the police station until she told the truth. She cried when he finally convinced her to lie about her mother. She hugged me and asked if I was going to get into trouble. I was devastated. I didn't know what to say or how to help her or myself. If I confronted him, he would deny it and be angry with the her. I'd have to wait and see what happened. I encouraged her to continue telling the truth and promised her I wasn't upset with her. She was protecting me from her father. I was sad that my daughter felt she had to lie to the police.

The courts said that AJ had to pick up the children from daycare on Fridays so we would have minimal contact. One Monday, my provider asked to talk with me. She seemed distraught. She said a couple of weeks earlier; Shawna had hit her tailbone on her sandbox and had bruised her tailbone and a small area around it. The provider explained this to AJ so if it was still swollen or bruised; he could put ice on it over the weekend. Instead, AJ brought Shawna to the police station and had them take pictures and reported that I had harmed her.

This made no sense. I was dazed and confused. She said AJ asked her to testify against me in court and say that I was not a good mother. She was worried that he would use the pictures to try to obtain custody of the girls. Thankfully, she told him that she thought I was a very good mother. She informed him that I was always on time and always concerned about the children. She made it clear to him she would not testify against me and called him on his lying. He said that his attorney might subpoena her to court. She advised against it because if she testified, it would be to criticize *his* parenting. I was grateful for her honesty and support and willingness to provide childcare despite the chaos AJ brought into her life. I felt ashamed that my childcare provider was now involved in my messy divorce.

The day my divorce was finalized, AJ dropped my car insurance. I had no idea how to buy insurance. The next day at work, I asked John what to do and he referred me to an agent. My coworkers advised me about car tabs and maintenance. I purchased the tabs but had no idea what to do with them. As a result, I was pulled over by a police officer. It was the first time I had ever been stopped and I was scared. The officer was kind and offered instructions on how to apply them. As he looked at my license, he began to laugh. He asked if I was the person on the license. Nervously I told him yes. He said, "I've seen your husband a great deal over the past few months and the way he described you, I thought you weighed 350 pounds and were one mean woman." He returned my license and laughed all the way back to his car. I was relieved, while at the same time scared because now I knew that AJ was a constant visitor at the police station. This realization made me very sad. I didn't understand how someone who wanted me to return home and be his wife could spread lies about me. I was confused and emotionally drained.

I stopped at my father's in the morning to check on him and have coffee. One morning my mother was there, and they were both extremely intoxicated. I was concerned about them, so I stopped on my lunch hour to see how they were doing. They were both passed out. I stopped again on my way home from work and before I picked up my daughters. They were awake but feeling quite tough. They were out of booze and money.

I dropped off some food later that night. I didn't feel like seeing this scene before work again. The next day mother asked me if I would help her enter a chemical dependency treatment center. I offered to help, but with the stipulation that she had to be serious about sobriety. Mother had been in treatment numerous times to no avail. Nothing ever changed it seemed. Liquor controlled her life. When we were children, the county had encouraged treatment, but now that we were adults, no one pushed treatment anymore. Her life was her own. She said she was serious this time and wanted my help and support. I said nothing would make me happier than to see her sober.

John recommended a treatment center about forty-five miles away.

Her boyfriend had dropped her off at father's place with only the clothes on her back. She borrowed a few of my father's shirts that didn't fit her very well. It didn't bother her because she was never concerned about material possessions. Our childhood consisted of multiple moves due to her inability to pay rent. We never packed any of our belongings, we just left. She was used to having nothing.

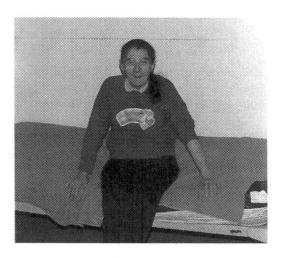

Her lifestyle was the same, only she was older. For the first time, I sensed she wanted seriously to accept sobriety. I vowed to support her any way I could. I was hopeful we could actually have a real mother-daughter relationship. That thought was a happy one, but I was realistically cautious. Life wasn't that simple.

John found a treatment center willing to take mother the next day. One the way there, she requested that we stop at a bar so she could have one last drink. I honored her request. Mother didn't like to drink alone and asked me to have one with her. I explained to her that my sobriety was very important to me and I would support her in any way except that. She was very nervous but I found her actions to be brave. I felt sad for her at the center when she had to answer personal questions about her chemical dependency. She tried to make light of some of the questions. I knew my presence also made her nervous.

I stayed with her most of the day while she was shown her room and introduced to her roommate. I went over the paperwork with her regarding expectations and the need to be respectful of others and the surrounding property. We studied the agenda together. I made a note of visiting times because I wanted to support her the best I could.

I was grateful that AJ couldn't prevent me from assisting my mother at this critical time. It was hard to leave her at the treatment center. She appeared so vulnerable and alone, but I felt more hopeful for her than I had in a long time. I promised to visit her on the weekend when AJ had the girls.

I earned about $800 a month take-home pay, but money was short even with rental and childcare assistance. I spent over half my paycheck on clothes for my mother—most were on sale and nothing fancy—but I felt honored to buy them for her. I had to put some bills on hold, but it felt wonderful to buy for my mother, another new experience.

The following weeks were financially difficult, and I didn't think I would have enough gas to visit my mother on the weekend. Cal sold his used TV and contributed the money so I could visit.

I was extremely grateful for his generosity and kindness. I felt we worked well together in understanding what was important to each other. He understood what it meant for me to visit her. I loved our together times at the treatment center. Mother and I laughed a lot and I found myself truly enjoying getting to know her. I liked her. We were different women with different life experiences. I realized that I would never have an emotionally close relationship with her like I had with my daughters, but we could be close in a different way nonetheless. While mother's recovery was new, I couldn't help but hope that this time it would different, that she would remain a part of each other's lives. It felt good to tell coworkers that I was going to see my mother on the weekend much like many of them did. Sadly, I didn't feel I could mention that she was in a treatment center.

I received a call that mother had a heart attack and was in intensive care. However, they said she was doing fine. When I went to visit, mother said that the treatment staff didn't believe her when she told them about her physical symptoms. They felt her symptoms were a result of the chemicals coming out of her body. She was grateful for the one staff person who insisted she get to the hospital, and so was I.

My brothers were angry with mother and had limited contact with her. They were stuck in their anger and blamed her for their current struggles. Mother never complained about her lack of contact from them, but I'm sure it bothered her because they all resided in the same town. When I attempted to tell them how well mother was doing, they angrily responded by saying, "Oh yeah," and walked away. They weren't as hopeful as I was.

In July 1986, the sandbox incident was investigated by Social Services. The allegation of child abuse was brought to my attention, at my place of work, by a Child Protection Social Worker. I was devastated emotionally. I was embarrassed and ashamed. This nightmare never seemed to end.

Social Service staff knew me due to their school visits. They were as uncomfortable as I was. They gently explained that they had to investigate all reports and were apologetic about visiting me at work. They didn't feel there were any concerns about my parenting; however they were mandated to follow up. They were forbidden by data privacy laws to reveal who the reporter was.

After the appointment, I laid my head on the table and sobbed. I told John I would understand if he wanted to fire me. I didn't want him to have any doubts about my working with kids that were already struggling. He gave me a big hug and said he wasn't going to fire me. In fact, he thought I handled myself very professionally during a very painful situation. He reiterated that he had no doubts about my character or my skills and wanted me to stay on. At that moment, it felt like it would be easier to go back to my husband than continue to try and defend who I was. John sent me home. I thanked him for his kindness and his belief in me.

My mother was at my house when I arrived home. I looked and felt defeated. I laid my head on the table and cried. I explained to her what had happened. Then Cal came by to say he had been laid off from his job. Fortunately, the girls were still I daycare. As I wept at the table, my mother walked up behind me and placed her hand on my shoulder. I will never forget what she said to me. "You are a good person, and don't let anyone tell you any different." With that she left to make a pot of coffee. My mother had never complimented me in any way before. I will always remember her words. I could have used a hug, but that wasn't her style. I cried tears of joy that my mother thought I was a good person. This memory still lifts my heart and helps me when I'm feeling low.

Later, after I was over the tears, all I felt was anger. I called AJ and demanded an explanation. Did he truly believe I could hurt our children? Again he reiterated his belief that I needed to return to his home where I belonged. It would stop he said, but only if I returned to him, that the children and I belonged with him. I asked him why he wanted me back if he thought I was such a danger to his children. "You asked for it, now you can live with it," she said. He ordered me to come home immediately and forget all my crazy notions of trying to make it on my own. If I did as he requested, he would forgive me for all that I had done to our family.

I hung up the phone and put my head in my arms and cried at the table. Everything was so complicated. I hadn't left him to be vindictive or mean. I just couldn't live with him anymore. My mental health was on the line and I simply wanted out. I wanted an opportunity to live my life like other people did. I wanted the freedom to love my children and learn what life was truly about.

I wanted Shawna and Sandy to grow up to be kind to those less fortunate than themselves, to be compassionate, and not see money as the most important part of their lives. I wanted them to have empathy for people like me. While people are more important than possessions, the sad fact of life is that money is needed to provide the necessities of live. I worried and prayed that I could provide for my children financially. I hoped that parenting my children from my heart was as important as the money I earned. Now, after many years of being a single parent, I realize how idealistic this belief actually was.

The custody study continued for an additional eight months. I walked on eggshells, and my heart was very heavy. I worried that I wouldn't gain custody of my daughters. I often wondered what chances I had – a woman with physical and sexual abuse in her past against a man who had money, a house, and all kinds of relatives as a support system. If I was the judge, who would I pick for the children to live with? If I wasn't awarded custody of my children, I wanted them to know that at least I tried. If I failed, I didn't know what I would do or what would become of me. It was too painful to think about.

In early 1987, the hearing was held. John and Marie attended at my request and testified on my behalf. They testified about my character, dependability, and the love I had for my children in spite of some weaknesses due to my childhood. AJ had his parents, a great aunt, and some of his siblings testify for him. He and I also testified. Repeatedly, my childhood abuse was brought up, which was very painful.

I remember the judge asking AJ to clarify the term "running around" as he referred to my activities away from the house. He said I was visiting my grandmother and father before work and taking the children with me when I should be content to stay home. The judge stated that this was not recognized as "running around" and went on to ask him other questions. The hearing with all the legal terminology was extremely scary, and again I felt like a small child with no control over my future. At the end of the hearing, the judge stated that he was going against his better judgment and awarded me custody of the girls. He rejected AJ because he felt he harbored too much anger and resentment over the divorce, and this would be an unhealthy environment for the children. The judge looked at me and said he had no doubt that my children would be in foster care within two years due to my own history of physical and sexual abuse. This, he said, was almost certain based on statistics.

I was angry that he questioned my ability as a parent. How did he know my potential when I didn't? Why did I feel so confused?

I felt like I wanted to celebrate, and then I felt deep shame and anxiety at the same time. This was a bittersweet victory. I was elated that my children would be living with me. I prayed there would be no more court hearings or legal issues. Hopefully, it was all over and we could move on.

I couldn't have been more wrong. It was far from over. AJ continued to harass me, continued manipulating the children and continued to bring me to court to have his child support lowered.

AJ was awarded visitation, including one month in the summer. It was very difficult and painful to go one month without seeing the girls. I worried he would keep them. I sent self-addressed stamped envelopes and asked them to keep in touch. AJ found the envelopes and ripped them up. I called to tell them I loved them and missed them, but AJ refused to put them on the line. He would hang up and never inform them. When they returned, they said they had worried I had forgotten about them. I tried to reassure them, but it pained my heart.

Shawna, Sandy and I decided to wear matching bracelets when they left for visitation. This would be a reminder to each of us that we would not forget one another while we were apart. They always checked to make sure I had my bracelet on before they left. We all found this to be therapeutic during our separations.

My daughters taught me a great deal about parenting. I tried to make sure they looked just right for school. For example, when Sandy was in kindergarten, there was a period of time when she insisted on putting her shoes on the wrong feet. I changed them to the correct feet before she left the house, then she switched them back to the wrong feet in the car. I changed the shoes again before dropping the girls off at school. I was concerned what the teacher might think of me if she saw my child wearing her shoes the wrong way. Finally, in frustration of the shoe ritual and battle of wills in the morning, I decided to allow her to wear her shoes on the wrong feet. She came home from school with her shoes on the correct feet. I asked her why. She simply stated that they hurt the other way. This incident taught me a memorable lesson in natural consequences and to pick my battles wisely.

Cal asked me to spend time with his family. He spoke highly of them and felt deep regret about his past behavior. He spoke of his mother's emotional support and how proud he was of her for raising him and his siblings. With great pride he spoke of how she had worked herself off welfare. His parents were divorced, and he didn't see his father much because he had moved out of state.

His mother had young children at home. I still had concerns about our age difference and the fact I had two young children. He was certain that they would accept us because we were important to him.

I had a deep desire for acceptance because I cared so much about him and I hoped they would see that. I was very nervous, but the initial visit went very well. I didn't bring my girls along because I was worried that his family might not be as excited about them. They asked about the girls and truly seemed interested.

When I met his grandmother, acceptance came easily. Her eyes were very kind, and she gave me a gentle hug. Cal's grandmother was a beautiful woman. The first time she met Shawna and Sandy, she treated them as if they were her own. Her love knew no boundaries. She called often just to say hi or to see when we were coming to visit. I enjoyed her company and her deep compassion for life. She was a wonderful role model of unconditional love.

Over time, my desire to become a social worker increased. I checked into college options. The small, two-year college offered a warm, personable fit, but the drawback was I would have to move twice. Social work would provide financial stability, and while the prospect thrilled me, the fear of my personal limitations paralyzed me. The change would be difficult for my daughters, and housing remained a barrier.

In the summer of 1987, Jerry assisted my father with getting his driver's license. Father had lost his license in 1968. Jerry felt he would drink less if he felt more like a man and could move about independently. Jerry and I disagreed about this. I was concerned that dad would drink and drive. Dad had seizures from his alcohol binges and was in the process of being certified for disability payments. Besides his physical limitations, his mental health was poor. Jerry saw an emotionally broken-down man who had lost his family, turned to drinking, and couldn't be the man he once was.

I knew my father had lost his family, but his relationship with my mother always hinged on drinking, which affected his ability to work, maintain relationships and parent his children. I was angry with him because I believed he gave up on us. In a way, both Jerry and I were right.

Once dad obtained his license, Jerry helped him buy a small used car. This made dad happy. However, this did not change his drinking habits, nor did it alter his lifestyle.

I remember one Saturday my father drove up to the house. Dad honked his car horn and staggered out from behind the wheel. A little girl about four years old jumped out from the front seat where she had been standing. She had mousy brown, tousled hair, and her clothes didn't fit. She was dirty and unkempt. Her eyes were big as she stood by my father. She didn't appear to be afraid to enter a total stranger's home. She was a little girl in the trailer park who asked him for a ride in the car. I was taken aback by her appearance. Twenty years earlier, I was that little girl, longing to go anywhere my father would take me. I offered her a Popsicle and gave my father some coffee. He reeked of alcohol, while his unstable gait told me he shouldn't be behind the wheel of a car. I was tearful as I looked at the two of them. It didn't seem so long ago when I was her.

Suddenly, I was flooded with old and painful memories. I found it difficult to speak. I scolded him for driving drunk with a child in the vehicle. He became angry and abruptly rose. He said he was sorry he stopped, and they left. I cried for a long time, knowing he was thinking back in time to when I was the little girl in the car with him. The reality was that neither of us could go back to that time and place. This was a powerful reminder that we needed to do things differently rather than ignore the poor choices made in our youth. My father kept his license, but never drove to my house again.

Cal and I were asked to speak at church. I enjoyed sharing parts of my history with others in hopes they would see that there was potential for people like me and not to give us on us. I wanted people to see it wasn't ability we lacked, but mentoring.

In the spring of 1987, I received a call at work from my mother's landlord. Mother had been badly beaten. She was so disfigured he barely recognized her. I asked the landlord to call the police. He balked, saying that he didn't want to get involved so I called myself. They called back later to say she refused medical attention. The officer said she was badly beaten but still coherent, so they couldn't make her go. In the meantime, they would search for her boyfriend, Bud, the likely suspect. Eventually they called back to report that the mother didn't want to press charges so they were dropping it.

I was concerned she had suffered serious internal injuries. Also, it was likely her boyfriend would return. Unfortunately, I knew I wouldn't be able to convince her to return to my home. Regardless of how painful it was, I reminded myself that this was her lifestyle.

In the fall of 1987, my mother married Bud, the man who had badly beaten her. I feared he would kill her. He was older than she was plus he was an ex-convict. I didn't know much about him other than he was very physically abusive to her. Just when I dared to hope that mother might follow through on her sobriety, she retreated to her familiar lifestyle. She had been sober one year. I seldom heard from her after this incident. I lost my desire to visit her because I didn't know what condition I would find her in. If she was out of money, she'd ask to borrow some, and my money was limited as it was. I was sad that our year together was over which caused my anger to resurface. I felt foolish that I believed I would be a part of mother's life and that she would quit drinking. I was wrong and knew better than to have false hopes. I wasn't a child. What was wrong with me?

In November, Cal resumed chemical use. I was totally unaware of this and didn't discover it until later. Our relationship had grown strained over the summer. His behavior seemed out of character. I felt something was wrong with me and so I tried hard to change things about me that I thought would make him happy. Nothing I did improved our relationship, so I focused my energy solely on my daughters. Shawna and Sandy were excited about the prospect of me attending college. Cal would soon graduate from school. I could sense he was nervous about the financial responsibility of supporting all four of us. I assured him that my children were my responsibility and he didn't have to feel like he was responsible for a ready-made family. Also, my children had a father; they were not needing or wanting him to be their father. Our communication dwindled, but I felt we would somehow work our differences out.

In January of 1988, I took the entrance examination for college. I completed only one math problem on the test. I felt deep shame. Again I felt incompetent in comparison to others. I asked Cal to assist me with the financial aid packet, but he refused. He told me it was my duty and responsibility and not his. He had become increasingly distant and was no longer supportive of me attending college. I was twenty-nine years old and scared to make this giant step. I had graduated from high school, though I didn't remember much of it. I was a B student through high school although I wasn't certain I was smart enough for college. Despite such hesitation, I felt a commitment to this goal and was certain our lives would improve if I attended school.

Cal was very intelligent. He never studied, yet he received A's in his classes. He often talked of his classmates, many of whom were young and female. This was an insecure time for me. He obtained a driver's permit for the first time and enjoyed his freedom.

He began to spend more and more time with his classmates and was irritable around us. When I asked him what was wrong, he belittled me and returned to his apartment. I was confused. Other times he was kind and understanding. I felt that our relationship might end because he had found a woman his own age, someone who didn't have the responsibilities that I had. Life never seemed simple.

I maintained communication as best I could, but it was shaky at best. He visited us less often, and when he was around, I could sense his inner turmoil. For the first time in our relationship, I felt at a loss in how to assist him. I found him difficult to be around as his presence added additional stress to our household. We rarely talked of our future together.

I completed the paperwork for college and Section 8 housing. There was a two-year waiting list for housing. The plan was that Cal would move with us to the college town. The girls and I would go to school during the day while Cal worked, and we'd all be together at night. As the time drew near, I wasn't sure if Cal would join us. I hoped he would, but that was his decision.

I experienced many firsts as an adult during this time:

1. Went sledding (Christmas 1985).
2. Learned to ice skate with Cal and children (winter of 1986).
3. Cal's father passed away. We drove to Nebraska for the funeral (July 1987).
4. Christmas with my mother, who was sober. She tried to make fudge for the holidays, and she called me at work because the fudge was boiling over. She wanted to know what to do. I didn't know. We laughed and laughed—a beautiful memory.
5. Holidays spent with my children, my mother, my father, and brothers with their families—so wonderful.
6. Bought my children and myself new bicycles (with divorce settlement).
7. Bought myself a microwave, VCR, and phone answering machine with my first income tax money—so excited.
8. I could afford to take Cal and the girls to a motel occasionally (wonderful fun).

IN 1988, MY MOTHER MOVED TO Spokane, Washington. She left me a voice message informing me of the change. She sounded very happy and encouraged me to keep in contact. She said she hoped that I wasn't too disappointed in her and that she would write. Her message angered me. Her life was her own, but I called her and tried to convince her to stay. I was afraid Bud would kill her or she would drink herself to death. Plus, I wanted her to have a relationship with her grandchildren. I shared with her our childhood experiences in foster care. I asked her why she never contacted us or tried to regain custody. I sensed she was uncomfortable with the conversation, but I had so many questions and couldn't stop myself. She changed the subject. I tried to tell myself to be grateful for the time we had together over the past year. She was uncomfortable talking about or past which I understood but I needed for her to empathize with her children who had to live through it.

I found housing about 35 miles from the college. My name still hadn't come up on the HUD housing list. This caused me concern but the agency was certain that it would come up within the next couple of months.

The timing would be perfect if I moved in July and started college in September. The thought of leaving my job, where I felt competent and liked was difficult. This was a very painful decision. I had come to value the students, John and coworkers. Here I was, 29 years old, and I had finally found a safe place where people accepted me for who I was. My history of abuse and out-of-home placement was an asset on my job. My coworkers and John supported me during my painful divorce.

Once or twice a week John sent me to the bakery to buy treats for the staff. On one of these visits, the clerk asked me about college. I beamed and told her how excited I was. I was floored when she said that one of my coworkers had speculated to her that I wouldn't last six months. I felt like I had been hit in the stomach. I couldn't catch my breath. I numbly walked out of the bakery. Again someone had made an assumption without really knowing me. I knew I could accomplish anything I set my mind to. My children depended on me. I could not afford to fail. I vowed at that moment that I would try harder than I ever tried before. Besides, John thought I could do it; he believed in me and he knew me better than anyone. I would not let him or my children down. I wanted a better life and I would work damn hard for it!

Although it pained me, I applied for AFDC/welfare. This was difficult emotionally. I wanted no part of the system and preferred to make a living on my own. However, I couldn't quit my job and start college without some financial assistance.

Cal was emotionally distant. He planned to make the move with us so he was busy looking for work. I wanted to live in a house that I could rent with a HUD voucher to avoid the stigma of living in low-income housing. That way no one would realize that I was on rental assistance and I wouldn't stand out.

John and my coworkers gave me a going away party. It was a beautiful event and I questioned whether I was making the right choice. However, it was too late to change my mind. I had given my notice at work. I was deathly afraid of all these new transitions, but slowly things seemed to be coming together.

When AJ heard that I was leaving for school, he hauled me back into court. I was as sick of seeing the judge as I'm sure he was as sick of seeing me. The judge reprimanded me for leaving the county and distancing the girls from their father. He felt it was important for them to remain physically close to their father, so he ordered me to be responsible for visitation.

I attempted to explain the importance of an education to the judge, but he was not swayed by my arguments. He sided with AJ and ordered that I needed to have the girls to their father by 5:00 a.m. on Fridays and pick them up by 8:00 p.m. on Sundays. Also, I was responsible to drive them on holidays and summer vacation. I had no idea how grueling a schedule this would be.

My brothers didn't understand my decision to attend college. They felt I should stay at my job, raise my children, and reconcile with AJ. They accepted Cal but felt I belonged with AJ. Despite this, they helped us move, and Jerry lent me $250 for the deposit.

Cal found a job in computer programming. He was moody, but I had too many of my own irons in the fire to worry about what was bothering him. I didn't know a thing about colleges or the expectations and didn't have anyone to ask without sounding stupid. I was very relieved when Cal offered to accompany me to orientation. When the day came, Cal backed out of his commitment because he said he wanted to spend the day with friends instead. I was devastated. I was very hurt that he didn't see the importance of it. I could have used his support and encouragement.

He didn't seem to recognize how difficult a transition this was for the three of us. He was more into what was important to him. His behavior was confusing and painful. He made his own plans with little thought to any of us. He seemed disinterested in what was going on and very lethargic.

On my way to orientation, I got lost. I pulled the car over and cried. How was I going to make it in college if I had trouble driving to it? I wished I was back at my previous job. I kept hearing my mother's voice saying I would never amount to anything. Did I think for some reason I was special, she would say, and then more emphatically she would say, I was not! I had left early primarily because I didn't want to be late and have to walk in and have everyone look at me. So I relied on my anger and determination to motivate me. I dried my eyes and found a gas station and asked for directions. I was only about ten miles away. I knew the decision to go to college would not be easy, and this was the first test of my courage and commitment. When I finally arrived, there were cars parked everywhere. I didn't know where to park, so I took the first open spot I could find. I was a few minutes late and everyone looked at me when I entered the room. I took an available chair halfway to the front. Feelings of doubt and severe anxiety started to overwhelm me. I felt so out of place tears started welling in my eyes. I felt so incompetent, so overwhelmed, and I had the strong feeling I didn't belong and wouldn't fit in. There wasn't another person my age in attendance. Maybe I was at the wrong orientation. I decided I would ask the speaker during the break.

The parents talked proudly of their children; rubbing their children's backs as they offered them words of encouragement. The parents discussed the money, lunch payment, and transportation concerns. They expressed their desire for their children to come home and visit on weekends. It felt uplifting and encouraging to watch parents take an interest in their children. I knew someday I would do this with my children.

I waited until the speaker was free before asking him if I was in the right orientation, if maybe there was a separate one for older students. The speaker confirmed there was only one orientation. He seemed a bit confused by my question and quickly turned to talk to another parent. *Well,* I told myself, *at least I'm not lost again.* This made me smile. I just wasn't sure if that was a good thing or not.

I was exhausted by the end of the day. There was a lot to learn I quickly realized. I had to learn where my classes were, how to register, where to park, where to buy books and how to obtain a student ID. The registrar told me it was a requirement I take classes that seemed to have nothing to do with social work. This confused me because I didn't understand why I had to spend money on classes totally unrelated to social work.

When I raised the question, the registrar seemed irritated with me and said everyone was required to take general classes. I could tell he thought I was being argumentative, so I quit asking. I signed up for (1) College Introduction; (2) Written Compos I (English); (3) Modern Technology and Civilization; and (4) Modern America. I left the registration session quite confused. None of these classed seemed at all relevant to me. Panic slowly set in. I realized that at this rate, it could take me forever to complete the social work program.

When I walked to my car at the end of this difficult and frustrating day, I found a parking ticket on my windshield. Sarcastically I thought, *perfect closing to an almost perfect day!*

Chapter Eight
College

IN 1988, I STARTED COLLEGE. I quickly realized I had entered an environment I knew absolutely nothing about. My coping skills were put to the test daily. The limitations of my knowledge and life experiences came to the forefront. My self-created safe environment was strongly challenged. I believed I had made a grave mistake entering this unknown world. College was not for people like me.

Money was exceptionally tight. My name had still not come up on the housing list. After paying $350 for rent, there was little left for other expenses. I received $90 in food stamps. However, once my financial aid came through, I would no longer be eligible for food stamps. To a certain extent, I was okay with that. Food stamps couldn't buy toilet paper, shampoo, toothpaste or gas. Because I received AFDC, the county kept my child support. With expenses for car insurance, gas, heating fuel, groceries and utilities, the $532 was stretched very thin.

I used my rent rebate to buy my daughters their school supplies and clothing. Shawna and Sandy were anxious about entering a new school, residing in a new community, and making friends. I tried to reassure them that they would make friends very quickly. Considering they were in first and third grade, they adjusted well and quickly made friends. I was happy and relieved that they were able to make this transition so easily.

Towards the end of August, I still had not received my financial aid. School was only one week away. I needed the money to buy books and pay bills. I checked with the college and I discovered that financial aid checks weren't issued until three or four weeks after school started. This realization was another adjustment for me.

I signed up for 12 credits plus work study. I rented a parking spot, but it was so far away, I had to take a shuttle bus. I quickly realized I needed Student ID card because without it there wasn't much on campus I could do. Every day was a new challenge in and out of the classroom.

At the time I didn't understand why I was forced to take classes which had absolutely no bearing on social work. In order to graduate, I needed credits in Math, English, Music, and Physical Education. Only later did I discover why. The purpose of college is to make a person well-rounded. Though this made sense, I didn't have the time or money.

Without my financial aid I couldn't purchase textbooks. I couldn't cash a check. I couldn't even find a bathroom to cry in! I felt deep anxiety which caused me to doubt myself. I was angry that I had left a paying job, my coworkers, my support group and counseling. I couldn't afford to return to the town I just left. Plus, John had already hired my replacement, so my only option was to continue on.

I was extremely distraught. There were no easy answers. I prayed a great deal and often. I prayed that God would guide me through what I didn't know and to help me to learn as quickly as possible. My daughters were proud of me for going to school which help me immensely because I knew they would be disappointed if said I was quitting. My daughters and I liked to dream about our lives after I received my degree. We looked forward to having enough money to stop at the Dairy Queen or to visit department stores and buy clothes. I wanted to be a good role model for my children, and if I quit, I would send the wrong message. I envisioned a future where someday they would attend college. If that dream was to come true, I knew I had to tough it out. I had to be strong to save them from feelings of doubt and inadequacy that overwhelmed me.

CAL LIVED IN HIS OWN WORLD. He disliked his work and disliked where we lived. My daughters and I kept to ourselves due to his moodiness, his lack of patience and angry outbursts. I hoped his attitude would improve, but it didn't. I couldn't focus on what was causing his behavior as I had my own overwhelming obligations. I prayed he would come around.

One of my most memorable classes was English. The instructor looked as if he had just crawled out of bed. His hair and clothes were a mess. I was amazed he was a teacher. I had envisioned someone with a more professional presence. I thought an instructor would look like he had wisdom and education. He was nothing like what I expected.

Although I took good notes, I found it difficult to study at night. The girls were anxious for my time and there was dinner to prepare and chores to do.

I was overwhelmed the first quarter of school. Besides the problems with Cal, the transition was difficult. We lived in a different house in a new town, plus there was the financial stress I was continually under. I did not have emotional support and felt so alone. I had to transport the girls to their father's every other weekend. On top of that, I had to adjust to school life.

The third day of class, my English instructor asked for our completed assignment. I was stunned. I raised my hand and said, "I've been in class these past three days, and I don't remember hearing that we were to write a paper and turn it in." The instructor looked at me with disbelief and disgust. He asked a student to tell me where the assignment was located. His voice was very patronizing and sarcastic. I was sorry I had asked the question. The student said the assignment was in the syllabus, which was handed out the first day of class. I didn't know what a syllabus was. I vowed to look through my class materials when I got home. I felt embarrassed. Before class ended, the instructor confronted me in front of the students and said that I could hand in my paper the next day, but I would be docked points for being late. If my paper was later than that, I shouldn't bother handing it in. I felt my eyes filling with tears as I looked down at my desk. He made direct eye contact with me, his gaze firm. Shame-faced, I felt the other students' eyes on me. I promised myself that I would be more prepared before returning to my classes.

I was stretched so thin for money it was difficult to focus on school. One morning after I had used my final three dollars for gas, I went into the women's restroom and cried. I challenged myself to take one day at a time. It was too overwhelming to think past today.

That evening, I found the syllabus the instructor had referred to. In fact, each of my classes had a syllabus with the entire quarter's worth of assignments. I felt ashamed that I had not been more prepared.

Cal and I purchased a computer before we moved. It proved to be a life saver. I was able to do my homework at home instead of at the computer lab at school. I wasn't very computer savvy, but I learned as I went.

Towards the end of the first week of classes, another instructor gave a pop quiz. She had doubts that we were doing the assigned reading. I failed that quiz; I still didn't have my textbooks and couldn't' read the material. I made a mental note that in the future, I would purchase my books as soon as I received my class schedule. I often thought returning to work would be easier than tolerating four years of this kind of stress and humiliation. I knew how to work; attending college was very difficult. The language was different, there were different expectations and the majority of students were younger. Other students seemed to understand the rules and expectations. None of this felt easy to me at 29 years old. It seemed that I was reminded hourly of my lack of knowledge and limitations.

I received a zero on my English paper. He made so many corrections in red that I could barely see the words I had typed. At the end of the paper there was a note in red that said I should listen to the cassette tape. On the cassette tape the instructor chastised me with crude verbal remarks about my limited writing ability, pointing out my improper use of the English language, improper sentence structure, and many other faults. He said he was surprised that I was a high school graduate and suggested that I was not college material. It was his opinion that I should drop out of college and work in a factory. I listened to the tape over and over and cried. I didn't understand what would make an instructor so cruel. He could have said what he wanted about my paper, but he didn't have to attach me personally. I felt so defeated.

I talked to Cal about how hurtful all of this was. He encouraged me to keep working and try harder. I had hoped for more support from him. I didn't know how to try harder; I was trying as hard as I knew how! I was exhausted and overwhelmed with doubts about myself. I realized I couldn't turn to Cal for emotional support of any kind. He was stressed about his own situation and had little empathy for my college struggles. It was clear he didn't want me bothering him.

The more I looked over the paper and listened to the tape, the angrier and more determined I became. I was not a quitter. I didn't understand why the instructor was so unkind. He didn't know my abilities or me. John had suggested college which meant he knew I had the capability. I made my mind up that I would pass the class with or without textbooks. I contacted the English Resource Center for guidance.

The staff was very helpful and said many students of this English instructor used their services and were able to pass his class successfully. I was relieved. While my writing improved, the instructor's disposition towards me never did. However, his corrections became less and less intense. He tolerated my presence unless he needed to make a point of what not to do on writing a paper for his class. I cried many nights over this and my inability to understand what he wanted in a paper. I tried to tell myself I would improve.

Finally my financial aid came in. When I went to the college bookstore to buy books, all the used ones were gone, so I had to pay full price. They encouraged me to buy earlier in the quarter next time. Another lesson learned. My financial aid allowed me to buy textbooks, pay up bills, purchase fuel oil, and buy a few items for the girls. After paying on my attorney bill, I saved the rest for gas money.

One evening I needed to borrow Cal's calculator. It was in his jacket pocket. When I reached in to retrieve it, I found a small plastic baggie with marijuana and a pipe. I was floored. It was like someone had knocked the wind out of me. He had disrespected the agreement we had made. We had agreed that neither one of us would use chemicals or be dishonest with each other. I felt deep betrayal. I felt the familiar emotional sting of a chemical that had come between a loved one and me.

Cal's behavior made more sense now – his moodiness, how quickly he became angry over little things, his coming and going at all hours, his lack of communication and intimacy. Why hadn't I guessed what was going on. I was familiar with chemicals and how people behaved while using them. I had believed in something that wasn't real. He kept secrets and now I could understand why he was difficult to be around. I was angry and very, very hurt. How were we to start a new life with lies, secrets and emotional detachment? My goals obviously weren't his.

I called John later that night when Cal was gone. I was crying so hard I had difficulty explaining what had happened. John said he was willing to do an intervention without Cal's knowledge. Cal and I were planning on stopping to see John on our next visit to town and he agreed to meet us at the park. I was to have a bag of clothes packed for Cal. John would confront Cal about his chemical use. I asked him to tell Cal he could not be around my children if he used chemicals.

This was a very painful time. I assumed Cal would want his freedom so I was ready for our relationship to end. In the past eight months, our relationship had been non-existent. I missed his friendship, gentle manner, and kind treatment of my daughters. Now the girls kept their distance due to his angry behavior and lack of patience. This was no way to live. I had quit my work-study job because his moods were so unpredictable. I chose to take out student loans so I wouldn't have to count on Cal to watch my daughters. Life was hard enough with all the changes we were going through. Now we had to decide if Cal was to remain a part of our family. This meant more anger and pain. Damn, how I hated chemicals and how they turned my loved ones into people I didn't know.

Cal was extremely angry about the intervention. I told him that we couldn't be a family if he was going to use chemicals. Our relationship could not tolerate lies and secrets. He wasn't thinking of the family, only himself. Cal fought the idea of treatment. I had cosigned for his car and if he entered treatment, he couldn't make the car payments. He knew I couldn't afford to make them. He said he felt trapped and I didn't realize the stress he was going through. I reiterated that doing drugs around my girls was not an option. He needed to make a decision if he wanted to be part of our family or not. He knew what the expectations were. Cal and I parted after our confrontation. I hugged and thanked John for his support. There were tears in his eyes too.

I left the girls at their father's and went home. The next day Cal showed up. He was teary-eyed. He said he was sorry he had betrayed me and wanted another chance. He agreed to enter treatment. I was leery. He said he wanted to be part of our family, however, based on past experience I knew this was questionable because my parents had chosen alcohol over family. I was willing to help him, but only if we worked together as a couple. I agreed to be supportive and assist him in any way I could. While I knew that the draw to use chemicals was strong, I wanted him to know that love and a family could fight the strong addiction.

Without Cal's income, my financial struggles worsened. I was driving 70 miles round trip to school, traveling 200 miles every other weekend to drop the girls off at their father's and visiting Cal in treatment, which was another 70 miles. With the added stress of school, I was emotionally and physically exhausted.

On top of that, AJ continued to take me into court over child support. I attempted to have the court hearing moved closer to where I lived, but the court said no. This meant I had to miss school. If I missed two times or more in one quarter, I was dropped a letter grade. It was difficult to prioritize the importance of these two needs. He was unrelenting in his attempts to have his support payments lowered. Sometimes he was successful, sometimes not. By this time, I was so exhausted, I really didn't care anymore. The girls said very little of what went on at their father's house. I was tired of being angry all the time. All I really wanted was to make sure the girls felt safe while they were at AJ's. I had some concerns about his parenting. He was careless about safety. He would take the girls out on his motorcycle without helmets. While AJ no longer took the girls to the police station to report me, he continued to tell them that I had ripped the family apart.

I believe AJ wanted to make life so difficult I would return home. During the first three months of college, I gave this serious consideration. With Cal in treatment, I lacked emotional support. School was a difficult transition, plus I was strapped financially. It was all so overwhelming; I struggled to get out of bed some mornings. I often asked myself why I was doing this. I could only come up with one answer. I wanted a better life and future for my children and myself. On more positive days, I asked myself why I couldn't do this. Any discomfort was temporary. Life will get better. I had to believe life would improve. I knew it couldn't get any worse. I also knew my ability and heart even if I didn't know anyone else's. I could always count on me.

I met another single mother, Linda. We became friends. We met through our daughters, who went to school together. She too was a single parent who had struggled financially. She offered support and encouragement, which I was thankful for.

CAL COMPLETED TREATMENT, which reduced my travel time somewhat. I was still logging over 1, 840 miles per month between school, court hearings, and visits to AJ. This amounted to 42 hours in the car. When my car insurance came due, I didn't have the money to pay the premium of $80.

One night over dinner with Linda, I shared this with her. As we left, she handed me an envelope. I opened it to find $100 inside. She said it was for the car insurance. I was stunned by her kindness. She said she wasn't worried about being paid back but asked if I would pay it forward to someone else who might need financial assistance. I gave her a big hub, and we both cried. We remain good friends to this day. I continue to assist others when I can in memory of her kindness and caring about my family at such a difficult time.

Cal chose not to return to his job. He felt it had contributed to his relapse. He worked hard on his sobriety, and I did my best to support him. After treatment, the girls and I still felt isolated from him. He had a support group he was active in which meant less time for us. There always seemed to be something interfering with our family relationship, something that took the focus away from the bonding we all desperately needed. It felt like we were all going in different directions with different needs.

My name still had not come up on the housing list. Soon I would need to move into less expensive housing or I would sink financially. If I was able to secure low-income housing, Cal wouldn't be allowed to join us due to housing rules. With the major upheavals in both our lives, it was impossible to support each other like we needed.

My ability to support him during this difficult transition weighed heavily on my mind. I found it difficult to be emotionally supportive to Cal when I was financially and emotionally stressed. I felt so alone and helpless. Quitting school seemed like my only viable option. I was exhausted and desperate.

At Thanksgiving, we stayed home and played cards because we couldn't afford to go anywhere. We made do, but the thought of a bleak Christmas depressed me. I felt sad that I had very little to offer my children. I didn't mind going without, but I longed to buy them a few gifts for the holidays. My daughters never complained. I watched other families prepare for the holidays and this made my heart heavy. I tried to tell myself that this was only one Christmas and future holidays would be better. However, I couldn't envision a better holiday, so I tried not to show my daughters how painful all of this was to me.

I completed my first quarter of college. I received an S in College Introduction, B in English, B in Modern Technology and Civilization, and C in Modern America. I had passed all my classes with a C or better. I had done it! I was not stupid! I realized I had a lot to learn outside the classroom, but most importantly, I *could* learn! I was elated!

I wished I had family members or someone to share the exciting news with. Education came easy to Cal, so he had no perception of how hard I had worked to succeed. He didn't realize what kind of an accomplishment this was for me personally. I became sad when I realized I had no one to share this small victory with. Finally, I thought of John and he was thrilled for me. I truly wanted to share this news with my parents or my brothers, but I knew none of them understood why I was going to college.

My relationship with my brothers was difficult already, but when I discovered that Cal had been using drugs with them prior to entering treatment, I was furious. I felt betrayed by them. When I called them out their retort was, "Who did I think I was and why did I think I was better than they were just because I was going to college." They had no idea how difficult it was to be a single parent and support children on minimum-wage jobs. I found it futile to try and explain. I felt isolated from my brothers. I missed our easy-going relationship.

My mother remained in contact with me. She no longer called me collect. I shared with her my college struggles. She didn't understand my goal, but she was slightly supportive and wished me well. It may have been a lukewarm endorsement, but it meant the world to me.

I visited my father when I could. If he was sober, I stayed. If not, our visits were short. Due to the travel, my daughter's time with their grandfather was limited. It was difficult when AJ wouldn't be there at 8:00 for me to pick up the children. His normal routine was to take them to a movie, out to eat, or over to his mother's. He didn't worry about having the girls to me on time. His lack of respect for me and the children made a difficult situation even more trying.

I moved into a two-bedroom low-income apartment my landlady managed in a town nearby. I saved about $150 a month on rent and utilities. She waived the deposit until I could afford it. The downside of the move was that Cal could not join us due to housing regulations. I hoped we would reunite within a year. While I detested the thought of living in low-income housing, I really had no choice. There were too many unhappy memories from my childhood.

Cal was emotionally distant and distraught. He was helpful during the move with packing and transporting; however, he didn't want to discuss our relationship or future together. I had detached emotionally in order to survive our separation.

Again, thoughts of quitting school entered my mind. Cal was angry and upset with me. He blamed me for the separation. He felt I had made too hasty a decision in moving out of our shared housing. We agreed to continue our relationship, but the physical separation made it difficult. Cal found housing and a job. Fortunately, the girls were able to attend their same school. I was grateful they had the fewest changes to adjust to.

Cal usually rode with me to pick up the girls from their father's. I was grateful for the company on the three-hour journey. On our trip home, I tried not to feel hurt when the girls talked about going to the movies or shopping, activities I could not afford to provide them. AJ forbid them from bringing anything he had purchased for them to my apartment. I felt sad for them because they longed to share their new items with their friends and me.

I took out student loans to pay the attorney for the divorce and custody study. Half of my financial aid went to pay these bills. When I contacted my divorce attorney about making smaller payments, he stated he was a Vietnam Vet and didn't receive any special treatment so neither would I. He said I needed to pay my bill in full immediately. I explained my situation, but there was no flexibility on his part. I paid him off in two payments. I contacted my therapist and asked if I could delay payment on my therapy bills. Marie said I didn't owe her a cent and wished me well.

In my second quarter of college, I enrolled in one social work class – Introduction to Social Work. I was docked one grade, from and A to a B, due to missing class because of a blizzard. I prayed my car would continue to run, and we would all stay healthy.

By spring, it was clear that my car was dying. I needed to secure a more reliable vehicle, but on AFDC, it was impossible. The only solution was to find a job.

During the summer when the girls were with their father, I worked as a Certified Nursing Assistant. I applied at a nursing home and was immediately hired. I was assigned to the night shift (10:00 p.m. to 6:30 a.m.). By working nights I was able to attend school, meet the court requirements for visitation and earn enough money to buy a car. The downside was I was spreading myself thin and missing sleep. Due to the 100-hour AFDC rule, I needed to keep my work hours under 100 per month. I purchased two uniforms for $25, notified my financial worker and commenced my $5.15 per hour job.

There were no medical or dental benefits. However, I did earn sick time. I had worked as a Certified Nursing Assistant in my late teens so I was familiar with the job duties. My only concern was working the graveyard shift and going to college during the day – could I stay awake? It would be extremely important for our family to work together as a team, as this would add another variable to our already busy and stressful schedules.

I showed up for my first night on the job and had to knock on the door to gain entry. My coworkers didn't know that I was starting. This made for an interesting first night with them. They had been working short-handed and had difficulty filling the graveyard position. However, this didn't make any of them friendlier. The graveyard shift was a revolving door. As soon as someone was trained, they often quit. Understandably, they were not receptive to my presence.

I was assigned to work with a woman in her early fifties. She had worked for the nursing home for over ten years. The air was tense. I was told to sit at a table and wait. I sat there for a very long time. Finally, the woman walked by and I asked her if I was going to start my training soon. She told me to sit where I was. She said she was busy catching up on work that the college students from the shift before didn't do. I assured her that my intention was not to come and do my homework, but to work. She said the breaks were few and far between on the night shift and, if we got one, it wasn't because of a scheduled time.

I worked closely with this woman during the first few months. Over time we became close. She shared her life with me and how essential her job was to her. She had a husband, but he tended to drink too much and offered her little in emotional or financial support. I had never met a woman who worked so hard and was so compassionate towards the people who lived in the nursing home. She was a wonderful role model. She was a strong woman whom I deeply respected and admired. She taught me more than how to be a good nursing assistant. She had a wonderful sense of humor. Over time she became interested in my schooling. It felt good to talk with another woman about my days in class. She was a wonderful support and it didn't take me long to share my history with her – I trusted her. As we talked, her eyes filled with tears. She hugged me and encouraged me to continue to follow my dreams. She said she had a dream job once, but the wage didn't pay enough to support her family, so she returned to being a nursing assistant.

I grew close to many of the elderly residents. We laughed a lot and enjoyed each other's company. Both the residents and the staff were in it together and needed to make the most of it.

The job was difficult with a great deal of physical lifting and speed. Strong communication skills were essential in order to offer compassion, understanding and kindness in very delicate situations. I often had to tell staff and family of the death of a resident. I also had to make sure the combative residents were not physically violent and offer encouragement and compassion when the elderly felt deep shame about their current physical condition.

The job provided excellent social work training. I had deep compassion and respect for the elderly. Although I knew I was combating fatigue much of the time, I was appreciative of the fact that I was still young and healthy enough to roll over in bed without assistance, walk to the bathroom unassisted and could visit loved ones. The residents didn't have those choices. There wasn't one resident who wouldn't have changed places with me in a heartbeat. I felt blessed and did my best to treat the people with the respect and kindness that they deserved.

Occasionally I worked a day shift. During a break, a woman from another wing asked me if I was Catholic. I told her I was spiritual but didn't have a church affiliation. She began to talk a little louder, so others in the break room could hear our conversation. She said if I wasn't Catholic, the residents wouldn't allow me to give them baths. I became angry and suggested that maybe she would like to the bathe four people I was assigned to, and I would take an extended break. Her mouth dropped open and before I walked away, I told her I was here to make a buck not friends. My religious background was never questioned again.

I quickly realized that the nursing home was short-staffed on all shifts. On weekends when the girls visited their father, I worked double shifts. I earned double wages, but I was exhausted. I resolved that if I worked every shift for the first six months, I would become valuable to the nursing home staff. That way, I would be called to pick up extra shifts. I needed the money and so I picked up hours when I could, but I had to stay under the 100 hours so I wouldn't jeopardize my AFDC. With a full school and workload, it didn't take long for my system to revolt.

I found I couldn't sleep, I had difficulty eating, and my body couldn't adjust to the change from day to night shifts. I eventually chose to work strictly nights. One time a woman who worked the day shift told me she didn't think people on the night shift worked as hard, and she challenged me to switch shifts. I accepted her challenge. The following week, she admitted that the night shift was just as hard, if not harder, than the day shift. We agreed that both our jobs were important – one was not more important than the other.

I was not invited to any staff activities. With work, school, and my dislike for social events, I wouldn't have attended anyway. A friend confided to me that I was not invited because I was divorced. Others worried that I might be looking for a husband. Apparently, they also thought I was odd because I wanted to work nights. It was clear that some of my coworkers felt threatened by my independence and goal setting. My lifestyle definitely challenged my coworker's belief and value systems. However, taking time to figure out their belief system was not a luxury I had.

My financial aid was considered income and therefore, I was not eligible for food stamps. I decided to take out student loans to ease some of the financial stress. I was notified by the county that it was mandatory I attend a Stride eligibility workshop or I would lose my monthly grant. I argued that I should be exempt due to work and school, but my financial worker said those were not exemptions. Failure to attend would mean the end of my cash. So I took two hours out of my school day and attended, only to be told I didn't meet the criteria for Stride. I felt like I was caught in the middle of two very confusing cultures.

That December I met Margie. She lived in the same apartment building. We visited in the laundry room and became friends. AJ had the girls for Christmas, so I was alone. Margie asked if I would like to accompany her to her parents' home for Christmas dinner. When I questioned her as to whether it would be okay with her parents, she said they were used to her bringing home strays. She had done it since she was very young. Her intent was not to be mean, but the statement hurt. I gently declined the invitation. The term "stray" seemed to fit how I felt about myself, and it was a painful realization.

Chapter Nine
Parent Loss

MARGIE OFFERED TO WATCH the girls on some of the nights I worked. She was on public assistance too. She felt ashamed of being on welfare. She said many times she didn't use the food stamps, and if she did, she drove out of town to buy her groceries so no one she knew would see her using them. I could sense her shame and it brought tears to my eyes.

I knew the feeling too well – shame and how the eyes of others seemed to brand me with incompetence. I tried to convince her that there was no shame in using food stamps because she was not abusing them. She was using them for what they were intended – to buy food for her children. I said it took great courage to be on public assistance and to know when to ask for help for her children. She was tearful and hugged me.

We began a very close friendship that remains today. We built a friendship of trust and honesty. We lived a lifestyle of difficult decisions and shared a common bond of poverty. She became my cheerleader and offered a hug when I was hurting. I offered the same in return. I was blessed to have found such a friend. I didn't feel I had to be anyone but myself when I was with her, and I know she felt the same.

IN JANUARY OF 1990, I purchased a car through the dealership that had done all the maintenance on my vehicles. They didn't know much about the car so they recommended a warranty that cost me $20 per month. Although $20 was a lot for me, I couldn't risk not having it. That was the best decision I made. It turned out the car had serious mechanical problems. Due to the warranty, it was repaired at no cost to me. Once fixed, the car proved to be reliable and dependable. It was my primary vehicle until 2003, when it had over 250,000 miles on it.

THAT SAME MONTH, Jerry called to say our father died. I could tell he was hurting. He told me our brothers were struggling as well. My parents' presence was powerful. It didn't seem conceivable that they could die. Jerry said dad didn't have any alcohol at his residence. Jerry and I believe that dad went into withdrawal from lack of alcohol, which caused the heart attack.

I felt angry and a deep sadness for my brothers because they liked to visit with dad. They fed him, drank with him and took him to the liquor store. I refused to take him to the liquor store because I didn't want to be an enabler. Jerry disagreed and said that I should accept him the way he was. He felt I was judgmental. This angered me. I wanted a father and a grandfather for my children; he offered nothing. When he was sober, my children and I spent time with him; but, I had stopped wasting my time trying to build a relationship with him. That ceased being a priority long before.

Father was 59 years old. So much had been lost over the years for all of us. Making arrangements for the funeral was difficult with my schedule. The loss of income from work was a concern. Coupled with the funeral expenses, I was pinched financially. There never seemed to be an easy answer to life's complexities. Two of my class instructors were helpful regarding the lost time, but one was not supportive. He said if I missed assignments I couldn't make them up. By now, this didn't faze me.

Jerry picked out the coffin before I arrived, which was fine with me. He had been sober for a few years, but Jesse and Lenny drowned their grief in alcohol. Jerry and I worked out a payment schedule. We both worked hard, but neither of us had much money. We all went through father's personal things, meager as they were. A great sense of sadness came over all of us looking at his possessions.

Part of me was happy because he no longer had to struggle with life's rules or feel shame or grief over the decisions he'd made. His heart was free, and he was no longer a slave to alcohol. He was at peace and for that I was grateful.

That evening Jerry took out his anger on me. He asked me who I thought I was, driving such a fancy car and attending college instead of spending time with our father. He asked me if I thought I was too good for the rest of the family. I was shocked at his words. I angrily responded that I needed dependable transportation for work, school and my children. I most certainly did not feel like I was better than anyone else. I made a choice not to visit with him when he was drunk because I refused to listen to his belligerent language and sexual comments. I was his daughter whether he was drunk or sober. Jerry felt I should have been more tolerant of him and his behavior, good or bad.

I tried to explain to Jerry that I was not everyone else. He refused to ride back to the motel with me. I threatened to leave if we were not going to support each other during this difficult time. He responded that I should do whatever I damn well pleased because I always did.

I cried all the way back to the motel. I sat in my car for a long time because the tears kept flowing. I tried to tell myself that Jerry was angry over our father's death and wasn't angry at me. I didn't want to believe that he felt I was behaving as if I were better than anyone else, and that I was being judgmental of our father. I had grown weary of the alcoholism and the behavior. After the funeral, Jerry softened and talked with me.

I tried to reach mother about his death, but she had no phone. I contacted the police department to see if they could stop by her apartment. However, I never heard back from them. I decided to send mother a letter. Would she have come? In her alcoholic state, it was impossible to predict. At least I tried to let her know and that was all I could do.

My brothers and I knew nothing about death, or about funerals. Nothing, absolutely nothing. No one taught us about living, about being children, about parenting, about anything. In death we tried to be good children and do what was respectful and right for our father. What was the right thing to do? We picked out a coffin and the funeral home prepared him for his final destination. There we sat, his five children, viewing his casket and grieving his death and all the losses of years gone by when he was alive.

At the cemetery, there was a military gun salute with a flag-draped coffin. Another piece of my father I wasn't aware of. My father was shown more respect at his funeral than he ever received when he was alive.

After the funeral I stopped at father's house. I opened a letter from the Social Security office. He had been approved for Social Security after two years of waiting.

I thought back to his Psychological Evaluation, when I waited for him in the lobby. When father left to use the restroom, the psychologist asked me to clarify a few facts. He said that on father's paperwork it stated that he had five children; however, during the evaluation father could only remember having three. He'd forgotten two of us. That is still a very painful memory.

There were times when I bought my father's food stamps from him because I knew he felt shame in using them. I ripped them up and threw them away. Although I knew he used the cash to buy alcohol, I felt it was the right thing to do.

His Social Security lump sum was used to pay the funeral costs. The bill was paid in full. This was a financial relief to Jerry and me.

A coworker asked me to work her shift. I knew this would put me over 100 hours for the month, but because I didn't want her to know I was on public assistance, I agreed. I contacted my financial worker the next morning and informed her. I explained this was a one-time deal, and I would keep my hours under the limit from then on. My financial worker said I'd be suspended for two months, which meant that I would lose my grant, and they would keep my child support. Angry, I told her to close my case and have my child support sent to me. No income for two months! How was I supposed to keep up with my monthly bills? AFDC was a meager amount, but it helped with my car payment.

I immediately called the head nurse and asked for more hours. I was able to pick up hours, but because I was classified as part-time, no matter how many extra hours I picked up, my part-time status would remain, and I would not be eligible for medical benefits.

I decided I could be a better mother tired than a mother with no self-esteem. I would have to be extra careful not to get sick or hurt because I no longer had any medical benefits.

I worked as many double shifts and holidays as I could for time-and-a-half pay. AJ had the girls every holiday, so it was easy to pick up extra shifts. The difficult part was finding time for school, work, parenting, commuting, and driving the girls to and from their father's. I slept whenever I could. My motto quickly became – put on your cleanest dirty shirt and get on with the day.

My daughters brightened up my day when I'd open my folder at work and find one of their colored drawings. The pictures reminded me that no matter how exhausted I was, that life would be simpler soon. It kept my spirits up and I remained hopeful even on those especially difficult days.

I SPOKE WITH THE OWNER of the gas station I frequented and asked him if I could open up an account. I agreed to pay my balance on paydays. Thankfully, he allowed me this option. I was better able to manage my money plus I avoided overdrafts.

A car repair shop also set up an account for me. Eventually, it was no longer offered as an option for customers. I made the decision to obtain a credit card. I learned over time that credit cards are high risk. Debt occurs with sky-high interest rates. I suffered serious financial consequences because of credit cards. It was another lesson learned in my never-ending education.

In the spring of 1990, I signed my children up for the Big Brothers/Big Sister program. During the interview they asked me if my children smoked or used drugs, if they swore, or if they stole things. My children were eight and ten years old. They needed Big Sisters not because of their behavior but because I worked nights and attended school during the day. With my schedule there was no time for ice skating, sledding, or any other family activities. They needed appropriate role models and guidance from another adult until my life became less stressful and more manageable. Twenty-four hours a day just didn't seem to be enough. I was contacted about six months later that there was a Big Sister for Shawna. Christine was a part-time social work student at my college.

Shawna enjoyed this one-on-one relationship with Christine and looked forward to the visits. Christine took Shawna shopping to buy me a few small gifts for special occasions like Mother's Day or Christmas. I could tell Shawna felt special, and I was grateful. However, I was often tearful after they left knowing I should be doing these activities with her. I longed for the day I would be able to do activities with my daughters again.

Sandy was eventually assigned a Big Sister too. Kelly was a first-year college student. She took Sandy to Disney on Ice, hosted sleepovers and helped her construct a gingerbread house. My daughters truly enjoyed their Big Sisters because their personalities were very well matched. I was very grateful for these young women. They were very respectful and caring of my children and our personal situation.

THE TOILET IN OUR APARTMENT OVERFLOWED. A plumber came over to repair it while I was out of the apartment. In order to clean up the mess in the bathroom, he grabbed my two work uniforms off the shower rod. Try as I could, I couldn't remove the grease stains. I sat on the stool and cried. I didn't have the money to buy new ones.

I borrowed two uniforms from a coworker. On payday I was able to purchase new ones. My landlady eventually reimbursed me for the cost of the two uniforms. I longed for the day when such an incident wouldn't cause such financial and personal crises.

While I was grateful for our housing, low-income apartments have their drawbacks. The building had a minimal number of washers and dryers and often, several of them were broken. I liked to nap while doing laundry, but I learned early on that I had to be vigilant. Several times my towels were stolen. I learned to be alert or risk losing the few possessions we owned.

I found that working nights was physically demanding, while going to school was mentally demanding. Though both were exhausting, I wasn't overusing one part of my body more than the other. My mother's nightly rampages when I was a child proved to be good training for me during this period of time in my life when sleep was a luxury. Sleep deprivation was common during my childhood and I was able to utilize that skill to assist me during a difficult time.

IN OCTOBER 1990, the *St. Paul Pioneer Press* contacted me, requesting an interview. They were doing a series of articles titled "The Working Poor," and they wanted my input. The reporter said a friend of mine had given him my name. I was naïve. When they told me their paper was in St. Paul, I thought that meant the article would be circulated only in St. Paul. I asked if this was to be an article of pity or of encouragement. I was told it would be a realistic depiction of the working poor and their struggles.

I soon discovered that the *Pioneer Press* was a well-distributed paper. I went to the gas station after work and the paper was there. When I paid, the attendant said he liked my interview and that I should be proud of my efforts. I was embarrassed and worried about who else had read it. I worried that my daughters might be treated differently at school.

When I arrived home, I had numerous messages from people I didn't know on my answering machine. All the messages were very positive and encouraging. I was surprised how the article touched so many people and how differently I was perceived after that. I received a great deal of attention from coworkers and several of my college professors. I received clothing for my daughters in the mail from people I didn't know. A man called offering me a bike for one of my daughters. He asked if I was dating. I did not want this attention, my life was complicated enough!

Another man called to commend me for attending school. Before the phone call ended, he said he couldn't help but notice that I didn't sound mentally handicapped or mentally retarded. Angry at his ignorance, I told him that having a low income was not directly related to being mentally handicapped. I would prefer a sizable wage, but that was not an option.

One coworker commended that I didn't walk poorly. She said she never would have guessed that my life was so stressful. In anger, I suggested that maybe I should hold my head down and walk with a limp so others could pick me out easier!

Other coworkers brought me furniture or clothing. I was treated differently, as if I was fragile; and, many looked at me with pity in their eyes. That was a very difficult time for me. My work was my social outlet. I had worked hard at being a dependable employee to earn the respect of my coworkers. I hoped the article would soon be forgotten, so I could get back to being just me.

Several of the social worker professors treated me differently from then on. They asked my thoughts more often in class and took more of an interest in my goal. This was a positive aspect.

I have stayed in touch with two of the families I came to know because of the article. One family consisted of adult twin sisters and the other an older couple with grown children. Both have been very generous and kind to me. Over the years, the twin sisters have been a constant in our lives. They've assisted us financially and emotionally. They ran a consignment shop for wealthy women and we often benefited from their business. We affectionately referred to them as "the Grandmas." They paid for my daughters to go to summer camp. One Christmas, they sent all three of us matching black velvet dresses. Along with the dresses, they sent money requesting we have our picture taken and to send them a copy. We felt like princesses.

These two women offered a great deal of emotional support during a time I felt isolated and alone. They took an avid interest in my schooling and often called or sent cards of encouragement. They thought I should receive something in the mail besides bills.

When our towels were stolen out of the laundry room, they sent replacements. They sent me $80 to buy good shoes, worried that I might develop chronic foot and back injuries due to wearing $6 sneakers.

The relationship with the Grandmas gave me something to look forward to. I began to feel like we really mattered to someone. They sent us round-trip tickets to visit them one weekend after they convinced me to take a few days off. They insisted I sleep in while they took my daughters out to eat.

The Grandmas saved my spirit. We loved each other in return. I hoped to repay some of their favors once I graduated from college.

I knew they expected nothing from me, but I dreamed about surprising them and doing for them what they had done for us.

We were very blessed to have both of these families in our lives. Without their emotional support, I'm not sure I would have completed college. While their financial assistance was an immense help, the laughter, hugs and sharing was what I truly treasured the most.

The Grandmas never complained. When I asked them how they were, they always replied, "Perfect, just perfect." They didn't mind if I was sad or exhausted. They always made me laugh and before long, I too agreed that everything was perfect, just perfect. They taught me a useful coping skill.

Today when I'm down or sad, I remember what they told us – overall, life is perfect, just perfect! I know some days are more perfect than others, and I think the Grandmas would agree. They shared many wonderful gifts with us – their heart, their time, and their love for life. My heart will never forget the two of them.

IN JULY OF 1991, my mother died in Spokane, Washington. She was 52 years old. On my answering machine there was a message from mother's husband, drunkenly informing me of her death. He said he found her dead at the apartment. That was all the information his message provided.

I was very sad and angry. I was angry that she was dead and that I hadn't seen her in over five years. I remembered the year of sobriety we had shared and the memories we had made. Her last letter stated that she was divorcing her husband and coming back to Minnesota. I regretted that I hadn't driven out to Washington to pick her up, but I had neither the time or the money.

The next day I received a phone call from the funeral home. They said my mother had been brought there without any clothes on. How odd was that? Although it was costly, Jerry and I agreed that mother belonged in Minnesota. We arranged to have her body flown back.

I felt abandoned. I wanted her to see my college diploma and be proud of me. I was angry that future opportunities for us to become close were now gone forever. She would never know her grandchildren, or see how special they were. I had always wanted more than she could offer. Life was so unfair.

My brothers had mixed emotions. Some were angry with her for their unhappy childhoods; others were angry that she didn't quit drinking. They felt anger that her behavior remained selfish until death. I believe they had higher expectations of our mother than our father. Duane was very close to mother and he seemed to take her death the hardest. He shared his feelings with me because I was the least angry with her. I also believe society has higher expectations of mothers than fathers in raising children.

Jerry and I felt that her four sons should carry the casket. Lenny and Jesse disagreed. They felt they didn't really know her, due to entering foster care at such a young age. Jerry and I insisted that we all show her respect in death.

Finances were tight but we agreed to worry about the expenses once the immediate grief and ceremonial piece of mother's death was completed. It was too much to think about during this emotional time.

My coworkers volunteered to cover my shifts during this difficult time. I was awestruck by their generosity.

The Grandmas helped me work through my grief. I told them I thought I was over wanting my mother in my life when she really had never been there anyway. They pointed out that my mother was my mother, good or bad, and that we all have feelings of regret, sadness, anger, love and hope. They were convinced that my mother had these feelings about her life as well.

They never judged me and felt I possessed the wisdom to do the right thing no matter the situation or circumstances. They mailed me $200 to help with expenses, which was a godsend. Unexpectedly, I received a letter from mother two days after she died which provided a bit of closure. It gave me a little something to hold onto.

After the funeral, I met two of mother's sisters for the first time. They inquired as to who I was. I angrily asked them who they were. I felt disgusted. They had no relationship with their sister or her children when she was alive, yet they had the gall to show up at her funeral.

The day of mother's funeral was very hot and humid. I remember hearing loud whispers that were critical of mother's behavior. Jerry stood up, faced mother's casket and firmly requested that no one discuss her failures in life. He also asked that anyone not wanting to be respectful during her funeral service to leave.

The room became silent and there was no more muttering about our mother. I was proud of him demanding respect for her. At the gravesite, it began to storm. I found it difficult to leave her there alone because she had always been afraid of storms. Often when drunk she told me the story that when they buried my infant sister, snakes crawled in and out of the hole they had dug for the casket. Mother was afraid of snakes and she said that was why she never visited her daughter's grave.

Jerry came and stood by me and said it was time to leave. "She can rest now, and no one will hurt her anymore. She won't feel the alcoholic addiction grab hold of her anymore." I sat in my car and cried for a long time.

Much to my chagrin, Jerry invited mother's two sisters over after the funeral. Over coffee, we talked about what each of us was doing. They felt we had turned out well, considering where we came from. They said that they had visited us when we were small children and were shocked by what they saw. We were unkempt and dirty, running around the apartment while mother was passed out on the sofa. It was too painful so they walked out and never returned.

They thought looking at our environment was difficult; did they have any idea what it was like to *live* in it? They walked away from five small children that needed assistance and protection. I was not impressed with them. Jerry gave me a stern look as if he knew what I was thinking, warning me not to say anything out loud.

One of the aunts asked me if I remembered receiving a birthday gift signed by my mother at one of our foster homes. It was a necklace with my birthstone and a matching ring. I responded that I had. She said she had sent it to me and signed mother's name because she felt I should receive something from her. I knew it hadn't come from mother; she never acknowledged my birthday. Anything of value would have been pawned for alcohol rather than spent on a gift. I knew my mother and her behavior. I never knew her to buy a gift, borrow money, yes, but not buy anyone a gift.

I felt different after mother died and things I considered important, no longer seemed to matter. I began to question why I pushed myself so hard when I could die tomorrow. As I look back now, I believe I was depressed.

ONE WEEKEND THERE WAS A SNOWSTORM. I called AJ to tell him I wouldn't transport the girls in a blizzard. He demanded I bring the children per the court order and if I didn't, he would report me to the court and have me incarcerated. He was not concerned about the children's safety, but only interested in making me jump through hoops.

Within 30 minutes of his call, a police officer arrived at my door with a copy of the divorce decree. He encouraged me to drive the children to their father. It didn't appear that anyone was concerned about the children's safety. Against my better judgment, we packed up and drove safely to his home.

I encouraged me daughters to join at least one extracurricular activity at school. On AJ's weekends with the girls, they were unable to participate because he refused to be flexible on the times. He maintained that the divorce was my fault and there would be no scheduling difficulties if I reconciled with him.

After one visit, Shawna forgot a book at her father's. I called AJ and asked if he would mail it or meet me halfway so I could retrieve it. He refused. He said I was the mother so it was my responsibility to pick it up. His contention was that if I hadn't divorced him, this wouldn't have happened. I drove 110 miles to pick up the book before I started my 10:00 p.m. shift at the nursing home.

The visitation schedule was grueling. AJ wasn't always home when I dropped the girls off which meant I had to wait for him. This resulted in some very late nights for all three of us. In fact, some Mondays the girls were so exhausted they stayed home from school to sleep.

Early one Saturday when the girls were at their father's, I received a call from a woman at the Sears store. She said Sandy had given her my number. Sandy asked her to tell me I needed to come right away. She didn't know if Sandy was hurt, but Sandy said she couldn't call herself because her father wouldn't allow it.

I called Jerry and asked him to check on the girls and assure them that I was on my way. When I arrived, I discovered AJ had been suffering from migraine headaches through the night and had become physically ill. He told the girls he felt as if he was dying. The girls had been up all night worried that their father might die. They didn't know what to do, yet their dad said they couldn't call me. When the Sears woman called the house to say AJ's order was in, Sandy answered the phone and quietly gave her my phone number. It angered me that he had worried them needlessly.

AJ was controlling and manipulative, even with his daughters. He didn't care how this affected our children. I found his behavior pathetic.

COLLEGE WAS MUCH LESS INTIMIDATING THE LONGER I ATTENDED. However, my Political Science class was challenging. The first day of class the professor asked all the Business majors to raise their hands. Then he asked all the Social Work students to raise their hands. He said those of us in Social Work must have a desire to be poor. He laughed at us. I felt his statement was demeaning. I received a D in the class because I chose to put little effort into it. His arrogant attitude turned me off from day one.

In one of my Social Work classes, the instructor asked us to write to our legislators concerning an issue of importance to us. I picked the topic of Medical Assistance. I was without medical coverage. Because I was fearful of being hurt, my cautiousness greatly impacted what activities I could do with my girls. I couldn't afford to be off of work.

Our local legislator came to our class to answer questions. He said he had received so many letters, he decided to come and answer our questions in person. When I asked him how many letters that was, he said six. It seemed odd to me he would think six letters was a lot, but my perception of things was often different from others.

When I inquired about AFDC, FS, and MA, he was puzzled and asked me what the acronyms meant. It was clear to me he had little idea what these programs were. This angered me, so I chose not to participate further.

From that experience I learned that six letters piqued a politician's interest, yet legislators were virtually clueless when it came to the struggles of poor families.

Chapter Ten
End of a Relationship

ONE CLASS ASSIGNMENT CALLED FOR US to write a three-page paper on our life experiences. I had to make a decision whether I should reveal the truth about myself. The truth would probably cause discomfort for both the instructor and me. After much thought, I decided to write an open and honest paper. If I was to be a social worker, then I needed to be honest about who I was.

After class the instructor approached me. She said she had never met an incest victim before. I pointed out that the abuser was not my biological father. I suggested that she had met many incest victims before – she just didn't know it.

Later I felt badly about how I reacted to her comment. I knew her intent was to be kind and gentle, but I wasn't fragile. I could think, walk and talk. My abuse was only a small part of who I was. I loathed the pity I saw in others eyes when they heard about my past. With role models and honest teachers, I was as capable as the next person of reaching my potential. I needed the opportunity. Like everyone, I have certain strengths and certain weaknesses. I love my children, work hard, pay taxes and try to be a better person every day. I am a person, a real person.

A CULTURE CLASS WAS QUITE MEMORABLE. The instructor wore dress slacks held up with suspenders and a flannel plaid shirt. He had a scruffy gray beard matched his thinning hair. He was short but built rather robustly and often took a stance with his thumbs under his suspenders. Our class was rather large. The classroom was set up so that the instructor was down in the center with a few desks of students on the level close to him and everyone else angled upward.

On the first day of class, the instructor walked over to a student's desk and took a large drink of the student's pop. He replaced the can of pop on the desk, stepped back, stretched out his suspenders and emitted a large belch. As he wiped his mouth with the back of his hand, he said he had been thirsty all morning. Some students thought it was funny and others whispered their disgust for his uncouthness.

I overheard many students state that they would not sit in front the next day. I was grateful I had sat near the back. *Get a grade and get out,* I told myself. I had to repeat this self-talk often as I found his behavior disrespectful and class discussion absolutely irrelevant to anything we needed to learn in reference to other countries.

Sometimes the discussion was about how American men were attracted to women with large breasts, or how in other cultures, men were more attracted to a women's legs. Most of the men found these discussions humorous. I observed the changing dynamics of the classroom seating arrangement each day, with most of the young women slowly moving to the back of the room and the men of the class moving to the front.

As negative comments about women increased, I noticed the class was shrinking. I found it a challenge not to express my disgust. I reminded myself that I didn't have time to repeat the class, which was a possibility if I challenged the instructor's behavior and etiquette. I reminded myself that I needed to stay focused on my social worker goal, and nothing I could say or do likely would change his teaching practices.

One morning before class, I struck up a conversation with another female student. She was tearful and nervous about class and worried that the instructor might single her out. I tried to reassure her that it was just one class and it would be over soon. Several days went by and the instructor's inappropriate comments continued. I decided I was older and needed to speak up. The next time he brought up the subject of the female anatomy, I raised my hand. When he called on me I asked him how this discussion could possibly be helpful to any student. The room grew quiet as the anger spread over his face. I was wearing a pair of glasses that medical assistance paid for. They had a small decal on the lower left lens. The instructor asked me if it was dirt on my glasses or bird shit. Some students laughed, others flinched. With that he resumed his lecturing. The girl who had been so fearful of him turned and smiled at me. I was frustrated at the instructor's obvious power play in the classroom and his total disregard for his students.

I left in the middle of the class and went to the instructor's department where I spoke with one of his peers. I shared with him what had happened and he suggested that I share my concerns with the head of the department, although honestly, he felt it would be a waste of time. Many students had complained, but the instructor was tenured, so there was nothing that could be done. He suggested I let the matter drop, which I did. I was too overwhelmed to take that challenge on.

SANDY HAD TO HAVE HER TONSILS REMOVED. Due to the surgery, I missed class. The doctor gave me a note to give to my instructor. I had missed a test and asked to make it up. The instructor refused. He said I had to decide between being a parent or a student. I angrily informed him that my children came first. I received a zero on the test.

MY LACK OF SLEEP CAUGHT UP TO ME. I was taking an exam when I realized I didn't have a #2 pencil with me. I walked up to the instructor and asked to borrow one. He said he didn't want me in his class and asked me to leave. Confused, I asked him why. My eyes were red and my speech slow due to lack of exhaustion and he presumed I was on drugs. It took some explaining on my part to convince him otherwise.

I SIGNED UP FOR WHAT I THOUGHT would be the easiest Physical Education course. It was something about studying the human body. Much to my surprise, after two weeks of classroom lectures, we walked three miles every day! My big plan to enroll in an easy class backfired.

I WAS REQURIED TO TAKE a computer class. My knowledge of computers was minimal, so I asked Cal to assist me. Although we no longer lived together, we still maintained a relationship. After working with computers all day, he said he had no interest in working on them at night. I lined up a tutor who charged $5 an hour. While it was a lot of money to me at the time, it was money well spent. I received a "B" in the class.

ONE INSTRUCTOR IN THE SOCIAL WORK department I particularly liked. She didn't just teach from the front of the room, she walked amongst her students. She welcomed discussion and truly wanted the student's thoughts and feelings. She asked questions that made us think long after our class was over. I enjoyed her classes no matter how tired I was. She was gentle and had a habit of putting her hand on my shoulder if we talked. She listened to everyone's perspective on poverty, government programs and life situations.

During a discussion on money and privilege, she spoke of a bus trip she took with several poor families. She spoke of the songs they sang on the bus and how heartfelt the words were. As she clenched her fist to her chest and with tears in her eyes, she slowly began to sing one of the songs. It was beautiful! We all had tears in our eyes. It was clear that she possessed compassion for less fortunate individuals and families. She had a deep passion for teaching her students more than what was contained in textbooks. I found her to be a wonderful role model. She was sincere, honest and compassionate. To this day, I treasure her wisdom and friendship.

When I arrived home from school one day, I found my neighbor Margie helping Shawna into the apartment. She had a temperature of 102°. Shawna had asked the school nurse to call me so I could pick her up, but the nurse refused. Her explanation to Shawna was that a good parent would be home for her child and not at school. I called the school several times to set up an appointment with the school nurse, but she never returned my calls. After speaking with several other low-income mothers in the neighborhood, I realized they had had similar experiences with the nurse. Upset over the lack of respect for poor families, I called the principal and asked for a joint meeting. He said he'd set it up and get back to me, but he never did. I continued to call but to no avail. Finally, I threatened him with legal action. From that point forward, the school nurse always called my neighbors or me if one of our children was ill.

AT ONE POINT WHEN I WAS STRUGGLING financially, I swallowed my pride and went to the food shelf. I vowed this would be a one-time occurrence because I felt the food shelf was for families who had less than me. I felt very self-conscious. They gave me noodles and potatoes and a coupon to go the creamery for milk. They also provided a jar of cherries and a bag of peanuts, which didn't seem like the most practical items. Before I left, they asked if I would like some microwave popcorn. I said yes, my children would love it. An elderly female volunteer angrily said it was a rarity for people who use the food shelf to own a microwave. I felt ashamed that I had a microwave, even though I had purchased it many years before. I decided that I would rather scrimp on my budget and do without before experiencing another episode like that. My belief is that people who donate to food shelves should only donate items they themselves use, not just items they want to get rid of. Chances are if they don't use it, neither does a needy family. When coworkers told me that I looked like I was losing weight, I'd smile and say I was dieting. This way, no one felt uncomfortable. If I honestly replied that sometimes I only had enough food for my two children, it would have been awkward. I had plenty of those as it was – no need to create more.

DUE TO MY SCHEDULE, there was little time to develop meaningful friendships. My friends were primarily my coworkers and the residents. Music became important to me. Mainly I listened to music that encouraged me, made me feel blessed and reminded me how much I loved my children. I liked Garth Brooks "If Tomorrow Never Comes, Will They Know How Much I Loved Them", "The River", and "The Dance." I loved songs that told a story, touched my heart, and connected with me emotionally; music that tapped into my need for encouragement or motivated me even by anger, like, "Fast Car" by Tracy Chapman. Still, my mother's messages that I was incompetent and worthless remained constant, thus propelling me to work even harder out of fear that I too might fail my own children.

My daughters and I often did our homework together. Shawna seemed to understand college math much better than I did. She was quite proud to assist me. Both my daughters took turns quizzing me. We'd compete in our grades. They opened my grades when they came in the mail, and I opened theirs. We had many discussions about our grades reflecting our efforts. I enjoyed these times with my children. They spoke frequently about going to college after graduation. It pleased to know they had dreams for themselves. I encouraged them always to work up to their potential.

If my children were too ill to go to school, I gave them Tylenol and brought them to class with me, so I wouldn't get docked for lack of attendance.

My children did a wonderful job keeping our apartment clean. They vacuumed and dusted, helped cook meals, and assisted with the laundry. They slept in the bunk beds that I received in the divorce settlement, while I slept in the other bedroom. Shawna asked for an allowance and I agreed. We kept track on the back of an envelope. I agreed to pay up once I received my first social work check. When the total neared $1,000, we threw away the envelope and started over.

My daughters were very forgiving and understanding of our financial situation. However, there were times when Shawna was discouraged and yearned for extras. She worried we would always be poor. I too was discouraged, but I tried to relay my hope that brighter days were imminent. Hope was all we had. As a family, we couldn't afford to lose that.

I remember one time, lying on the bathroom floor before work after the children were tucked into bed. I had my feet hanging in the tub and a cold washcloth over my face. In my head I was repeating, "I am somebody, I will make it," as tears slid down my face. I tried to convince myself that my lifestyle was only temporary, but it was the longest temporary I had ever faced! I prayed for strength and guidance to make it through to my goal of a better life for my children like I had promised them.

One night after supper, I was resting on the couch for a few minutes before leaving for work. Suddenly I felt a warm liquid on my feet. I looked up and saw Shawna crying. I asked her what was wrong. She said, "I'll be so glad when I don't have to see you looking so tired anymore." I felt such deep sadness that my eyes welled with tears. Though I tried hard not to let them think I was tired or exhausted, they were maturing and much more perceptive. I held Shawna and promised her it wouldn't be long before our lives improved. I vowed to look less tired so my children wouldn't worry. Because of my love for them, there was nothing I couldn't do. Our lifestyle forced them to grow up quickly.

I felt deep shame the night Sandy became ill in bed and I only had one set of sheets. I brought her in to sleep with me the rest of the night. After the girls left for school the next morning, I sat down on the floor and cried. I had been crying for some time when I heard a knock on the door. It was a middle-aged woman who was a Jehovah Witness. I attempted to dismiss her quickly, but she sensed my hurt. Through my tears I explained how I didn't have money to wash my dirty sheets. She reached into her purse and gently placed $20 in my hand. As she rubbed the top of my hand, she said she would stop by at a more convenient time in the future. Then she left. People truly do come into our lives when we need them.

IN FEBRUARY, I NOTICED a dull pain on my right side. It seemed more painful when I lifted things at work or carried my book bag. I tried to lie down before work, but I was unable to sleep. For days this pattern continued.

When I shifted gears in my car and I noticed a dull ache in my side. I decided I must have pulled a muscle. Margie, my friend across the hall, noticed I was holding my right side. She encouraged me to go to the emergency room; but because I was without health insurance, I was hesitant to do so. I called the charge nurse at work who also suggested I go in. I called Cal for a ride, but he said he'd had a bad day and didn't want to. Margie drove me instead. I was having an appendicitis attack so emergency surgery was performed. The next day I asked the doctor if I could go to work that weekend. He said absolutely not, that it might be weeks before I could drive.

I lay back on my pillow devastated. How would I care for my children? How would I make my car payment and rent? How would I go to school and keep up my attendance? I'd have to take the quarter over again. I was overwhelmed with fear and doubt.

The next day, the doctor asked if I had been abused as a child. I was surprised. He said I had a very high level of pain tolerance, much higher than most people.

AJ unexpectedly showed up at the hospital with the girls. He said his weekend was over and left. I looked into my daughters eyes and I could tell they thought I was dying. I attempted to calm their fears by telling them I would heal quickly and we could resume our regular routine soon. I declined pain pills because I didn't want to be groggy while they were with me. Margie offered to take the girls but with her limited income, I didn't want to burden her.

Later that day Cal stopped by. He said he only came because his mother and grandmother wanted to know how I was. I asked if he could stay with the girls but he became irritated, so I dropped the subject. Cal was still in the room when the two Grandmas came in. Everyone picked up on Cal's foul mood. He reluctantly volunteered to take the girls for one night. The girls said they would rather stay with Margie.

After everyone left, I felt overwhelmed. I couldn't work, attend school or drive. I cried most of the night, wondering how to sort everything out.

Several days after my hospitalization, the social work instructor I particularly liked and several students came to visit. I was down emotionally and it must have been transparent because she looked me in the eye and said, "You're not going to give up, are you?" I looked away, tears in my eyes. *She doesn't know how hard these past few years have been and what it takes emotionally, mentally and physically not to give up. I probably should have given up long ago!* The words "giving up" felt so harsh. I had never given up on anything. My heart hurt worse than my body after surgery.

Margie called later to say the two Grandmas had given her money for groceries and gas. I don't know why the Grandmas chose us, but they were truly lifesavers.

Once home, I expected to hear from Cal but I didn't. Besides his usual moodiness, he was now angry whenever I saw him. This worried me so I tried to contact him. After several failed attempts, I called his phone to check his messages. He had given me prior permission to do this if I couldn't reach him. Much to my surprise, there was a message from a woman thanking him for the good time. From her message it was obvious they were in an intimate relationship. His unpredictable behavior now made sense. He was seeing someone else.

I was angry and hurt. Throughout our six-year relationship, I had been financially responsible for my children. I hadn't asked him to be their father, only a friend. I had made every effort to be independent and not lean on him emotionally or financially. Occasionally, he purchased a few groceries or treated us out to eat, but mostly we split the bill for any activity. I felt deep sadness that he hadn't been honest with me about this other relationship. When I shared with Margie my predicament, she told me that her husband had cheated on her with two women at the same time. And I thought I had problems! Margie and I shared many laughs over that.

My hospital bill totaled $6,000. Margie urged me to apply for medical assistance. I had been denied previously for being $10 over the income limits. I swallowed my pride and applied. Thankfully I met the income guidelines and my bill was paid in full.

I was chomping at the bit to return to work. Only after I signed a waiver would my doctor release me earlier than he recommended. Fortunately, I had no complications.

I received a letter from Cal saying he needed a new relationship. The letter made me sad in one respect, angry in another. Apparently, he didn't have the courage to tell me in person. Six years was a long time with a partner, especially considering the many trials we had encountered together.

Chapter Eleven
My Cleanest Dirty Shirt

Dreams and Hopes Die Very Painful Deaths

I RECEIVED MANY SUPPORTIVE PHONE CALLS from Cal's family. Our breakup played like an old tape of loss and grief. The mental message of not being good enough no matter how hard I tried resurfaced. The Grandmas kept in close contact with me and continued to encourage me about a brighter future for my children and myself.

Cal's family was as confused by his behavior as I was. However, they were his family and his support. It seemed best for everyone to have some closure with them, but this would require time. We agreed we would say our goodbyes later.

There were too many emotions and responsibilities to mentally and emotionally grasp. I needed to engage my automatic pilot mode and shut off the overwhelming mental static in my mind. I had to take care of what I could, take care of the needs of my children, and shut down my emotions as I had done as a child to cope. The hope of coming together as a family was no longer a possibility. Another life lesson about the realization that we have no control over others, no matter how beautiful the long-term dream we have built, and at times, we have no control over our physical health, our environment or our financial situation. We have to make the best of what we have and who we are. This is a painful lesson each and every time we face it. Dreams and hopes die very painful deaths.

About two weeks after surgery, I noticed I had some leakage from my breasts. The doctor at the student clinic suggested I quit taking birth control pills. He scheduled another appointment to run more tests. He wanted to rule out a tumor or a pituitary gland problem. I was terrified when I left the clinic.

Going off birth control was not a big deal. I was no longer in a meaningful relationship and had no need for birth control. At the age of 33, my sexual relationships had consisted of a total of three men – my foster father, AJ and Cal.

I disliked not being in control of my situation. My children depended on me and needed me to be there for them. I knew only too well what life was like without a mother or family support. I couldn't be sick again. I had no time to be sick. Again, I tapped into the anger that always surfaced when I felt helpless and hopeless. I vowed to channel this anger into deep motivation and reach my goal of being a social worker. I had approximately one year of school remaining. Both personally and professionally I had to succeed.

I had people in my life who believed in me, so who was I to argue with them? I continued to pray for strength and guidance when I was exhausted and felt as if I had no more to give. When I was sad or discouraged and wanted to quit or when I heard my mother's voice telling me I was worthless and would never amount to anything, then I wanted more than anything to prove my mother's predictions were wrong. Thoughts of my mother made my anger rise from inside me and gave me energy and strength to continue to move in the direction of the dream my daughters and I had built for a better life. I would not settle for less as my mother had done. I wanted more for my children than I had – a loving and caring parent they could take for granted – they deserved the best I could give.

AS PART OF A CLASS ASSIGNMENT, I had to develop a support group. I asked the Women's Center about the possibility of forming a group for non-traditional students who wanted to further their education. The Center was supportive. The group went well and the director asked me to volunteer at the Center on a regular basis.

This was a good match professionally. It felt good to offer the students' shortcuts to community and county services that they were not aware of. The students I worked with were deeply appreciative of the support and encouragement I provided. While it was time consuming, I wanted to help other students achieve their hopes and dreams as well.

Besides hugs and encouraging words, they needed sincere and honest answers and to know that they were in control of their own lives. Many of their choices were not easy, but they had choices. I advised them, "It is time to put on your cleanest dirty shirt and get on with your life the best you can. Always do your best and you will like the person you see in the mirror looking back at you!"

The arrangement of holding sessions with the students at the technical college worked for a while, although I sensed friction between the college and the Women's Center. The technical school administrators didn't feel I was qualified to meet with the students because I had not received my Social Work degree. They were concerned about the number of students who came to see me when the technical college offered degreed, paid employees to assist students with the services I provided. The school barred us from meeting in their facility so we met at the Women's Center.

Why were the students coming to see me when the technical college provided the same service? The question was raised and the students were asked. The students said it was easier to speak with someone if they didn't have to make an appointment three weeks in advance, especially when their crisis was now. One student said she didn't feel ashamed to talk to someone who dressed the same as she did. Due to my own personal situation, students felt comfortable sharing their struggles and looked to me for information on available resources. Many of the school counselors had never lived in poverty or struggled themselves. The women said they felt shame and intimidation when dealing with professionals. Many of the students did not feel comfortable sharing their personal struggles of domestic abuse, chemical dependency and financial issues with those who had never experienced them personally. I derived a great deal of satisfaction from this work and hopefully I helped others on their life journey.

CAL ASKED TO RESUME OUR RELATIONSHIP. He apologized about his affair and said he had made a mistake. He said he still cared about me but had grown tired of my rigid schedule. I still cared about him deeply; however, his attitude angered me. If he felt my schedule was so difficult, he could have offered financial or emotional support. Why did he think engaging in a relationship with someone else was the solution? He admitted he felt he had gone about things the wrong way and understood if I no longer wanted anything to do with him.

Although I still loved him very much, the pain of his actions was very fresh. It would take time. Besides, my responsibilities had not lessened, and my schedule remained the same. I had one y ear of school left.

We decided to resume our relationship slowly. Shawna and Sandy were very angry with Cal and wanted nothing to do with him. They were very protective of me. The three of us talked about not throwing people away due to mistakes made because we'd never have loved ones in our lives if that was the case. Cal needed to find out for himself what he valued and felt important. I couldn't do that for him. Everything in life is a lesson. Unfortunately, some lessons need to be repeated before we understand the meaning clearly.

During this time, Cal was sad and talked about the shame and guilt he felt. One day he was unusually quiet and tearful. He gave me a letter he had written. He said he had caused my children and me enough pain, and he didn't want to cause any more. He revealed that his ex-girlfriend was pregnant with his child. I felt like the wind had been knocked out of me. I had always hoped and dreamed that we would come together as a family, build a home together and maybe even add onto our family. I was numb. I didn't know what to feel or do. I cried over the loss of my dreams.

The next day I called him to say that we needed to talk about our future. I didn't hate him, but I needed time to process our situation and there was very little time or energy for that.

Our time together was limited. At times we seemed to be able to move past the crisis and focus on the strengths of our relationship, other times he remained moody and distant. I tried not to stress him to allow him time to absorb his situation. I found it difficult to watch him struggle, but I also knew I couldn't fix it for him. As time went on and the woman's pregnancy was drawing to a close, he became more emotionally distant. It was time to focus on my own responsibilities.

MY FINAL YEAR OF SCHOOL, I was hired at the Children's Home. They had many cottages filled with children with various disabilities and barriers, both behavioral and legal.

I worked from 12:00 noon to 9:00 p.m. in addition to my job at the nursing home. This schedule soon became too much and I resigned from the nursing home. I found leaving the residents and my coworkers very difficult. They had become my family. During my final two days, many tears were shed. My coworkers said I was the best certified nursing assistant/social worker they had ever had. I reminded them that I was the only one, and we laughed. I still look back at this time in my life and smile. I learned a great deal and came to bond with everyone. Most importantly, I felt loved.

Shortly after I started my new position, I noticed I was more tired than usual. I had leakage from my breasts again. I panicked, believing whatever I had before was back! I tried to convince myself it was nothing, but then, I started feeling nauseous and having headaches. I had insurance through work but it took 30 days to activate. I thought, *this is my luck, with only ten months to complete my Social Work degree, I'm probably dying and then what was all of this for!*

After my insurance became valid, I went to a doctor. As I sat waiting, I began to cry. I prayed that I didn't have some terrible disease. Who would care for my children? I was distraught. When the doctor returned, I asked him if I had cancer. He said no, but he had concerns because I was very underweight. I was floored when he said I was pregnant.

Pregnant! I was 33 years old. I had children about to be teenagers. I had just started a new job plus my relationship with Cal was far from stable or secure. We had been together only one time during an emotional moment. How could this be? I had planned my life so carefully, trying to simplify my future and eliminate barriers –

now what was I going to do? I loved babies; however I wasn't certain my children and Cal would feel the same way? Could I complete college? Could I cover the cost of childcare? I was in shock when I walked out of the doctor's office. I was overwhelmed.

My life had taken another drastic turn. I called the Grandmas and confessed to them that I had made a mistake. As always, they were supportive and insisted it wasn't the end of the world. I would be done with school in seven months, so at least the baby would be born after that.

I felt so ashamed it was difficult for me to share the news. I wanted my child's birth to be happy and I wasn't sure that was possible during this stressful and confusing time. Like I had done many times in my life, I decided to put on my cleanest dirty shirt and to get on with life as I had always done. I would love this baby as I loved the baby's father. I could not predict anything else.

Cal was not pleased. He was still dealing with his girlfriend and her pregnancy. My children had mixed reactions. Shawna was very upset, partially because I wasn't married and partially because my condition might embarrass her in front of her friends. She was very moody anyway due to her age, and my pregnancy didn't help the situation. She made it very clear she didn't want to hear about the baby. Conversely, Sandy was very excited about the prospect of a newborn in the house. She asked to go to the doctor's appointments with me and was very gentle and kind.

I talked with Cal's family and initially they were cool. My brothers were disgusted with me. There would be limited support for me during this pregnancy. I repeatedly told myself, *I can do this. I've done it before, and life will be easier for this baby as I will have completed college and hopefully be working at a day job, with benefits, dependable transportation, and a living wage!*

A baby made the goal of completing college more intense and necessary. Although loved ones accepted the fact that I was pregnant, no one seemed to think it was a joyous occasion. I knew that I had wanted a child with Cal, just not at this time. The pregnancy wasn't something I had planned; however, it was wanted and loved. Because I had two daughters, I hoped this child would be a boy. Cal was emotionally distant and didn't share the same excitement I did.

I made doctor's appointments around Cal's schedule because he said he would accompany me. When the day arrived, he would make up some excuse and not go. Eventually, I quit asking him. The Grandmas sent us train tickets to visit them one weekend. They bought me maternity clothes and special treats for the girls. They made it seem as if this baby was a wonderful blessing. Their positive attitude helped the girls to adjust.

When I was six months along, I developed complications with my pregnancy. My doctor strongly advised me to stay off my feet as much as possible. This meant I had to leave my job at the Children's Home. I secured an internship through the Women's Center that paid $20 an hour. The wage allowed me to pay for my health insurance.

In June, one month before the baby was due; Cal agreed to move in with us. We rented a house together. During June I took the state test for licensure as a social worker. I had bronchitis and wasn't feeling well, which raised my stress level. I did not feel confident after completing the test. It took six weeks to find out the results.

Shawna was not happy that Cal lived with us. He was sullen or angry most of the time. After four weeks of living together I knew I'd made a mistake. If Cal didn't want to be part of a family, I wasn't going to force him. I didn't know why he was so angry and silent. I felt overwhelmed most of the time and hoped he would adjust to family life after our son was born. However, his behavior added more stress. The three of us mainly stayed out of his way.

I was five days past my due date when I started having contractions. Shawna called Cal. I thought if Cal was there for the birth of his child, he might feel a bond or connection with him. We barely made it to the hospital in time. Adam was born very quickly. Shawna and Sandy left the birthing room just minutes before he arrived. Shawna, who was initially upset about the pregnancy, used her own money to buy him a sleeper and blanket. My daughters quickly bonded with him. Cal held him, but I could see the concern and nervousness in his eyes. It was apparent he wasn't sure what his responsibilities were.

I delivered Adam on a Friday afternoon and was released from the hospital on Sunday at noon. I returned to my job on Monday. I brought all three children to work with me. There was a corner room where I nursed Adam. Shawna and Sandy were a tremendous help during this time of adjustment.

After six months, Cal had still not taken much interest in Adam. Cal disliked the baby crying during the night because he didn't feel rested enough to work on his computer projects. After about a week, Adam and I moved downstairs so we wouldn't disrupt his sleep. I hoped this would improve his mood; however, his behavior didn't change. His words and actions remained angry. We all were grateful when he wasn't home. Life was less tense and stressful in his absence.

Cal and I split household bills, except that he paid for his additional work phone. Adam's expenses were my responsibility. The only communication we had was when he complained of lack of sleep or some behavior he disliked in my daughters.

Adam continued to disrupt his sleep even though we were sleeping downstairs in the living room. There was no pleasing him. When he came home, we avoided him. We could do nothing right in his eyes. I found myself becoming angry at his lack of disregard for the family. I felt that our home belonged to all of us, yet we continued to walk on eggshells for one person. I paid more than my share of the household bills and our son's expenses. It felt like we were bad roommates instead of parents and partners.

One morning his anger flared when he wrote out his child support check for his other child. His financial obligations were taking a toll on him. I didn't feel that our family deserved to feel his anger and resentment when we had nothing to do with the choices he had made. His lack of communication and continued complaints made daily life very difficult for us all.

When Adam was about three months old, I took him to visit Grandmother Elma. Due to a stroke, she now lived in a nursing home. The stroke affected her speech. When I entered her room, she was sitting in her wheelchair and had a little tray above her lap. Her eyes twinkled as she looked at me. My grandmother was a woman of few words before her stroke – her eyes said it all. You could look in grandma's eyes and know if she was sad, happy or angry. I could tell she was happy to see me. I set Adam on her tray. I opened the blanket so she could look at him. He had a t-shirt and diaper on. My grandma ever so gently touched his legs, toes, arms and fingers. Then she touched his cheek. Her eyes twinkled in approval as she looked into my eyes. I asked her if I could comb her hair like I had done when I was a small child. She nodded. She sat very still as I gently combed her hair and talked to her. My eyes filled with tears because it felt so good being close to her again. We went for a walk, Adam perched on her tray. Grandma gently held her hand on his stomach. When it was time to leave, I hugged her for a long time while she stroked my arm. As I held her face in my hands to kiss her cheek and to tell her how much I loved her, I noticed there were tears in her eyes. She gently rubbed Adam's forehead and cheek. I kissed her and left with a heavy heart.

I received notification that I had passed my licensure exam. My goal was complete. I was a social worker. I didn't attend graduation due to the cost. The Grandmas and my daughters were elated with the news, while Cal was silent.

I started to apply for social work positions. I had earned a major in Social Work and a minor in Human Relations, with an emphasis in Women's Studies. At the bottom of my resume I put the date of my Social Work licensure. I was quite proud of my work history and the date I became a professional. My goal was to work as a Child Protection Social Worker.

I received a job offer from the Women's Shelter. The starting wage was $8.50 per hour. I found this difficult to believe. I was certain with my degree and licensure I could earn a better wage. I had taken out approximately $20,000 in student loans and needed more income to meet all my expenses. I accepted the job on a temporary basis.

I worked as an advocate for approximately three months. I interviewed for a county Social Services job 67 miles away. The county agency was hiring social workers in a pilot program related to welfare reform.

My brother Lenny accompanied me on the interview because I needed someone to watch Adam. The position paid $10.50 an hour with benefits. The downside was the lengthy drive, but the upside was I could meet the additional licensure requirements after two years. I was offered the job and accepted it.

Cal left most weekends, so I took the girls and Adam to work on Saturdays. They watched Adam while I worked.

My training at the agency was limited at best. The supervisor was moody and difficult to approach. I assisted families the best I could, despite my lack of guidance.

Adam had numerous ear infections and had to have tubes put in his ears. Life remained a juggling act. That had not changed.

In the spring of 1994, my grandmother Elma passed away. The world always seemed a more pleasant place because she was in it. However, I knew she was ready to leave this world because she had spoken of her desire many times. She had felt much pain and sadness in her lifetime. Her health was failing and she was tired. She said many times she was ready whenever God called her home. Her strong faith carried me through many difficult times. I missed her deeply, but I was happy that she no longer felt emotional or physical pain. I wished my daughters had a woman like her in their lives for strength, encouragement, guidance and faith. Her life represented all that is good in the world. She will remain forever close to me in my heart, in my prayers, and as a role model to always strive to be a better person.

TENSION EXISTED WITH MY BROTHERS because I no longer drank and I had a college degree. They often referred to me as "perfect." Jesse's wife sarcastically mentioned to me that she was surprised that Cal and I lived together, especially considering the fact he used drugs with my brothers. Her statement knocked the wind out of me. Why didn't I see it? Or didn't I want to see it? I felt so used and dumb. He knew where I stood with his using. Why didn't he have the courage to talk to me. His using could jeopardize my job as a social worker. I was tired of his lies and deceit. I was angry with his behavior and how he treated all of us. I no longer hoped we would be a family. I was sick of how he controlled the home. I made the decision to leave. This meant I had to find money for the deposit and rent but I would find a way. Shawna and Sandy asked if they could finish the school year before the move, and I agreed.

I received a phone call from my childcare provider. She was concerned about Cal's behavior, which she described as odd, when he picked up Adam. Cal's mood was erratic and his behavior unpredictable. My concern wasn't if he loved Adam, it was how appropriate was his behavior around him. If he wasn't alert or preoccupied then he wasn't capable of making rational and appropriate parenting decisions.

Eventually, Cal's anger exploded without warning. Shawna called me at work. She was crying so hard I could hardly understand her. Shawna said she offered to take Adam upstairs with her because he was crying when Cal tried to change his diaper. Cal went ballistic and came after her. He backed her up against a window and wiped the dirty diaper on her. Shawna threatened to call the police and Cal retaliated by wiping the diaper on her again. He told her she better be quiet if she knew what was good for her. He then took Adam and left the house.

I called Lenny. He offered to pick up the girls and bring them to his house. He cautioned me about taking any action while I was angry. I was furious that I had failed to protect my children. I was angry with Cal for making my children feel ashamed and afraid. I was angry that I wasn't there for my children. I called the childcare provider who confirmed that Cal had returned Adam. From now on I would be the only parent picking him up.

Later, when I spoke with Shawna and Sandy, they expressed how scared they were. Neither wanted Cal to live with us anymore. I promised them our living arrangement would change soon. I felt deeply ashamed, part of me knowing I could have prevented this situation.

When Cal came home that night, he was tearful. He felt the girls had been disrespectful and he reacted to it. I reminded him that he was the adult and he needed to be in control of his emotions. I told him I planned to move out in the spring. He offered to move out instead if that was what I wanted. He tried to rationalize his angry outbursts and behavior. In the past I might have given him a free pass but I wasn't interested in his lies anymore. I knew he was smoking marijuana and seeing his girlfriend again. I still loved him; however, I no longer could take his lies and deceit.

He said he loved me and didn't want to split up. Yet he never took an active interest in my daughters, he rarely paid for anything beyond the bare necessities, and he was absent most of the time. I'd had enough. If he wanted to be with someone else, he could have her. No longer would my children have to be afraid of a man I lived with. I would allow him visitation with Adam, but only if he was sober. Cal packed up a few of his belongings and left.

My daughters healed from the crisis with Cal, but they never forgave him. He never apologized to them about his abusive behavior nor did he explain why he was so angry with them. This anger still remains today. We worked out an arrangement where I allowed Cal to visit and spend time with his son, and his behavior was appropriate. The first few times he visited, we were uncomfortable. He said he felt badly about the episode with my daughters and he missed having our family around. He was tearful and I felt my heart go out to him. I still loved him but I knew he couldn't come back. We didn't even made good roommates. Our path was no longer the same. I didn't want to live with someone using drugs or alcohol. His life was his own. From now on he could choose how he wanted to live it. Likewise, I deserved a choice in my life and how I wanted to live it.

He felt marijuana should be legal and a person shouldn't feel shame because of it. All I knew was he wasn't the same person I fell in love with. He could believe what he wanted about drugs. Alcohol had stolen the hearts and minds of my loved ones. I wasn't going to expose my children or myself to this ongoing heartache. I had lost a great deal over the years emotionally and financially because of loved ones drug use. That was why I gave up alcohol, hoping never again to fall victim to a false reality that alcohol and drugs provide. My choice was to stop the cycle of physical and chemical abuse from continuing with my children. I hoped to visit a park with my grandchildren instead of having them visit me at a treatment center, detoxification unit, or my funeral. Life is very fragile and every decision is based on the one before it.

Through a friend, I leaned about FMHA housing loans. I applied and was approved. We found a house with a fenced in yard. I thought it would be perfect for Adam who loved being outside. The home had three bedrooms, a partially finished basement and a dishwasher. We all loved the house but I doubted we could afford it. Fortunately, the home had been approved for an FMHA loan before, so it was accepted.

To finance it, I needed to put a small amount of money down. I called my bank to ask them how much money I actually had in my checking account. To my surprise, I had over $800. When I wrote a check, I always rounded it to the next highest dollar in the register. I had a savings plan without realizing it.

I needed to be out of the rental home before the house was available. While I didn't like to impose, friends were gracious enough to house us until the process was finalized. We stored our belongings in their garage and lived with this generous couple for eight weeks. I assisted with groceries and in some small ways financially. They never acted as if we were in their way and were always helpful in making this transition comfortable for everyone.

On August 10, 1995, we moved into our spacious new home. What a dream it was! Adam's childcare provider and the couple we stayed with had put a beautiful sandbox in our backyard with a red ribbon on it with the word "Welcome" written in the sand.

Cal followed and rented a home near us. I was uneasy about him being so close. Even though he assisted in the move, he was angry about our separation. I kept my distance because so much emotional damage had been done. When we were together he had no interest in building a bond with his son. Now that we weren't together, he was all of a sudden interested. If he truly was interested in building relationships, why didn't he work on it when we were all living together? I didn't trust him, nor did I believe he knew what commitment was all about. What was his relationship with the other woman and the child they shared? It was more work to be in the relationship than out of it. I wanted peace and stability.

At the same time, I yearned for Adam to have a relationship with his father, if his father truly wanted one with him.

I drove 67 miles one way to work. At a meeting, I met a supervisor from the town I resided in who had an opening in his agency. Shortly thereafter, I went to work for him at Rural Minnesota CEP. I saved on mileage and childcare costs.

Before I left my previous job, I asked how close I was to licensure. The supervisor admitted there was no one on staff who could license me. My 134 mile commute meant nothing. At the new job, my supervisor David was a licensed social worker, and he promised to assist me.

David was wonderful. He was very helpful in teaching me about office expectations. He was always available to answer questions. He never made me feel inadequate when I expressed my feelings or thoughts. He asked about my children and was delighted if they stopped to see me at work. It didn't take long to being to feel productive and part of the team. I truly enjoyed going to work and brainstorming with my coworkers about how best to assist our families. I developed some very close relationships with my coworkers. This was a healthy and enjoyable setting to grow personally and professionally.

David was a strong emotional support as I struggled with parenting my teenage children. I trusted him; he was always kind and gently reassuring. He offered hugs and knowing smile s to my children and me when times were difficult. I treasured his friendship and deeply respected him as a professional. I witnessed him many time showing the same compassion to the families we worked with that he offered to my coworkers and me.

The state dictated that employment was the goal for the families on the new MFIP program. I agreed that employment was beneficial – it helped with self-esteem, developed confidence, improved self-worth, opened awareness of other resources through coworkers, developed friendships and allowed families to achieve financial independence. However, my professional conflict with employment as the ultimate cure for our families living in poverty was that many of the employment positions had low wages. The low wage was the result of the parents not having a work history, not completing high school nor having a GED. Some families had serious, active, chemical dependency issues, undiagnosed mental health concerns, behavioral issues, legal issues, and no driver's license. These families were not ready for employment, nor could they keep a job if one was found. I would not set these families up for failure by telling them a job would fix their problems. They needed to resolve their current barriers before they would be work ready.

There were families that had their lives in order and were work ready. However, I felt that every family was as unique as the individuals within it. The uniqueness of each family's needs meant that, as their social worker, my goal was to assist the families in becoming financially independent and less dependent on public assistance.

It soon became clear that we were overlooking the families that needed other resources. We were asked to sanction families for lack of follow-through when they were not capable of that due to personal barriers. It was not reasonable to expect families to go off public assistance and become financially self-sufficient. There remained a serious gap in understanding poverty and the barriers families had to overcome in combination with realistic and attainable goals.

In my personal life, I found parenting my teenage daughters to be a challenge. We had a home we loved where we felt safe and stable. I no longer worked nights, weekends, and holidays plus I no longer commuted many miles to work. However, I was not prepared for adolescent rebellion. I thought if I was sober, worked hard, provided food and was not an abusive parent, our lives should run smoothly. I had done my best to eliminate barriers for my family. I was confused when I discovered my daughters sneaking out of the house. At times they were verbally disrespectful. I caught them in lies and found out they were experimenting with drugs and alcohol.

Average teenage behavior is what my friends called it. Adolescents rebel and challenge a parent's control, they said. I had no desire to control them; I merely wanted to guide them into safe environments and respectful behavior. At times, I hardly recognized them. They seemed more like strangers than my children. I admit that our life hadn't been easy, yet we had worked together and succeeded. What were my daughters rebelling against? Our lives were so much smoother. We had accomplished a great deal together. Our life was good. I still struggled financially, but as a single parent, that was a fact of life.

Through their teenage years, my daughters taught me a great deal about parenting. We dealt with a lot of issues – dating, curfews, truancy, teen pregnancy, chemical dependency/treatment, disrespectful behavior, and dishonesty.

I found myself challenging other parents. I challenged local professionals and the legal system on their follow-through because I felt they enabled dangerous behavior.

I will not share the intimate details of my daughter's adolescent struggles or my deep emotional concerns trying to keep them safe in an unsafe society. Out of respect for my daughter's privacy, this is their story to tell if they ever wish to share it. However, I will relate that there was a time in each of my daughter's lives that I almost lost them. I can return to this pain quite easily as the thought and fear of burying my children can leave me paralyzed.

My children are my greatest blessing. Without them, my life would have no meaning. I continue to stand beside my children, yet they know that if I feel they are in the wrong, I will be the first to tell them. My children know I strongly believe in natural consequences. They know I believe in honesty and expect this from them. It will not enable, make excuses, or condone bad behavior. I am honest with them whether they want to hear it or not. I will always support them.

Chapter Twelve
What Shall I Do?

Dying is easy. Living is hard; and yes,
I will accept this challenge daily.

IN THE SPRING OF 1997, Cal's grandmother became very ill and was hospitalized. She and I had been very close. I brought Shawna, Sandy and Adam to visit her. Her eyes lit up when she saw the children and especially when she received a big hug from Adam. She always treated my children and me as if we were her own. She loved us and we loved her. I felt blessed to have known her and honored to be a part of her life.

Eventually, the hospital could do no more for her and they sent her home. She wanted to die in her own bed.

Because of my certified nursing experience, I was privileged to provide some of her final care. I turned her as needed, offered her frequent sips of water, assisted with her oxygen, checked her bedding, powdered her skin, freshened up her face and hands with a washcloth and applied lotion to her feet. Oftentimes, comfort care is difficult for a family to provide, so I was honored to do it. I was able to repay her a little for all the years of love and kindness she had shown me and my children.

When she died, I dressed her in her favorite nightgown, put booties on her feet, and dabbed her with her favorite perfume. I gently washed her, changed her bedding and fixed her hair. She looked so peaceful and beautiful. I hoped my efforts in her final hours offered her a glimmer of dignity, pride and respect.

How quickly time passes in this world when one is trying to survive. My children are now seventeen, fifteen, and five years of age. Financially, I was never able to take them to Disneyland or the Black Hills, but I feel I did the best I could do with what I had. I am very proud of my three children. They've taught me much about this world and inspired a desire in my heart I didn't know existed. There were many things as an abused child and single parent I had never known. There was much I could not offer my children, but I gave them myself and somehow, by the Grace of God, they blossomed into beautiful people right before my eyes.

I received a call on a Sunday morning from Jerry. I was sitting in my recliner, crocheting a blanket. I could not comprehend what he was saying. His voice was very non-affect and he kept repeating: "Bobby is dead, Bobby is dead. My son, Bobby is dead." I was certain Jerry must be mistaken. I prayed the whole way to his house that he was wrong, but he wasn't. Bobby was dead, killed in a freak accident.

The police investigated the suspicious nature of Bobby's death. After a week-long investigation, it was determined that Bobby had an argument with his girlfriend and had used his fist to hit a glass window in his trailer home. In bringing his arm back in, the jagged edges of the glass cut a main artery in his inner arm. He bled to death in three minutes. How often I have seen men in my family in a fit of anger hit windows, walls, or other people. A simple act of anger cost this young man his life, forever changing the lives of his father, brother, cousins and all those that loved and cared about him.

I could not offer Jerry any solutions or suggestions that would lighten the pain in his heart. His grief was immense and rightly so. All the love and support could not change what had happened and I could not tell him life would improve – his son was gone. I felt my own grief at the loss of my nephew, but my brother needed my strength. I grieved later.

After the police investigation was complete, Jerry went to the trailer where Bobby died. He cut a piece of blood-stained carpet out of the floor. Weeping, he held the carpet up and said, "This is all I have of my son. This is all I have!" I stroked his back and cried with him. Life is so fragile. My brother's sadness was very deep, but the openness of his grief gave him a change to heal rather than to pretend he was fine. Grief makes most people uncomfortable. Many of his coworkers struggled seeing the pain he was experiencing. This was a difficult time for our family. We have suffered many losses in our lives; however, they never become any easier.

I hug my children often, grateful that I didn't have to experience the loss of a child. I can't even comprehend the thought. I visited Jerry on weekends, sometimes by myself, and sometimes with the children. I listened to his thoughts and memories as he struggled to regain some type of normalcy to his life. I knew he didn't share much with others as he felt they thought he should be over his grief.

Shortly after Bobby's death, one of the Grandmas called me to say her twin sister had died. She had become such a loving part of my family. I longed to be with her, but I didn't have any vacation time left at work. I had used it up to spend time with Jerry after Bobby's death. Grandma and I cried together on the phone. A few weeks later, we were able to get together and share our grief.

In the spring of 1998, Shawna graduated from high school with honors. I was so proud of her. She had challenged my parenting a great deal during her adolescence. However, I must admit she has a few of my traits — stubbornness, independence, self-sufficiency and pride. Therefore, we struggled a bit in our relationship over the years. However, we loved each other a great deal and we overcame many obstacles as a family, which made us emotionally closer.

Shawna wanted to invite her father and his family to her graduation party. This caused me great distress. I had been divorced from her father for approximately 13 years. Communication between us was strained. However, this was her day of celebrating and her party. I said she could invite whomever she wanted. She was elated.

I inquired of friends and coworkers about graduation parties. I had no idea what to do. Putting on parties was not something I was familiar with or felt comfortable doing, plus I preferred avoiding crowds. But for Shawna's big day, I wanted to do it right. I was adamant about one thing, no alcoholic beverages.

AJ came with his girlfriend and his family. It had been many years since I had seen them and interestingly, the tension between us did not seem to be there. We were just people who hadn't seen each other in a long time.

Because Shawna and Adam were close, her leaving home was hard on him. She treated him as if he were a special gift to her and vice versa. She never minded him tagging along and always made a point to take him someplace special. He waited for her to call or to come home; it didn't matter the day or time. I knew once she moved, that would change. I also know I would struggle emotionally with her absence.

The night before she left, she asked to sleep with me like she had as a child. We talked about her day in school. She held my hand all night and I was grateful for her presence. This remains a bittersweet memory.

I gave her Old Blue, my dependable car from college.

Shawna and Adam wrote back and forth to each other often. After Halloween, he insisted that I mail her half of his Halloween candy. She had always taken him trick or treating, and they had shared the candy afterwards. Adam had a stuffed animal, a cat named Al. He bought Shawna an identical stuffed animal. They each slept with their matching cats.

My son missed her deeply and when he started kindergarten, I spoke with the school social worker to see if they had a support group for children with loss and grief issues. Fortunately, they had the Rainbow Group. He liked being able to talk about his sister. Their relationship remains close to this day.

I had approximately six credit cards I was paying on. I paid off three of them but the other three companies refused to work with me. I visited a budgeting counselor who recommended that I file bankruptcy. I was devastated. I had hoped he would be able to negotiate with the companies on my behalf. The credit counselor said my income could not absorb the costs, thus he felt bankruptcy was my only answer. I cried in his office. I took pride in paying my bills. At times I could only afford a partial payment, but I always paid. He said I had no other options.

I attempted to keep up the payments, but in time I realized bankruptcy was my only option. This memory remains a painful long-term reminder of my financial incompetence at that time. Financial stress will always be a barrier for single parents and families on limited incomes. Good credit ratings for single parents or families with limited resources and income is highly unrealistic.

My daughters were very angry that I filed for bankruptcy. They felt that if Cal paid child support, this wouldn't have occurred. What little support I received was applied to household bills, still our household income was inadequate to cover all of our expenses.

In 2000, Sandy graduated from high school. I threw a graduation party for her as well. The second time was easier.

I felt she was not as focused on her future goals as she should be. However, it was her future and I assured her I would always be there for her.

Surprisingly, AJ took more of a financial interest in Shawna and Sandy once they left home. I'm happy that they have built a relationship with their father. Although they are still angry with him, they have matured and realize people make mistakes but can change. None of us can have enough people to love us. I am grateful that he has become a supportive father to his daughters.

IN NOVEMBER 2000, I accepted a child protection position in a county. This meant a $600 a month reduction in pay, but my heart's desire was to work with at risk children. I wanted to be in a position to offer support and guidance to families. I struggled financially with the cut in pay and increased insurance premiums. Eventually I was forced to cash out my retirement benefits to pay off my truck. Cal picked up Adam's share of the health insurance, which helped.

I worked with three women who had been in the child protection department for almost 20 years. The supervisor had been there almost the same amount of time. They knew what each other was thinking because they had shared personal struggles and triumphs over the years. They were very professionally and emotionally bonded.

During a regional training session, I met and developed a relationship with the facilitator. The facilitator asked us to make a list of our adolescent behavior including dating. During a break I asked the facilitator if I could be assigned a different assignment. Due to the sexual abuse in my foster home, my adolescent experiences were quite limited. I also knew from previous experience that if I were to share my sexual abuse, then the focus would be on the sexual abuse which was not something I preferred to share with the group.

The facilitator agreed and gave me a separate assignment. During a break later in the day, she asked me if I ever thought of putting my memories on paper. She suggested I might be able to assist professionals in understanding the dynamics of sexual abuse, alcoholism and physical abuse because of my personal experiences.

Although I had not considered this, her suggestion sparked an interest. She suggested that if I decided to pursue such a project, I should enter individual counseling with a therapist I trusted. This person could safely walk me through the return to my childhood, which undoubtedly would bring back many painful memories.

Her suggestion lingered in my mind. Perhaps I could offer professional insights to those working with families like mine. This could prove beneficial to both the victims and the professionals. To make this a reality, I would have to return to the depths of my childhood in my mind and heart. I questioned myself, asking if I had the emotional strength to go back and relive the painful memories. If I moved forward with the project, I wanted it to be as accurate and honest as possible. This also meant writing about my mistakes and the poor decisions made.

Choosing a counselor was easy. I picked Marie, the counselor who had assisted me on my journey of emotional growth. She had been one of the first professionals who believed in me. She saw me as a competent person and parent and encouraged me to take risks. It had been 14 years since I saw her.

Marie remembered me and was the perfect fit again. She helped me deal with the end of my relationship with Cal – he was now seeing another woman. I had lost hope that we would ever come together as a family, but I still felt emotionally attached. Loyalty, dreams, and hope die hard in my heart. This was the beginning of putting my memories on paper. This project took two and one-half years. My hope was to assist others, but unexpectedly, it has also helped to heal my heart.

IN THE SPRING OF 2001, Sandy told me she was pregnant. She was in her first year of college. She and the father wanted to raise the baby together and make a life and family.

I knew that her relationship with Joe had been emotionally rocky and I had some deep concerns for her. We discussed the possibility of adoption. She became tearful as I spoke to her bluntly about parenting. I reminded her that she was the daughter of a single parent and that life would not be easy if her partner choose not to contribute emotionally or financially. She should know this first hand as she had observed my struggles daily. Her child deserved unconditional love and commitment from both parents.

She had to realize that there was more to raising a child than playing house. A deep-hearted commitment from both parents was necessary regardless of their personal relationship. When she was a child some of the simplest pleasures we had to forgo. Yes, we survived, but there is more to life than survival. There should be a quality of life for oneself and one's children. I certainly would be a support to her and the child she was carrying, but I wanted to remind her there was more to parenting than just giving birth.

Being a parent is emotionally exhausting because there is limited time for self. A realistic commitment in parenting means the child always comes first. Always. I was fortunate I had the understanding employer I did.

Sandy felt she was ready to become a parent and wanted to have a child. The pregnancy went smoothly and I was with her for the delivery of my granddaughter, Kerri.

I fell in love with my granddaughter as they placed her in my arms. I made the same promise to God that very day that I had made on the birth of my own children. I would always do my best for her as I had done for my children. Immediately, this little bundle wrapped all of our hearts into hers. There was no question she would have our love, loyalty, and the best we could offer her in the years to come.

IN 2001, I MET A CHILD PROTECTION SUPERVISOR from another county. She encouraged me to apply for a social worker position in her county. The job involved working with families on cash assistance (MFIP).

I was very impressed with her gentle demeanor and extensive knowledge of children and families. However, I explained to her that my goal had always been to be a child protection worker. However, the more I thought about it, I found this position very tempting because it offered proactive services to families prior to child protection involvement. The downside was this was a grant position which meant the job might end when the funding did. She was certain I could move into another social work position if the grant ended.

My therapist encouraged me to consider the offer. Marie felt this position matched my personal and professional skills. I truly liked the idea of being proactive with families rather than coming in after a major crisis as happens in child protection. I made the decision to apply for the position and was hired. I could not have found a better job that matched my personal and professional skills. I loved this position from the start.

I have two supervisors, a child protection supervisor and a financial services supervisor. The communication between all departments is excellent. Most importantly, my coworkers and supervisors deeply and sincerely care about the families we work with. We have excellent teamwork and continually build on it. My supervisors encourage creativity to help families succeed, so when our services are discontinued, these families have built positive relationships with the professionals in their lives. Within a compassionate framework, we set realistic expectations that are as unique as the individuals we work with. We have developed good relationships with other community agencies. I find my job challenging and very positive. This county is very proactive and realistic concerning the current barriers of our families. I feel very proud of my job and look forward to going to work every day.

I HAVE GIVEN READERS a small glimpse of some of the strengths and weaknesses in my life. I do not believe I hold the corner on pain and suffering. My life has been better than some and worse than others. I have gained some very important strengths and insights from my childhood.

I hope the realization of how difficult like can be without emotional or financial support from family or friends, with limited resources, limited communication skills and understanding of our society rules, financial stress, feelings of being isolated and alone, and limited parenting skills can make a difference in the foundation of the decisions we make daily as adults and parents.

A frequent word used in my profession is RESILIENCE. The Webster Dictionary definition of resilience is: Power of springing back; elasticity; resilient quality of nature; cheerfulness. In other words, resilience says that one will bounce back after everything that has happened to a person in one's life and leave the past behind. This is unrealistic to believe of the families we work so closely with.

I was not resilient as a child. While professionals would like to think of children in seriously neglectful or abusive life situations as resilient, it just isn't accurate. I carry my childhood pain and confusion with me to this very day. I have tried to build on my strengths and to understand and lessen my weaknesses. I've also tried to understand the difference between learned behavior, which can be changed, and genetics that can only be understood. I cannot change my personal history, but I can learn from it. In writing this book, I hope I offer readers some insights and guidance. The rules of survival are ever changing to fit the needs of the day. There is no planning for the future and very little to look forward to. Hope and dreams are rarely a reality and come at a high emotional price.

I learned to tell adults what they wanted to hear at a very young age. I learned to act appropriately and not show sadness or vulnerability. I learned to behave with manners because it pleased the adults. I became a chameleon – whatever people wanted me to be I could be, and I became very good at it. This skill has proven to be a weakness and strength. I sadly admit today, it has been a difficult task to become Karen and be true to who she is, to like her with her weaknesses and limitations. The journey from youth to adulthood has been a difficult one; still I like the person I see in the mirror today. I am no longer interested in what others want me to be; instead I focus instead on what I want to be. I am still discovering who I am, but it is a more pleasant journey now. I celebrate today and my future. I enjoy watching it unfold as it is meant to be.

Families like the one in which I grew up need compassion and realistic expectations that are as individual and unique as our fingerprints. We share common characteristics; still there is no quick fix for any of us. Building trust and a gentle heart when we fall down takes time and patience. Do you have time and patience for me and others like me?

I wrote this book from my heart. Returning to my childhood caused me great pain, while at the same time it provided me with overwhelming healing. It took time to find all the pieces and some I could not find. I want to believe this book can offer hope to others like myself that struggle every day and insight to professionals that work with families similar to mine.

*A personal thought to professionals: Remember when you grow frustrated with families like the one I was born into; try to imagine what it must be like to live this lifestyle. The word frustration could not possibly describe it.

Take time to build relationships with your families, build trust and offer them your honesty. You may be the only lifeline this family has to living the quality of life they dared not even dream about.

You may have one of us as a coworker in the near future.

I have been very blessed with good friends and those whom I have come to know during my journey and have believed in me.

I remain eternally grateful for them all. Without them I wouldn't be here.

I remain blessed and grateful for my children and granddaughter, who kept my focus on what was important and stirred a love in my heart I am unable to describe. They are the wind beneath my wings!

I have a favorite poem given to me by the Grandmas from years ago, but the message will always be clear:

Oh, What Shall I Do?

"This is such an awesome place,
Oh, Lord, what shall I do?
God looked down and smiled and said,
Just build a better you!"

Visit Karen at www.karenwussow.com

Epilogue

I AM FIFTY ONE YEARS OLD as my dream, this book, goes into a second printing. It has been eleven years since I wrote the bulk of this book so a short update is necessary. I am a social worker at Crow Wing County Social Services in Brainerd, Minnesota. For the past nine years, I have worked with MFIP families. Crow Wing County has developed an innovative, proactive system designed to provide intensive services to families. With the emphasis on individual plans, incentives, and tools, I am able to identify the needs of all family members and target those needs.

I truly enjoy my job and look forward to going to work each day. I am honest and compassionate with the families I work with. My goal is to make a difference and prepare families for the time when they no longer are eligible for MFIP. Families in crisis need to develop trust, honesty, open communication, and healthy relationships. As I build trust with a family, it often becomes apparent that mine is the only healthy relationship they have. This provides a base for us to work on as they continue to grow and build healthier relationships.

I challenge families' thinking and lifestyles. I am honest about what changes need to be made and what can't be changed. Together we try to build a life for them; one that they only dreamed was possible. My personal history allows me to develop close and trusting relationships. As families open up about the trauma in their lives, we discuss the difficulties but also the good times that are possible. Life will not be perfect, but it will be manageable.

I am supervised and guided by two people who, in their heart, want to make positive changes within the families we work with. We offer realistic solutions to realistic problems that families face on a daily basis. I truly believe other agencies should follow the lead of Crow Wing County and adopt similar proactive programs for MFIP families.

On a more personal note, I no longer try to be what others want me to be. I enjoy my job, my children, and my grandchildren. I know I don't fit into the social norms but my mind and heart are okay with that.

I have a daily routine that brings me comfort and happiness. Most nights you'll find me in my sweatpants, reading, doing laundry, making supper, talking with my children and taking a bath before bed. Life is good.

Writing this book has been a very healthy journey for me. Though my childhood memories remain strong in my mind and heart, they no longer hold the intensity they once did. They are part of who I am and I am grateful for that, but they no longer define me.

Financially, I still struggle and continually juggle my budget. I still owe on my student loans. I deferred them for many years while raising my children and the original $20,000 has now ballooned to $85,000. This is a financial barrier and will be a challenge for me to pay off.

Shawna is 30 and earned her Master's Degree in Criminal Justice in 2007. She works as probation agent in central Minnesota. I was able to take my first vacation as she had a destination wedding on a tropical island. She and her husband are expecting their first baby. She lives nearby and we see each other often.

Sandy works in sales at a growing technology firm. She is 28 and the wonderful mother of my beautiful eight year old granddaughter, Kelly. She lives nearby and we see each other often.

Adam is an active 16 year old. As a teenager, he challenges my thinking and parenting daily. I've watched him grow into a compassionate and bright man. He is a very good student who looks forward to college. He is in speech, choir and loves animals.

I am proud of my children and their kind hearts. They continue to amaze me with their accomplishments and I am blessed that even with their busy lives they find time to make their mother a priority.

Kelly is in third grade and loves school. She has quite a strong personality. She shares my love of horses. We ride every chance we can. We enjoy our frequent hikes to Super America where I splurge and buy her too many treats.

I love being close to my children and granddaughter as they bring laughter and warmth to my heart. They don't seem to mind that I see the world through different lenses. They love me the way I am. There is no greater blessing for me than to watch them mature and grow into beautiful human beings. I feel very blessed.

My brother Jerry and I remain close. We make time to share about our lives and discuss our struggles and triumphs. His childhood dream of singing country music has come true. He has a band and spends many weekends on the road playing the classic country tunes that touched our family so much.

My relationship with Duane, Lenny and Jesse remains fragmented due to our different lifestyles. Their lives continue to include chemicals and the consequences of the choices they make. Although it is difficult not to be a part of their lives, they are adults now with the freedom to make their own decisions. I continue to hold them close to my heart.

Cal's lifestyle has distanced him from his son but he allows his son to set the boundaries and the pace to developing a relationship that is comfortable. Cal is aware that decision he's made has created difficult barriers between him and his son.

Although many positive strides have been made in society, families continue to face very difficult challenges and barriers. My family is not so different than many families today. Hopefully, this book is a reminder that we each need to be aware and take an interest in those children living in trauma in our towns, neighborhoods, and families. You can make a difference whether or not children grow into healthy or angry adults. I ask that you accept that challenge in your daily life.

A Dialogue with the Author

Why did you choose to tell your story?

In my early 20's I was an angry young woman. I was angry that my mother walked away from me. I was angry that I was judged about how I grew up when I had no control over the decisions that were or were not made on my behalf. I was labeled a problem child not because of my own actions but because of those of my parents and other adults. While it was my parents who abused chemicals and were physically abusive, I was wrongly viewed as a reflection of them. By telling my story, I am able to have a voice and express how it felt to be labeled and judged as a child and an adult. As a child I had no power to make decisions, change my surroundings or share my feeling with a trustworthy adult. Over time I learned to positively channel my anger and frustration and to become the person I knew I was capable of being. In a way I also wanted to honor those individuals who came into my life and believed in my heart.

On another level, my hope is that the book offers insight to professionals and support to victims. There are many of us who suffered as children who have gone on to become productive members in our communities. I wish to offer compassion and understanding to others who have suffered. I recognize the emotional toll this has taken on me and on others in similar situations. I want to be a voice for them as well.

How long did it take to write the book?

The book took me 5 years to write and it was an emotional and grueling journey. Because it forced me to delve into my childhood, I was flooded with emotions daily. For this reason, I started counseling to guide me as I once again felt the uncertainty, fear, shame, loss, and hopelessness of my childhood return to the surface. I found it difficult to balance work, parenting and writing a deeply personal and painful book all at the same time. Tapping into my childhood memories was relatively easy but only if I allowed myself a block of uninterrupted time to go back in time to an emotionally painful place. I was flooded with memories and it was emotionally impossible to just flip a switch to turn them off. I had to allow myself ample time to heal and return to my present world. This was a very emotionally draining project but very healing to my heart. Through this arduous process I learned that I was no longer a helpless child but a successful and competent adult and parent. While I felt sadness for my lost childhood, I discovered I no longer harbored the anger and resentment for those who did not protect me. Instead, I came to understand that people are not perfect and we all make mistakes. I realize now that the adults in my life didn't have the knowledge or tools to work with families such as mine. My hope is that I can assist and teach others. Most importantly, I want other adults who were hurt as children to know they are not alone. There is HOPE!

How have your children responded to the book?

My oldest daughter has read the book. She has accompanied me to several speaking engagements. She is very encouraging and proud that I shared my story. My younger daughter has chosen not to read the book. She feels it would be too painful to read. However, she is very approving and supports my efforts. My son is 16 and has no interest at this time in reading the book. Maybe when he is older he will have thoughts or questions but for right now his world is safe, structured, and consistent. He is surrounded by loving adults who encourage and nurture him. He is busy being a teenager and life revolves around him as it should. I gently try to guide him in what to expect from the world – my vision of the world is GREATLY different from his. For that, I am grateful.

How difficult was it to remain positive and move forward?

I knew if I had mentors and role models I could learn what I needed to. And I did. Over time I gained the tools necessary to set goals and to achieve them. I knew this was possible and so I continued to strive to make it happen. I could envision a future where life was better, happier and more positive. While I was painfully aware of my limitations, I learned to build on my strengths. I knew I had potential and I wanted to develop into the best person I possibly could be. When I had children this became especially important to me. I wanted their lives to be so much better than mine. My lack of knowledge or exposure to the world had nothing to do with my intelligence or ability to learn. However, it appeared to me that it was easier to pass judgment rather than to provide me the tools I needed to live in this world. At times this left me feeling helpless and hopeless. I was left on my own to flounder and try to find my own way. I desperately wanted to prove that I was not a statistic, doomed to failure. My heart was not willing to accept this predicted outcome. My anger proved to be a very valuable tool because it provided me the stamina, endurance and commitment I needed to be successful.

What happened to your cousin Lisa?

In the book I describe the time my foster father took me to visit Lisa. That was the last time I saw her. While I no longer know of her whereabouts, I always keep her in my prayers. The reality is sometimes some of us never get out.

What is your current relationship with your brothers?

My brothers and I have little contact with one another currently. We came together for one of their wedding this past summer. Before that, the last time we were all together was at my mother's funeral 20 years ago. It was nice to see them and to be together, but our lives are different. We are different. We shared a painful childhood but as adults we seem to have taken different paths in how we relate to one-another and what we took away from our childhood. This saddens me deeply but I've learned we are all on our own journey. I am hopeful they have found their place in this confusing world as I have done.

How were you able to develop parenting skills with no parent or significant adult to teach you?

As a child living in an unsafe environment, I quickly learned I needed fine tuned instincts and senses to keep my siblings and myself safe. This was essential due to the chaos and unpredictable behaviors of the adults around me. These skills allowed me to manage the best I could as a child. I became a strong observer of people. I read others by their body language and eye contact. I learned it wasn't so much what they said but what I sensed about them. Were there a threat? Would they help us? As a survival skill, I trusted no one. I followed my instincts and my heart. As I grew into adulthood, I recognized that due to my personal history I viewed the world very differently than my peers and others I was in contact with. I questioned everything and believed in no one but myself. I learned who could be trusted to get honest answers and necessary resources. I am a deep thinker and need time to process the information I gather about my surroundings. I found if I dressed like others I could fit in and learn by watching. The continual feeling that I need to be aware of my surroundings at all times is exhausting. But this is how I've learned and survived. And I must say I do find other people's actions and behaviors rather amusing at times.

What do you struggle most with as an adult?

I am keenly aware that my vision of the world is different from others. It is important for me to nurture and maintain healthy relationships with trusted friends. This provides balance and an appreciation for the power of friendship. I try to surround myself with people who accept and care for me despite my limitations. I feel somewhat isolated during the holidays. Our society falsely promotes family, loved ones and happy times. While I love the time I spend and share with my children and granddaughter, I am keenly aware that I don't have parents or siblings to share such special times with. It saddens me that my children do not have grandparents or any extended family from my side. There is a void because I don't have family to turn to for emotional or financial support. I have few positive memories of my childhood to share with my children. It's almost as if I didn't exist until age 20. When I do reflect on those early memories, I am left with a sense of melancholy. To this day I am uncomfortable in large crowds and avoid them when possible. I work hard to be a responsible citizen. I pay my bills, use credit wisely and maintain my home. I follow through on what I say I am going to do. My character, credibility and honesty are essential to me building good relationships. I am saddened at times that I do not have the financial ability to assist my children more. I know firsthand how difficult it is to financially stay afloat without additional support and guidance. My children are very independent and do not request this of me. The wish to offer my children more is the desire that comes from a mother's heart.

How has the child welfare system changed and is it better now?

Yes, as a professional I have witnessed many positive changes within the system. My book and speaking would not be possible if other professionals weren't interested in improving services and providing hope to families. One of the positive changes I have seen is the establishment of the MFIP cash program for families. In our county we provide resources to families, set goals, work on parenting skills and offer many other services. With the time limits in place it encourages families to take an active role in their future.

In the area of child protection, I support the time limits that foster children are now allowed to spend in foster care. There has been a focus on understanding reactive attachment disorder and the importance of building relationships for children. Case plans are now more realistic and the goals more attainable. The idea is to set people up to succeed, not to fail.

There is a better understanding now of how poverty affects people. It doesn't mean people are low functioning or unintelligent. By strengthening our listening skills and being open and honest in our communication with our families, they can convey to us what the needs are in their lives. This allows us to individually design a plan that truly works for them. The approach is much more strength based now than it's been in the past.

Fortunately, there has been movement away from cookie cutter programs. We better recognize now that each family has its own unique and individual needs. As an example, in the county I work for we have a program that truly works with families and builds on their strengths. We call it the Tier 3 program and it is about action not just talking about what should be done.

Do you ever share your background with the families you work with?

Some of the families I work with know of my personal history, especially since I wrote the book and started a website. Some of my families have requested the book and I give them a copy as long as they agree to critique it. I want them to know that I am interested in their thoughts and ideas. My wish is that it offers them encouragement and HOPE. While life may not be easy it is possible to build a healthy future.

What are some of your main talking points with families?

We talk a lot about choices and accepting responsibility for the decisions we make. There are consequences, some positive and some negative. I stress that we all make poor choices at times. It's a struggle for everyone to be successful in their own lives. But if you have a vision and a plan, then there is hope for a better future. There will always be bumps along the journey but no one is ever alone. However, each person alone must be responsible for the choices they make as our actions define each of us.

I stress that life is difficult for everyone. Everyone struggles in one area or another. We all have limitations but they are no excuse for making poor decisions. We need to reflect on past decisions and choose to make more positive ones in the future. Change is difficult because it will affect all aspects of a person's life. There will be feelings of hopelessness and helplessness that will remain but there are also many healthy resources available if we seek them out. There is individual counseling, support groups, healthy friendships and healthy family and individual activities. I ask them to focus on taking baby steps to make life more manageable.

Why do you think you made it when others in your situation may not have?

I had a grandmother who loved me. I can't emphasize enough how important her love was to me. Although she's no longer alive, I want her to be proud of who I am. I strive to be honest, trustworthy and act with good intentions. In respect to her memory, I want to show that I was worthy of the love and the time that she offered me unconditionally. I also want to show my appreciation to all the people who assisted me on my personal journey. Without them I would not be here today. I've certainly made mistakes but I've tried to learn and grow from each of them. I recognize the value in trying hard and believing in myself. I am not a statistic but a human being with the ability to learn and grow. When I became a parent I didn't want my children to be punished by society and be defined by who I was.

How has your personal history impacted you as a social worker?

There are positive and negatives. My style as a professional is a reflection of my personal history. As I have mentioned previously I believe I have a different vision of the world due to my personal history. My strengths are that I can connect quickly with families. I work particularly well with people who have anger issues. Also, I relate well with families who come from a background of generational poverty. I have no difficulty talking with my families about any topic. Nothing shocks me or scares me off. Loss and grief are two areas I can freely and openly discuss because I understand the impact that loss has on lives. I believe families have survived this long – they survived before me and they will survive after me. I trust they will make the right choices given the tools to do so. I challenge people in their way of thinking. If something hasn't worked in the past I challenge them to take the difficult step of trying something else. While it's difficult to learn new habits, it's essential in making that leap from a life of familiarity and easy choices to one of healthier and more positive choices. If something hasn't worked in the past, why continue doing it? Once they have other alternatives presented to them, I believe they are capable of making better choices.

In terms of limitations, I struggle with building relationships with co-workers because my style and view of the world tends to be different. I try to work with families the same way I wished professionals would have assisted my own family. I stress honest and open communication and accountability. There has to be consequences, positive or negative for families to learn and grow. At the same time I want the family to know that they are worthy of my time and that I will assist in any way to move them forward.

My definition of helping families is to reach the point where their children won't be in the system later. I believe we have capable and intelligent families. They can make wise choices if they are aware of all the choices available to them. At the same time, we can't do everything for our families. If we do, then we cripple them. We need to be a resource and a tool as they take steps to live a healthier lifestyle. This will take time and practice and there will be many bumps in the road. We need to encourage them and stand beside them. We must never judge.

In terms of my personal life, I differ from many of my co-workers. I prefer not to socialize with co-workers or attend work parties. I do not drink alcohol or go out. I enjoy going home after work and relax by watching TV or taking the dog for a walk. Coming from a history of chaos and uncertainty, I relish my down time. I work all day problem solving and being with people. The nights are my own. This is my time to recharge my batteries and parent my son. I like to keep my life simple. It takes a little bit of doing in a fast paced world.

How can professionals do a better job working with at risk families?

I see some professionals fearful of our families due to their life style and behavior. While safety of the professional is very important, I often see the fear simply based on the lifestyle differences, not any actual threat. I feel professionals and public and private agencies are working better together as a team, but we need to do better. When all the professionals involved in a family are on the same page as far as goals and services are concerned, the possibility of success is far more realistic. The key is good communication and a common goal. We have to check our egos at the door and avoid power struggles. We need to be on the same team so we can hold families accountable. If we can do that then everyone wins—our families, communities, children and society in general. As professionals we can't feel bad when families make choices we don't agree with. They have the right to disagree with us. Making mistakes is a good way for families to learn that all actions have consequences. If we make the mistake of doing everything for our families, then they always have someone to blame and there is no need for them to be accountable. They will only learn from their mistakes if they are allowed to make their own decisions, good or bad. If we always rescue them or save them from themselves, we are not doing them any favors. We are merely adding to the dysfunction. Families need to take responsibility for their own lives. I cannot live their life for them anymore than they can live mine for me. Everyone is on their own journey. Our job is merely to offer tools and supports. Our work is meaningless if families come to rely on us to do everything for them. The learning curve may be difficult for them, but it's essential.

While it's sometimes difficult and painful when they tell us they no longer desire our services, we need to be okay with their decision and not take it personally. Of course, we should point out the consequences of such an action but we need to let them go. It makes me sad to see families take the more complicated and painful path but it's their life and journey to take. These are lessons they will learn from much like we all do in our lives.

Have you ever met Peter Brinda, the Social Worker you refer to in the book?

Yes, I had the honor of meeting Mr. Brinda in 2008. I had spoken at the Minnesota Social Service Association conference and I made reference to him in my talk. I shared my heartfelt appreciation for his kindness and caring manner to the crowd and mentioned that I would love to meet him. The next week I received a voice mail from a Social Worker in another county who knew him and she provided me with a contact number. I was thrilled but nervous at the same time. Would he remember me? Would he want to hear from me? After a short deliberation I finally built up enough courage to call. He sounded the same as I remembered. His voice was gentle and kind. I thanked him for being a caring and loving professional in my emotionally chaotic childhood. When I asked him if he remembered my family he gently laughed and said he did. He described my mother as a colorful person. We both laughed at that. We set up a meeting at a restaurant. He was 87 years old when I met him. His gentle smile and kind demeanor were the same. Our meeting went well and in fact he and his beautiful wife invited me to dinner at their house. After a wonderful meal we had birthday cake to celebrate his special day. He looked at his wife and asked if I was to get a clean fork or not. She smiled and said I should keep my fork. Mr. Brinda put his hand on mine and said, "Family members keep their own fork." I became tearful and thanked them for their kindness. We remain in contact to this day. Meeting Mr. Brinda was one of the thrills of my life.

Questions for Discussion

My family

1. How would you get yourself in the door to meet this family?
2. What is the first thing you would assess when meeting the mother?
3. What is the first thing you would assess when meeting the five children?
4. What are the priorities/barriers?
5. Name any illegal activities.
6. List all the issues that need to be addressed.
7. What issues would you work on first? Make a list ranking each in order of importance.
8. What government services would this family qualify for?
9. After the initial appointment, what would you do differently for the second assessment appointment?
10. How many home visits are needed to make a clear assessment of needs?
11. Why?
12. How often would you meet with them?
13. What difficult situations might you encounter during a home visit?
14. How would you handle each of these situations?
15. When do you foresee accomplishing the goals you set?

Questions
1. What services do you have available within your community? County?
2. What are the strengths and weaknesses of each of these services?

3. How would you maintain appropriate communication with each professional involved with your family?
4. Which services are for the parent(s) and which are for the child(ren)?
5. What role does race, gender, economic status, religion, age, culture, etc., play in the services you will provide?
6. What is the likelihood of your families succeeding with the services?
7. If the likelihood is high, why? If the likelihood is low, why? What should you do differently?
8. Between you and your coworkers, are you the best "fit" to work with a certain family? Which families would be most difficult for you to work with?
9. Who is your support system professionally while working with difficult families?
10. How would you maintain professional boundaries with your assigned families?
11. What are some strategies you can utilize to build rapport with your families?
12. What are some strategies you can utilize to build rapport with your agency? Community?
13. How would you handle a conflict with a professional from another agency? Within your own agency?
14. How would you handle an uncooperative family member?